Britain's Locust Years

by the same author

★

THE WISEST FOOL IN CHRISTENDOM
THE MURDER OF SIR THOMAS OVERBURY
THE STORY OF ENGLAND

BRITAIN'S
LOCUST YEARS
1918—1940

★

by
William McElwee

FABER AND FABER
24 Russell Square
London

First published in mcmlxii
by Faber and Faber Limited
24 Russell Square London W.C.1
Printed in Great Britain by
Latimer Trend & Co Ltd Plymouth

Author's Note

I am conscious of an enormous temerity in venturing into the open on a period of what the French call 'contemporary history', and one around which passion and prejudice among historians and politicians still run dangerously high. It is time, nevertheless, that some attempt was made to assess this period objectively, and it has seemed to me that a great deal of recent scholarly work by, among others, Professor C. L. Mowat, Mr. R. Bassett, Mr. Julian Symons, Mr. Alan Bullock, and, of course, Mr. A. J. P. Taylor, has begun to make this possible. There is still much in the period which remains obscure and more that is hotly disputed. But the material is there for a dispassionate survey, and I hope that this is what I have achieved.

I owe so many debts of thanks to those who have allowed me to pillage their libraries and helped me with suggestions and advice, that it would be tedious to compile a list of them. I must, however, make personal acknowledgement to Mr. P. G. de Havilland who supplied me with the only authentic facts and figures of aircraft production in this country in the late thirties I could get hold of, and to Mr. A. J. P. Taylor for invaluable advice and help when I was planning this work, even though he may be exasperated by some of the conclusions I have drawn, which I have not given him an opportunity to criticise.

W. L. McElwee

Stowe,
Buckingham
September, 1961

Contents

CHAPTER 1

Armistice

The sudden, 11 o'clock silence of November 11th, 1918, which much of the world still commemorates, and which seemed unnerving at the time to the shell-shocked troops of the Western Front, fell upon a Europe whose civilisation most thoughtful men believed to be irretrievably in ruins. In the streets of London and in every city and town in Britain hysterical crowds shouted and sang and waved flags. Effigies of the Kaiser were burnt on innumerable village and preparatory school bonfires, while little bands of uniformed subalterns charged down Piccadilly shouting, only too prophetically for some, 'Now we're out of a job, Hurrah'. The plinth of Nelson's Column in Trafalgar Square bears to this day the marks of the victory bonfire kindled that evening from a watchman's hut, while another crowd in front of Buckingham Palace brought the King and Queen repeatedly to the balcony to acknowledge the wild cheering. Elsewhere the police stood back, instructed only to interfere to prevent damage to life or property; and it was not until the third night of peace, when deliberately disorderly elements began to appear, that they intervened, and the celebrations died away.

But even in the streets the rejoicing had for many a macabre quality admirably recaptured twelve years later by Noel Coward in *Cavalcade* with the spectacle of the bereaved mother, dazed with grief, mechanically waving her miniature union jack on the fringes of the intoxicated crowd. There were many who, like Stanley Baldwin, felt more like crying at the thought of 'the millions of dead, and the vision of Europe in ruins',[1] but all too few with the magnanimity of a Winston Churchill,

[1] A. W. Baldwin, *My Father: the True Story*, p. 89.

'divided between anxiety for the future and desire to help a fallen foe', and musing on 'the impossibility of rebuilding Europe without German aid'.[1] A later generation which has seen, not a continent merely, but a whole world in ruins, materially devastated, socially and spiritually disintegrated, is apt to feel that the damage of 1918 was trivial by comparison: that the sense of irretrievable loss and the despair for the future among responsible men were exaggerated and tinged with self-pity. But the men of 1918 were not inured to destruction as were those of 1945, and had no experience of the remarkable recuperative powers of a modern industrial society. The European wars of the XIX century had been comparatively gentlemanly affairs, fought by professional armies with little disturbance of civilian life outside the actual theatres of warfare. The total war of 1914 came as a nerve-shattering shock to a generation reared in security amid the comfortable Victorian certainties of steady and inevitable human progress, of rising dividends, improving standards of living, and freedom slowly broadening down 'from precedent to precedent'.

The sense of shock and of irretrievable loss was universal; but inevitably the people of Europe reacted differently and to different shocks. In Germany it was the shock of defeat: of seeing the sudden collapse of the militarist autocracy in which they had been trained to put all their faith and which had still been proclaiming its own invincibility in the spring of 1918. While Kaiser and Princes abdicated and fled from their responsibilities, and the generals set themselves at once to 'organise sympathy' and save the army at all costs for another day, the more energetic of the under-nourished, apathetic population turned, in despair rather than in hope, to revolution. In France the triumph of victory was swallowed up in mourning for the devastated provinces and the three million dead which represented a permanent and irreplaceable loss of wealth and power; and those groups of Allied officers who tried to celebrate the Armistice in Paris with noisy cheerfulness found themselves silenced and abashed by French gravity and grief. The collapse of the Austrian Empire left the whole of Central and South-Eastern Europe a prey to hysterical and self-assertive nationalisms which were to make political progress and economic recovery infinitely difficult; while further east again Russia, on the verge of starvation, was torn by

[1] Winston Churchill, *The World Crisis*, Vol. V, p. 20.

a civil war in which a Bolshevist victory seemed far from certain. In Great Britain the material damage inflicted by air raids and the bombardment of coastal towns had been slight and the losses in men far smaller in proportion to her population than those of France and Germany. Nevertheless the shock of the impact of war had been in some ways more severe. The Englishman had been spoilt by centuries of immunity from foreign invasion, and perhaps even more by the previous century of unparalleled commercial and industrial supremacy undisturbed by any major conflict. Except for the Crimea, wars had been small, highly professional affairs fought against uncivilised enemies on remote frontiers; and English opinion, guided by Mr. Kipling, was apt to regard even these as a sort of extension of the public school system. Thanks to the evolution of the international Red Cross organisation and to Hague Conventions, it had seemed that war itself was gradually being brought within rules which would eliminate the worst of its barbarities and sufferings. Soaked in the arts and conventions of peace and trade, with no memories of 1870 or 1859 to disturb him, the Englishman was quite unprepared for the ruthlessness which nations display when they believe that they are fighting for their very existence.

The effect of all this was to produce among Englishmen two successive reactions whose violence later generations often find very difficult to understand. First in point of time came a hatred of the Germans and all that they seemed to stand for: Prussian militarism and barbaric methods of conducting war such as the use of poison gas and the sinking without warning of unarmed merchant ships. It had been a German war, deliberately provoked—the Kaiser's war. Already, before the Armistice, the Cabinet had decided that there must be an immediate general election, so that the Coalition which had won the war should have a mandate from the people for making the peace; and shamelessly Lloyd George allowed it to be fought to the cries of 'Hang the Kaiser' and 'Make Germany Pay'. The *Daily Mail* caught the prevailing mood exactly with its headline of November 16th, when the Germans protested at the continuing blockade: 'Hun Food Snivel'. The Prime Minister himself knew that the Kaiser was securely in Holland beyond the reach of any treason trial and he publicly warned election crowds that Germany would not be able to pay anything like the vast sums in reparation which were being bandied about. But he allowed his followers to use the

slogans, and it was phrases like the famous Cambridge utterance of Sir
Eric Geddes that they would 'squeeze Germany like a lemon, until the
pips squeaked' which captivated the electorate and returned 528 Coalition members to the first peace-time Parliament.

The shamefaced reaction against this hysteria was remarkably swift,
and in due course almost equally hysterical. Those who had clamoured against Hun barbarity came to feel within a year or two that
the blockade with which, largely, we had won the war was an attack on
women and children less spectacular than the sinking of the *Lusitania*
but every bit as ruthless. The campaign to hang the Kaiser came to look
as silly as it was; and historians, groping tentatively among the events
leading up to 1914, began to find mistakes and hesitancies in the policies
of England and her allies which made it difficult to reiterate the simple
doctrine of Germany's exclusive war guilt. French truculence in the
following years and a skilful self-pitying German propaganda were to
exaggerate this tendency into a dangerous obsession which in the end
proved all but fatal. The very violence of the initial anti-Germanism
made the reaction against it all the more violent; and it produced a
refusal to face the facts of international affairs which was the British
people's largest and most specific contribution to the failure of a world
which they sincerely believed they had made safe for democracy.

Perhaps the main cause for the easy triumph of the cheap hysteria
which started all the damage was the void of creative thought or impulse
which so suddenly faced the world when the guns fell silent. The abrupt
cessation of the need for grim, dogged concentration on war tasks in the
teeth of discomfort and rationing, of endless military disappointments
and unthinkable casualty lists, left men—statesmen and voters alike—
at a loss. All the best of them had believed that they were fighting for a
saner and happier future; but the emergency of peace caught them unprepared and with little vitality for planning it. In H. G. Wells's phrase
war had become 'an atmosphere, a habit of life, a new social order'; and
there was a sad lack of definition about such attempts as had been made
to blueprint the land of 'Homes fit for Heroes' which Lloyd George had
promised the returning armies. Even when he came to try to define his
aims to his Conservative colleague, Bonar Law, as an election programme they still did not really come down to earth: 'the unity and
development of the British Empire and the nations of which it is com-

posed', and 'such conditions of living for all the inhabitants of the British Isles as will secure plenty and opportunity to all'. He did not, he went on, 'think it necessary to discuss in detail how this programme is to be carried out'.[1]

It must, of course, be remembered that the hysteria was not shared by the fighting troops who would pour back from France, demobilised at the rate of 50,000 a month, in a very different mood from that of the civilians. Hating the Germans was one relief sought by men and women at home to mitigate the shortages and discomforts, the constant anxieties and intolerable tedium of war, and the real agony of the casualty lists. They had grasped eagerly at every atrocity story put out by Lord Northcliffe's propaganda machine to bolster morale, and had invested every British soldier from the generals downwards with an artificial heroism, as crusaders against the Hun. Others, too level-headed or too civilised to find an outlet in hatred, had clung instead to a tattered remnant of the romantic idealism which had inspired the poetry of Rupert Brooke and had sent a whole generation of young men out to fight in 1914 for what they believed was honour and decency and the rights of the poor and the weak against naked force and brutality. Only the thought that out of it all there would emerge a better world kept them going.

On the whole the fighting troops shared neither the hatred nor the idealism. They knew that in general the enemy had fought as cleanly as the Allies, that there are brutal men in all armies, and that war is apt to be a long series of regrettable incidents. Prussian thinkers and soldiers might be held responsible, academically, for loosing on the world the doctrine of total war; but they had, after all, been defeated by a ruthless and more efficient application of their own doctrine. What capacity he had for hatred the British soldier had long since directed against his own leaders: fire-eating generals in safe dug-outs miles behind the lines, fumbling statesmen at home, and all those who had evaded military service and were doing very nicely out of the war. It was not Brooke, thanking God for 'matching him with this hour', but Siegfried Sassoon, 'cursing the staff for incompetent swine', who spoke for the soldier of 1918, in a mood of bitter disillusionment which left little room for romantic ideals. Actual mutiny, such as broke out among the French

[1] Robert Blake, *The Unknown Prime Minister*, p. 385.

after Nivelle's Champagne offensive, had been avoided. But the mood was perilously near to it.

The returning soldier of 1918, already disillusioned about war, was not prepared to nourish many illusions about the peace. For him Northcliffe's propaganda had turned back on itself and taught him to mistrust any statement or promise put out by his leaders. His mood was one of truculence. He had been told often enough while the fighting lasted that he was a hero, and he was not going to put up in civilian life with the sort of treatment meted out to him and his like before the war. Beyond that his vision of a new heaven and a new earth did not go. He wanted a decent job and a decent house and nobody to kick him around.

But as far as the 1918 election went, the fighting troops and their views were largely irrelevant, because few of them were given the chance to vote. An elaborate scheme for postal voting had been worked out for them; and they did indeed represent a large proportion of the newly enfranchised men over 21 whom Lloyd George was so eager to consult. Thanks to the incompetence of Hayes Fisher, an obscure Conservative who had been made President of the Local Government Board, the electoral registers were still incomplete in November, 1918, and the majority of serving soldiers found themselves disfranchised. Lloyd George sacked Hayes Fisher in a rage, nearly precipitating a quarrel with Bonar Law in the process, and a consolatory peerage was found for him. But this was one reason why, in the London Boroughs, only half those qualified went to the polls, so that the new House of Commons had little claim fairly to represent the opinion of the country.

Nevertheless there were, of course, men with clearly defined, if somewhat limited, aims. The miners were grimly determined to preserve the standard of living restored to them by Government control during the war years, and intent, therefore, to the exclusion of all else, on the nationalisation of their industry. Lord Cunliffe, Governor of the Bank of England, and Professor Pigou of Cambridge formulated for the Government Committee on Currency and Foreign Exchanges the panacea of 'the restoration of the gold standard without delay', and invoked for the purpose the principles of the Bank Charter Act of 1844.[1] There were many among the ruling classes who, without going so far back as that, merely hoped to restore as much as possible of Edwardian

[1] Sir Henry Clay, *Lord Norman*, p. 111.

England. Repelled by these, and equally by the mass of war profiteers determined at all costs to keep their ill-gotten gains, Baldwin, still a comparatively unknown Financial Secretary to the Treasury, was pondering rather more deeply the kind of leadership the country would need and how to pull it together—'to make them realise the brotherhood of the human family';[1] and the first practical fruit of his ponderings was to be a gift of £120,000 to the Exchequer towards war debts, as a thank-offering for the sacrifice of a generation.

The aspirations of Europe and America were as cloudy and ill-defined as those of Britain. Mostly they were concentrated on President Wilson's much publicised Fourteen Points, which had been the basis on which the Armistice had been signed. Forty years later some of them have an ironic ring: the third, for example, in which an American President calls for the removal, 'as far as possible', of all trade barriers; and the fifth which declares for 'unhampered opportunity of development of Russia under institutions of her own choosing'. But in November, 1918, nobody could know that hardly one of Wilson's Fourteen Points would survive intact the negotiations of Versailles. The dangers and difficulties of applying self-determination 'as a principle of action' had still to be explored, as well as the impossibility of determining Balkan relationships 'by friendly counsel along historically established lines of allegiance and nationality'. Nor could anyone in Europe guess that behind the fanfare of enthusiasm which had led even newspapers hostile to the President to acclaim his Points as 'the voice of 100 million Americans' there lurked the Republican old guard who felt with Theodore Roosevelt that the League of Nations merely embodied the ideas of men who wanted 'everyone to float to heaven on a sloppy sea of universal mush'; and this was the view which was ultimately to prevail in the United States.

Indeed, behind the almost mystical excitement with which Europe hailed the Fourteen Points and, when he came over in December, the President himself, there were hard-headed statesmen and generals whose aims were severely practical and wholly self-interested, and who had no intention of letting American idealism come between them and their objectives: Germans intent on evading the consequences of defeat and creating the conditions needed for a come-back—what even May-

[1] Baldwin, *op. cit.*, p. 327.

nard Keynes, who more than anyone set the pro-German tone of English feeling in the twenties, called 'immense delusion and reckless self-regard'; Frenchmen who saw a chance of keeping Germany permanently down which was never likely to recur—like Clemenceau who, as Keynes again accurately diagnosed, 'neither expects nor hopes that we are on the threshold of a new age'. Indeed, Clemenceau scarcely tried to conceal his cynicism. 'God gave us His Ten Commandments and we broke them,' he said. 'Wilson has given us his Fourteen Points —we shall see.' The Italians were quite determined that their frontiers should not, in accordance with Point No. 9, be adjusted 'along clearly recognisable lines of nationality'; and even the English rejected in advance the Freedom of the Seas proclaimed in Point No. 2 and had their reservations about self-determination as it might be applied in Ireland. General Smuts had been prophetically right when he said, at Glasgow in May, 1918, 'The old world is dead, and the new not ready to be born'; only, the old world was not so dead as he thought. Those who looked forward to a new world were without the power to build it, and the minds of the politicians still moved in the grooves of 1914.

Understandably, perhaps, the leaders of English thought fell back on the platitudes which were all that Lloyd George had been able to produce for Bonar Law as an election programme. It was easy for Lord Curzon, in the rotund oratory of which he was so superbly master, to extol the triumph of democracy over 'the great fabric of over-weening ambition and towering pride reared by the sovereigns and peoples of the Central Empires'. He was moving an Address of congratulation to King George on the victory a week after the Armistice, and he ended with a notable peroration, quoting from Shelley, 'the great romantic poet of our land', on the 'birth of a new Hellas':

> *The world's great age begins anew,*
> *The golden years return,*
> *The earth doth like a snake renew*
> *Her winter weeds outworn;*
> *Heaven smiles, and faiths and empires gleam*
> *Like wrecks of a dissolving dream.*

'A similar vision', he said, 'now rises above a far wider horizon.'[1] And

[1] Ronaldshay, *Life of Lord Curzon*, Vol. III, p. 99.

so long as statesmen refrained from considering too closely the actual perplexities of M. Venizelos in Athens, or the practical difficulties of demobilising many millions of men and reconciling the construction of a 'loftier Argo' and 'another Athens' with an astronomical American debt and an economy disrupted by four years of world war, it was possible for them to face a general election, and even the negotiation of a peace treaty, with equanimity. For even Curzon's 'brighter Hellas' was to be inaugurated by the condemnation of the Kaiser, the Crown Prince, and 'the other offenders' to a 'punishment signal, crushing, unheard of in history'; and he had already written to ask the Prime Minister and Mr. Balfour to consider this project seriously, quoting in support the cynical approval of M. Clemenceau. It was not until the following July, when he found himself faced with the practical difficulty of getting hold of the Kaiser and staging a trial in London, that he confessed to serious misgivings.[1]

The public for the moment was quite content to look no further than the politicians who held England's destinies in their hands, and their tone was set by the mysterious, controversial figure of David Lloyd George. This little Welsh solicitor, who had jockeyed his staid pre-war Liberal colleagues into radical policies to outbid the Socialists, and who had driven peers and landlords, royalty owners and the top-hatted classes in general, demented with rage by his urchin jibes, had emerged now as a national hero—the man who had won the war. As a war minister, John Buchan said, he put him 'in the class of Cromwell and Pitt';[2] and certainly he alone had been able to galvanise into activity lethargic supply departments and slothful industries, to infuse energy into the somewhat dilettante war effort of Asquithian politicians and, above all, to stand up to the generals and admirals. Probably no English statesman—not even Churchill in 1945—has enjoyed a greater prestige than Lloyd George did in 1918. Certainly none has provoked deeper and more bitter animosities. Behind the impish features there was a mixture of revivalist fervour which was wholly Welsh, and a cockney humour which made his every speech into a good music-hall turn; and behind that again a brain, often superficial, but lightning quick and infinitely fertile in schemes and formulas, charming colleagues and

[1] His two letters on this are printed in Beaverbrook, *Men and Power*, pp. 384–92.
[2] Robert Boothby, *I Fight to Live*.

opponents into agreements which they would subsequently find puzzling and regrettable. 'That strange little genius who presides over us', Baldwin called him, and Keynes 'the goat-footed bard'; and to his colleagues he was nearly always, in affectionate esteem or exasperated contempt, 'the Goat'. Neville Chamberlain, after one embittering wartime experience, wrote in 1920 that he would never put his 'head under the Goat's arm again'; and Bonar Law's answer to Chamberlain reveals much of what made Lloyd George so tricky a colleague: 'If a man is not successful he never stops to enquire the reasons, but tries to get rid of him at once.'[1] To the public he was just the Welsh wizard who had snatched victory from apparent defeat, and they were content to believe his large promises for the peace settlement without demanding much detail.

The Prime Minister's position in the country at large was much more securely based than his Parliamentary position. It was true, as Bonar Law, the Chancellor of the Exchequer, reminded his Conservative followers on November 12th, that 'Mr. Lloyd George commands an influence in every constituency as great as has ever been exercised by any Prime Minister in our time'; but he had no political party behind him. When, in 1916, Asquith had fallen victim to a combination of public duty and private spite, he had taken with him into the wilderness almost all the great names of the brilliant pre-war Liberal team: Grey and Crewe, Buckmaster and McKenna, Samuel, Runciman, and Montagu had all stood by their leader. Thus all the principal offices in the Coalition government which won the war were held by Conservatives. Dr. Addison held the Ministry of Munitions and from 1917 Churchill was at the Air Ministry. Otherwise the Liberals and Labour men held only minor offices. Its Parliamentary support, too, was predominantly Conservative and, after Labour broke away to fight the election on its own, overwhelmingly so. For the moment the Conservatives were to stand by Lloyd George. But their leaders, too, were rooted in the past, their minds formed and hardened in a world of suffragettes and House of Lords Reform and Home Rule for Ireland; and the memories of these would soon overlay the more or less harmonious co-operation of the war years.

Sir Walter Raleigh once described Bonar Law as being 'without unc-

[1] Keith Feiling, *Life of Neville Chamberlain*, p. 85.

tion'; and there was certainly an unyielding cragginess in the man's public aspect—a quality of harshness inherited from Ulster Presbyterians and hardened in the bitter fights for Irish unionism in the years before the war. As the memory of those bitter battles has receded, his public reputation, helped by a brilliantly sympathetic biography, has improved; and he can be seen now as a first-class Parliamentarian, impeccably honest, hard-working and able, courteous and fair to his opponents, and lovable and affectionate among his friends. But his prime loyalty was to the Conservative Party, and his wildest apologist could not claim that he was a creative statesman. Asquith, in a phrase which has stuck, called him 'the unknown Prime Minister'; and he himself once remarked rather charmingly: 'If I am a great man, then all great men are frauds.'[1] Balfour, the Foreign Secretary, whom Law had succeeded as Conservative leader in 1911, was even more decisively a figure of the past: an elder statesman who had never dealt at all in political visions, urbane, witty, and sceptical, and always, probably, happier giving the Gifford Lectures at Glasgow University on 'The Knowledge of God' than in the hurly-burly of politics, which he had only entered anyway as a matter of public duty and social habit.

Most of the other prominent Conservatives were also men of the past rather than of the future. Walter Long, one of the two men who had disputed the leadership of the Party with Bonar Law in 1911, was the last great survivor of a squirearchy whose social and economic position was already irretrievably damaged; the other, Austen Chamberlain, monocled and elegant, kind and wise and utterly trustworthy, had still some great moments to come, but was basically too much of a gentleman to be a wholly successful politician. At critical moments, fear of doing the wrong thing, of seeming self-interested or over-ambitious, would inhibit his action and justify the Churchillian epigram that 'he always played the game and always lost it'. Curzon, still wandering among the vanished splendours of his Indian Viceroyalty and waiting impatiently for the premiership to which he and others felt he had been born, lived not even in the XIX century, but in the XVIII. Derby outside the world of the Turf was a spent force; and the erratic genius of F. E. Smith was soon to be relegated to comparative impotence in the House of Lords. The Conservative contribution to the future was to be made

[1] Blake, *op. cit.*, p. 75.

by none of these, but by men still only emerging from the obscurity of minor office: Stanley Baldwin, an efficient and unspectacular Financial Secretary, and Neville Chamberlain, who was only about, at the age of 51, to enter Parliament for the first time.

In the case of the Liberals it was not so much the men as the doctrines themselves which were out of date. Even before 1914 the assumptions on which XIX century Liberalism had been based were ceasing to be true. Lloyd George's budgets and the intervention of the state to ensure a minimum of welfare and security for the worker already represented a compromise with Gladstonian principle. In the post-war world of cut-throat economic nationalism there was, for the time being at any rate, no room for the freedoms which they had proclaimed. Free Trade would spell ruin for the British manufacturer, and free enterprise would leave to starve men who were unemployed, not through thriftlessness or lack of enterprise, but because there was no work for them to do.

Labour, of course, had its visions for the future in plenty, and able men to work at them. But Labour was hampered still by being a movement rather than a political party. There were many, especially among the Trade Unionists, who hoped to implement their ideals by industrial action rather than by working patiently for a parliamentary majority. There were differences of opinion on matters like the capital levy and on financial policy generally. The I.L.P. stood aloof from the Parliamentary Party, and as late as 1922 we find Dalton writing in his diary: 'Lunch at the Webbs'. Henderson, Clynes, Snowden—who hadn't met Henderson for three years; what need for liaison in the Labour Movement.' These social cleavages were, indeed, characteristic of the Labour movement as a whole, and symptomatic of deeper cleavages still, theoretical and ideological. The Webbs and the young men who sat at their feet—Hugh Dalton in particular—had a deep mistrust of Ramsay MacDonald. They disliked the ease with which he had adapted himself to the social usages of a class system they detested, his weakness for duchesses, even his parliamentary skill in adapting ideas and ideals to the exigencies of political opportunism. To many in the movement the attempt to achieve reform through parliamentary action seemed in itself a betrayal—a compromise with the very institutions they were out to destroy. It was to take the Labour Movement twenty years to achieve

unity of purpose and a coherent structure, and meanwhile much creative thought and energy were to be wasted in internal bickering.

Ramsay MacDonald and Arthur Henderson, the surviving grand old
men of the political party, would have to work hard for a decade to
wean their followers from revolutionary concepts which were dangerously
out of date: from a conviction of the inevitability of a class war, and a
belief in the absolute efficacy of a general strike. Divided counsels during
the war, when Ramsay MacDonald had felt impelled to pacifist non-
co-operation while Henderson and two colleagues had joined the Coalition, had further retarded the development of the Party; and the men
who, after yet another world war, would get the first fair opportunity to
put their ideas into practice, had not yet appeared in Parliament at all.
Major Attlee, speedily demobilised, was making for Stepney 'to see
how things were moving in East London', and Hugh Dalton, back from
the Italian front, was picking up the threads of life as a lecturer at the
London School of Economics and preparing for the press his first major
work on *Inequality of Incomes*.

Asquithian Liberals then and after denounced the decision to hold an
election immediately after the Armistice as a characteristic Lloyd
George ramp: a 'khaki election', in which the government cynically exploited a still surviving war hysteria. So far as Coalition electioneering
methods were concerned the criticisms were largely justified. But the
decision itself was almost inescapable. A Reform Act earlier in the year
had, very properly, enfranchised all men over 21, since those who had
been conscripted to die for their country could scarcely be denied the
vote, and had also extended the privilege to women over 30 as a belated
response to the damaging suffragette campaign of the pre-war years.
The effect was to double the size of the electorate and to make even
more remote and valueless a mandate given as long ago as 1910. Of
course, once Asquith and his friends rejected the offer of some seats in
the Cabinet and went into official opposition, their defeat also became
inevitable, and the chance of healing the split in the Liberal Party
receded still further. Whether Liberalism as a major political force
was doomed anyway or not, if Asquith and Lloyd George could not
agree the immediate disintegration of the Party was scarcely to be
avoided.

For Asquith himself the result of the election, announced just after

Christmas, was certainly decisive. He and all his best-known supporters lost their seats, and Liberals mustered only 26 votes in an opposition totalling 222. Since the Irish Sinn Feiners refused to take their seats, Labour, with 56 members, was left as the largest opposition group, and the government, with over 500 supporters, had a dangerously overwhelming majority. But these figures concealed the fact that Lloyd George was ultimately doomed as surely as Asquith. With the best will in the world his Chief Whip, Captain Guest, had only been able to muster 150 suitable Coalition Liberal candidates. All these received the certificate signed by Lloyd George and Bonar Law authenticating them as official Coalition supporters, which Asquith contemptuously called 'the Coupon', and the rest of the government candidates were found from among the Conservatives. Thus the Prime Minister had in the Commons only 136 Liberal followers. He held office by virtue only of Tory votes, and would continue to do so only as long as his policy conformed to the wishes of their leaders.

This solid block of Conservative members was the final obstacle in the path of constructive statesmanship. The Coupon had brought to Westminster a great body of men who were wholly untouched by the dream of a new world or a new Britain which might provide at least some justification for the sufferings and sacrifices of the past four years. Baldwin, after one look at them, described them to Maynard Keynes as 'a lot of hard-faced men who look as if they have done very well out of the war'; and J. C. Davidson said much the same of them in a note to Lord Stamfordham, the King's Private Secretary, when he entered Parliament for the first time a year later: 'Hard-headed men mostly on the make', and 'unscrupulous characters'. As the King wrote in his marginal note, 'A great pity. G.R.I.'[1] For these men did not even suffer as their leaders did, from a devotion to principles rooted in a dead past and ideas which had lost all meaning amid the crumbling of a civilisation. They had few ideas and no principles at all. They did not look into the past beyond the opportunities for profit offered by a great war and they asked of the future only that what had been ill-gotten might be safely preserved. The House of Commons in which they sat, 'the wealthiest, the least intelligent, and the least representative since Waterloo', went far to justify the claim that the 1918 election brought 'a vulgarisation of

[1] Harold Nicolson, *King George V, His Life and Reign*, p. 333.

British public life',[1] from which it recovered only very slowly, and perhaps never completely.

This sudden spiritual bankruptcy of the politicians was one vital factor in the failure of the brave new world for which so many men had consciously died and into which so many, too young for military service, believed that they had been born. Another, harder to explain to the survivors of a quite different war, but one of which people were far more vividly aware at the time, was that of 'the missing generation'. In spite of all the ink that has been spilt in military history and controversy, the last historical word still remains to be said on the failure of the generals of 1914–18 to master their own art, to prevent battles becoming an endlessly repeated stalemate and war a mere struggle of attrition. The cause, whether a failure of imagination, or of technique, or of willpower in high places, does not directly concern the historian of the subsequent inter-war period. The consequence, measured in terms of casualties alone, is of cardinal importance. The great nations of Western Europe emerged from the struggle with a great gap in their male populations between the elderly and the very young. All those who had been most directly conscious of the shortcomings of the pre-war world, most vividly aware of the needs and possibilities of the future, and best equipped to work for them, were either dead or too exhausted by years of hammering in the trenches to look beyond the restoration of their private lives and fortunes.

Quantitatively the blow fell more hardly on France, Germany, and Italy than on Britain—hardest of all, perhaps, on France. The French, always obsessed with the problem of population, and conscious of declining strength relative to that of their neighbours, were never to forget the loss of a whole generation of potential fathers or waver in their determination to avoid such another blood bath at any price. But in Great Britain the blow seems to have fallen qualitatively more severely. The causes were various. A naïf enthusiasm and a fear of not being in at the death sent the adventurous and most disinterested of the young men into the ranks to die before even their potential value as officers had been exploited. Inept methods of recruitment and the long postponement of conscription had completed the destruction of what should have been the nation's leaders of the 1930's. In the murderous battles of 1916 and

[1] R. F. Harrod, *Life of John Maynard Keynes*, p. 269.

1917, though the German casualties were often higher than the British, they lost only three officers to every five of ours. The talk of a missing generation was thus not mere rhetoric. In terms of leadership and initiative it was hard fact. Every diary and every volume of memoirs of the period bears sad testimony to it, as the survivors looked round for the friends of Oxford or Cambridge, or those who had shared early struggles in the City or at the bar or in East End settlements; and the belief in the brilliant promise of so many of the missing was not just sentimental illusion.

The cardinal facts for the historian of the inter-war period are, firstly, that the second world war, as Churchill and a few others have constantly insisted, could have been avoided, and avoided by British action alone; and, secondly, that the progress of the past fifteen years, the ironing out of the worst of economic inequalities and a measure of social security for all, could have been achieved at infinitely less cost twenty years earlier to justify the faith of so many who had believed that was what they were fighting for. Of the generation which grew up immediately after the war, which in Oxford and Cambridge and Bloomsbury made up what Evelyn Waugh has called the 'roaring twenties', which enrolled enthusiastically in the League of Nations' Union, and which seemed for a few years to show such brilliant promise in so many spheres, many believed that they were going to achieve both these objectives. Contemptuous of the Victorian values which still dominated English public life, they did not even think it was going to be very difficult. Those who have survived must inevitably seek to account for their failure. It is probably too early still to give any final answer; and the allocation of blame and responsibility is, in any case, an unprofitable exercise. But it is becoming possible to disentangle the facts from the special pleading and to give some coherent account of how that failure came about; and it is indisputably true that the first steps towards the disaster of 1939 were being taken before the rejoicings over the Armistice of 1918 had died away.

For 1918 produced in Britain a great gulf between two kinds of thinking. There is, in trying to define it, a grave danger of over-simplification: to see the division between the advocates of socialism and of free enterprise, or the division between those who believed in all that the League of Nations stood for and those who were sceptical about it, or even quite simply the division between two social systems and out-looks as represented by the elderly and the young, as the important division. It was not any one of these, but all of them together which led in the end to the misunderstandings and failures of the thirties. For, though these distinctions did not ever precisely overlap, they did so nearly enough to produce a deep cleavage of outlook which left the nation at the critical moment incapable of action. The young people who reached maturity in the twenties and thirties had little sympathy with the nation's leaders who were struggling in every sphere—in politics, in industry, in commerce and finance and in the services—to re-create as nearly as might be what seemed in retrospect the golden age of before the war. It was from the critics and the debunkers of the *ancien régime* that the young took their tone. They learnt from Keynes to be ashamed of the Treaty of Versailles, to mistrust all politicians, and to perceive more and more clearly the fallacies which underlay the financial policies of the Lord Cunliffes and the Lord Normans. Their view of war they drew not from Kipling or Rupert Brooke, but from Sassoon and Wilfred Owen. If they read Mr. Churchill's great account of the World Crisis it was to underline the mistakes and muddles and wastage which it revealed; and when they looked around they saw the army and the navy, and even the R.A.F., still commanded by living replicas of the men so austerely condemned by Captain Liddell Hart as being directly responsible for the useless slaughter of their fathers at Loos, on the Somme, and at Passchendaele. But, though they drew their view of war and its heroism, of imperialism, and of patriotism from the disillusioned and the sceptical, they turned to the surviving idealists who had pre-served some of the faith of 1914 for their international politics: to Lord Grey and the Cecils, and to Professor Gilbert Murray. They looked to Geneva and not to Downing Street for a solution of the world's problems without, it must be said, considering very closely what action might be involved in enforcing international justice in a highly nationalistic age. For literary inspiration, too, they went to the rebels and the non-combatants, to D. H. Lawrence and the Irishmen and Aldous Huxley; and they shocked their elders with ideas culled from the pages of Havelock Ellis and Freud and Jung.

It was here that the virtual disappearance of a whole generation became of such cardinal importance. There was nobody to cushion the shock of the impact of the young on the old, or of the old on the young; to temper reforming enthusiasm with common sense, or force the need for change on a reluctant conservatism. Lower in the social and economic scale, in circles more or less immune from such literary influences, a similar process was none the less observable. It was from the truculent and disillusioned ex-service men that post-war industrial relations took their tone, so that the governing classes found themselves suddenly haunted by the unthinkable fear of revolution. A new and more terrifying Russian bogey replaced the old. The pitiably small English Communist Party, which numbered but 5,116 members in 1922, only 2,300 of whom actually paid their subscription of 6d. a week, assumed gigantic and sinister proportions in capitalist imaginations; and to lend point to these fears, the mismanagement of demobilisation led to the very mutinies in the army which had been avoided in the black days of 1917.

But all these deeper cleavages lay still in the future. Once the demobilisation muddle had been sorted out, the prevailing mood became one of apathy and exhaustion. The transition to peace seemed even more difficult than the transition to war. Wartime rationing and wartime shortages perforce continued while industry struggled to reorganise itself for the expected 'peace boom'. The newspapers even continued to publish wartime news. It was extremely cold and there was a shortage of coal, and the final blow—an epidemic of Spanish influenza which killed off 200,000 people in Britain alone—made the 1918-19 winter as cheerless as any wartime winter in London. It was with weary relief rather than any high hopes that England faced the coming peace.

CHAPTER 2

The Treaty of Versailles

The Coalition Election Manifesto had confidently announced that: 'the knell of military autocracy has sounded for ever'; and in the third week of January of 1919 Mr. Lloyd George, accompanied by a train-load of secretaries and advisers, arrived in Paris to discuss with the representatives of some twenty-six allied and associated powers the arrangements necessary to implement this promise. Just over a hundred years before Lord Castlereagh, setting off to Vienna on a not dissimilar mission, had summarised Great Britain's objects as 'Peace and a just equilibrium in Europe'. It would have been as well if Lloyd George's brief had been as severely confined within a vague and harmless generalisation and he had not had his supporters' pledge to 'Make Germany Pay' hung around his neck. He himself had been scrupulously careful to raise no false hopes. 'I have always said we will exact the last penny we can out of Germany', he had told his constituents, 'up to the limit of her capacity, but I am not going to mislead the public on the question of her capacity until I know more about it.' But he left behind him in Westminster some four hundred supporters who had specifically pledged that Germany should be made to pay, 'to the uttermost farthing', for the whole cost of the war. The megalomaniac Lord Northcliffe, outraged because he had been refused a seat on the British peace delegation, had gone over into opposition, and *The Times* and *Daily Mail* were at one with the Conservatives in Parliament that there should be no weakening on this demand; and it was out of this demand that there grew in the end almost all the troubles later associated with the Treaty of Versailles.

Reparations, however, were not the immediate problem confronting

Mr. Lloyd George; they did not come up for discussion until March. The real difficulty was to get any sort of conference organised at all. The break-up of the two great conglomerate empires of Austria-Hungary and Turkey had crowded Paris not only with the official delegations of their component parts, already half recognised as new sovereign states, but with innumerable bodies clamouring to represent special interests and splinter parties and every kind of racial minority. It had been assumed that President Wilson would arrive with a prepared agenda, which he failed to do; and none, in fact, was ever drawn up. The discussions, confined at first to the representatives of the five great powers present, Great Britain, the United States, France, Italy, and Japan, began in a void and followed a course as haphazard and meandering as that of a stream finding its way to the sea. For many months the majority of those present thought that they were merely clearing the ground for a final Congress at which, in accordance with historical precedent, the defeated powers would be represented and given an opportunity to state their case. Astoundingly, no formal decision was ever taken on this point. The various commissions and sub-committees, formed from among the delegates not engaged in the central discussions and the innumerable 'experts' who attended them, formulated their demands and proposals on the assumption that they would subsequently be whittled down in argument, only to find them uncritically incorporated in the sum total of demands finally presented to the enemy on a take-it-or-leave-it basis in almost embarrassing extremeness.

Possibly the task was beyond any single conference, and the chaos into which the Armistice had plunged Europe and the Near East was too complicated to be sorted out in the time available. Certainly it was a task far beyond the capacities of two out of the three men whose opinions were in the last resort decisive. Clemenceau, the French Prime Minister, sat pretty. The mere fact that the conference—mistakenly—was held in Paris and that he, by customary courtesy, therefore took the chair gave him one initial advantage. But he had others far more important. In discussions of this kind he was a professional where Wilson and Lloyd George were amateurs. He had lived at the centre of European politics for nearly fifty years; he was smooth and experienced and entirely ruthless. Furthermore he had the great advantage that he knew exactly what he wanted. By a miracle France had achieved what had seemed the unattainable: not merely a revenge for 1870, but the total and crippling defeat of Germany. For the moment in a military sense she dominated the continent, and he believed that her only safety lay in prolonging that domination for ever. If ever Germany were allowed to rearm, France, with her relatively smaller and static population, would be doomed; for it was unlikely that she would ever again be lucky enough to find allies with the strength to save her. A German, moreover, was a man who could never be trusted, who understood no argument but force, and respected no obligation to the weak. Therefore Germany, once defeated and disarmed, must be kept so for all time by every means, political, military, and economic. Obligations to humanity as a whole, the duty of magnanimity to a beaten foe, Clemenceau dismissed with cynical contempt. The only disinterested passion in his life was for French security; and to this single object, with a total disregard for the interests of anyone else, enemy or ally, he brought to bear the accumulated cunning of a lifetime in French politics and a ferocity which, even in that world, had earned him the nickname of the Tiger.

Nothing in Wilson's character or experience fitted him to deal with a man like Clemenceau. An Oxford don, with thirty years of common-room intrigue behind him, might have stood a chance. An American professor, wholly ignorant of European geography, politics, and behaviour, accustomed to pontificate to naïf audiences of students or still more naïf crowds of electors, and sincerely convinced of the fundamental goodwill of all men, had no technique for handling the men and situations which he found in Paris. Margot Asquith, watching him with an eye which could be acute when not blinded by political prejudice, as he responded to the toast at a Guildhall luncheon, noted the 'lanky face, egotistical, slightly sensual mouth, and charming, if too frequent smile', and remarked of his speech that 'each sentence was perfect in structure and he might have sat down after any one of them'.[1] His mind moved easily among large generalisations and declarations of principle, and nobody then living could have formulated more clearly the aspirations of every intelligent man in Europe than he did in his Fourteen Points and his explanatory addresses. But having once done that he had shot his bolt. A curious, Presbyterian rigidity of mind left him without the capacity to compromise and manœuvre, or to perceive and counter the

[1] *Autobiography*, Vol. ii, p. 294.

calculations of clever, dishonest men. Entangled by his quick-thinking colleagues in what Keynes called a 'web of sophistry and Jesuitical exegesis',[1] he let himself be talked into decision after decision flagrantly at variance with the general principles he still publicly professed. Had he but remained on his Olympian height in Washington and entrusted the negotiations to professional diplomats, he might have preserved his principles and faith intact. In Paris he was almost helplessly at the mercy of Clemenceau's ruthless, perverted logic and the quicksilver irresponsibility of Lloyd George. In Washington, moreover, he might have had a better chance of stemming the tide of American opinion which all the world knew to be running against him—another factor which at Paris weakened both his influence and his faith in himself.

'Wilson', Keynes wrote in his account of the conference, 'had not even much of that culture of the world which marks M. Clemenceau and Mr. Balfour as exquisitely cultivated gentlemen of their class and generation.' He might have said the same of Lloyd George. For, though Lloyd George could make rings round the President, he was for different reasons quite as unfitted for the sort of negotiations in which he found himself involved. His liberalism and his generosity of impulse were sincere enough, and once or twice during the conference, when his imagination was caught, he was to lash out in the cause of justice with a vigour and a force which defeated even Clemenceau's immobility. But he was not rooted in the authentic English Liberal tradition, nor had he any deep sense of responsibility to the European civilisation of which events had now made him a temporary custodian. Keynes, who was rooted in that tradition and in a culture which carried with it the immense Victorian sense of right and wrong, discerned in Lloyd George 'a flavour of final purposelessness, inner irresponsibility, existence outside or away from our Saxon good and evil, mixed with cunning, remorselessness, love of power',[2] all of which he found Celtic and alien; and certainly there was an absence of principle in the Prime Minister as Keynes understood principle. Lloyd George approached the business of a peace treaty as he would have approached a tricky contract or a political deal. So long as he kept within the letter of the law and satisfied his client, the general principles could go hang. He had to produce a peace

[1] J. M. Keynes, *The Economic Consequences of the Peace*, p. 47.
[2] J. M. Keynes, *Essays in Biography*, p. 36.

acceptable to the House of Commons and the electorate and he brought to the task, in a very high degree, the cleverness of a Welsh solicitor, but not the wisdom of a responsible statesman.

It was clear from the start that the points of view of Wilson and Clemenceau were irreconcilable. Yet it was to the task of reconciling them that Lloyd George devoted his great talents; and the Treaties of Versailles, St. Germain, The Trianon, and Sèvres are a monument to his skill if not to his intellectual integrity. From the moment they heard its terms, the Germans denounced the Treaty of Versailles, in particular, as a dishonest document—a fraud which in no way implemented the Armistice terms based on the Fourteen Points. Before very long, as they recovered from their war-time hysteria, Englishmen and Americans were to reach the same conclusion and to jockey the French into the indiscriminate abandonment of all its safeguards for the future, thus giving Hitler and the German militarists a straight run, and justifying to the minds of many Frenchmen every line of the Clemenceau thesis.[1]

It can, of course, and has been argued by apologists for Lloyd George that Clemenceau's and Wilson's visions of a peace with Germany were alike impossible, and that a detailed compromise between the two was the best which could be achieved in the circumstances, politics being the art of the attainable and the practical. It is easy, indeed, for anyone but a Frenchman to see that the Clemenceau solution offered in the long run no security for France at all. A Germany disarmed save for the 100,000 Reichswehr needed for internal order, deprived of her Rhine Provinces, and condemned by reparations to sixty years of economic servitude, would inevitably become a source of unbearable international tension. To Englishmen and to many others such a situation would very soon seem unthinkable, and would come to represent a French military tyranny as objectionable as the original threat of Prussianism which it was designed to meet.

Moreover, subsequent history suggests that there was no particular virtue in the Rhine frontier as such anyway. It had dazzled the French imagination for three centuries, and Foch and his generals talked as though its mere acquisition would solve the problem of French security out of hand. But the fate of the Maginot and Siegfried Lines, and indeed all the military events of 1939–45, suggest that a Rhine frontier,

[1] For this view see particularly Etienne Mantoux, *The Carthaginian Peace.*

C

33

especially with a large, disaffected German population inside it, would have been an obstacle no more insuperable than any other; and that the French dream of permanent safety by military means was a chimera. Nor is there any validity in the argument constantly put forward by the generals that a more thorough defeat of Germany could have done the trick: a full-scale invasion and a triumphal march through the Brandenburger Tor into Berlin. The plain fact is that in November, 1918, the generals were doubtful enough of their ability to defeat a German army standing desperately at bay on the frontiers of the Fatherland to grasp thankfully at an Armistice. Though later they said they would have gone on had they known how weak German morale really was, the fact remains that when Foch was asked, on June 15, 1919, to enforce the peace terms by making his march to Berlin with nothing but a disarmed and demoralised Germany in front of him he declared it impossible, and Pétain endorsed his opinion.[1] Three years later again he met a similar demand by pointing out that Berlin was further from the Rhine than Paris was, and such an operation, in the teeth of German passive resistance, would be 'to renew Napoleon's errors and follies'.[2]

But there was truth, too, in the French thesis that a Wilsonian solution was altogether too trusting and naïf. One of the main arguments put forward by Brockdorff-Rantzau and the German delegation against the terms of the Treaty when they were at last allowed to see it was that to sign so humiliating and vicious a document would fatally condemn the already precarious government of the Weimar Republic and open wide the road to power for either Communist or military dictatorship. The Clemenceau school would have turned this argument against itself and have retorted that German democracy and the Weimar government were a fake anyway: a façade set up to conciliate English and American opinion, existing only on sufferance until it was safe to set up something less palatable. In view of what has come to light since, of the indisputable evidence of the evasion of the disarmament clauses of the Treaty and the preservation of all that might assist a swift rearmament, it is impossible to say that it would have been safe to trust to a German change of heart in 1918. The generals, 'organising sympathy', and developing the legend of the 'stab in the back', were throughout perfectly confident

[1] Liddell Hart, *Foch, Man of Orleans*, Vol. II, p. 447 (Penguin Edn.).
[2] *Ib.*, p. 459.

that, with the alliance of the great industrialists, they could at any suitable moment resume control. The Weimar government was far more dependent on their sufferance than its champions and historians have been prepared to admit.

It can be seen now that it might have been possible to have the best of both these worlds: to underwrite the disarmament of Germany with the severest sanctions which could be devised, and at the same time to set about rehabilitating her and reinstalling her in the comity of civilized nations with all possible generosity. What was in fact achieved by the impact of these three so diverse personalities on each other in the overheated rooms of the Hotel Majestic was the worst of both worlds. Compromise all along the line meant only that every salutary severity was enfeebled by qualifying definitions and every generous intention vitiated by galling safeguards. The Germans were left with much real grievance and perfect material for manufacturing more. The French were cheated of the security to which they had sacrificed so much else. The Americans withdrew altogether from Europe for the time being in disgust; and the British people, as it came to its senses, allowed sympathy for German grievances and a feeling of shame for having helped to cause them to obscure all other aspects of the European situation for nearly twenty fatal years.

For the first month of the discussions things went slowly, but fairly smoothly. The Arab dream of a great united desert empire, sedulously fostered by Colonel Lawrence, was summarily dispelled, and the Arab states were handed over to the victorious powers to be held as mandated territories under the general supervision and responsibility of the League of Nations until they should be fit for self-government. The German colonies were declared forfeit, though no convincing evidence of misgovernment could be brought forward to justify the decision, and they were similarly mandated. But the great work of this first period was the Covenant of the League of Nations, which the President was anxious to take with him as some practical evidence of progress when he paid a short visit to Washington in February. Fortunately there was a draft to hand, thanks to General Smuts who, having started as a provincial and rebellious Boer, had transformed himself into a great imperialist, and was now fast becoming the first and greatest of what might one day be a new kind of man—a citizen of the world. Smuts had seized on the somewhat nebulous pronouncements scattered through Wilson's Fourteen Points and speeches, and in a 71-page memorandum hammered them into a form which might prove workable, and which Wilson himself had already approved.

A final form of Covenant, to be approved by a special plenary session of the delegates on the very eve of the President's departure, was not achieved without dispute. French logic insisted that the League, to be effective, must be equipped with an armed force of its own, and thereby brought British and Americans face to face with a problem which they were to do their best to dodge for the next twenty years. For Lloyd George dared not pledge the British fleet to foreign control in unforeseeable circumstances, and the President of the United States was constitutionally and specifically forbidden to pledge armed forces of any kind in this way. Wilson himself had written to Colonel House the previous March that, 'Any attempt to begin by putting executive authority into the hands of a group of powers would be to sow a harvest of jealousy and mistrust which would spring up and choke the whole thing. The United States Senate would never ratify such a treaty.'[1] Since then he had, nevertheless, allowed House to put out a tentative scheme and the immediately hostile reaction of American opinion had been shown clearly in the Congressional elections in November. The French and the League protagonists had therefore to be content with an emasculated 16th Article which laid down that the Council would, when necessary, 'recommend' to member states what 'effective military, naval or air force' they should contribute to deal with an aggressor, but which said nothing of any obligation on member states to comply with such a recommendation.

Thus, even in this early, comparatively halcyon phase, there were already signs of fundamental differences in outlook which, when Reparations came to be discussed in March, would go near to wrecking the conference altogether. The dispute which most decisively underlined the divergent points of view, and which was to give the Germans one of their most substantial and unanswerable grievances, came over the supply of food to the enemy's civilian population, already near starvation in November. The Armistice had provided for 'the provisioning of Germany to the extent that shall be deemed necessary',

[1] Quoted in D. C. Somervell, *The Reign of King George V*, p. 235.

and the blockade was theoretically relaxed. One of Winston Churchill's first thoughts had been 'to send six fat food ships to Hamburg'. But the French had blocked all Germany's reserve of gold marks and her remaining holdings of foreign investments as being earmarked for the first payments of Reparations; there were no other exportable resources in Germany with which food could be bought, and for two months she was left to starve. It was a cruel winter, bitterly cold, and there was no coal. Influenza was raging already when the Armistice was signed, and the sight of sick and dying children in the Rhineland so sickened the English occupation troops that some awareness of the scandal penetrated even to an England already sinking back into a comfortable remoteness from continental affairs. But Germany continued to starve for four months before Lloyd George was at last roused, on March 8th, to a passionate outburst against which even Clemenceau's imperturbability could not stand. It was decided to release the gold; but the French— and it was typical of much of their diplomatic method in this period— insisted that the Germans should not be informed of this until they had formally agreed to hand over their merchant navy, without which the food could not be transported. Fortunately at this point the French hope that the Germans, ignorant of the decision about the gold, would refuse the ships and so provoke further delays was frustrated by Keynes and the British Admiralty, and the Germans at last got their food.[1]

A complete account of negotiations so tortuous as those of Paris would need many volumes; but this mixture of ruthlessness and trickery in the French proceedings, which often baffled Lloyd George as well as Wilson, needs underlining for two reasons: it provided the Germans later with a mass of well-founded grievances; and it did much to alienate British sympathy in the following years as the facts became known. A similar technique can be seen at work on the question, perhaps even more important in its after-effects of the union of Austria with Germany —the Anschluss. Cut off suddenly from the rest of the Austrian Empire and saddled with a great imperial capital in Vienna which their territories could scarcely feed, the German Austrians were in an almost impossible position. King George V had foreseen the problem and had written anxiously to Balfour even before the Armistice, suggesting that Austria must be given a port on the Adriatic to prevent her from be-

[1] For an admirable account of these negotiations see Keynes, *Two Memoirs*.

coming wholly dependent on Germany. Balfour had answered that the Allies had so categorically proclaimed the principle of self-determination that he did not see how the Anschluss could be prevented if the Austrians really wanted it. Such compensation to the Germans in man-power and territory for their lost provinces of Alsace-Lorraine was wholly unacceptable to the French, but the issue was here so clear that their objections were overruled. Unfortunately, as the price of giving way, Clemenceau was able to obtain the concession—apparently inno-cuous—that the Anschluss should not go through until it had been formally approved by the Council of the League, which seemed to in-volve no more than an unimportant postponement. Only too late was it remembered that the Covenant required the Council's vote on such a matter to be unanimous, and that the French had provided themselves with an absolute veto on the Anschluss, and Hitler some years later with one of his most powerful weapons. Austria was left to struggle out of her difficulties as best she could, and as late as November, 1919, King George was again protesting to the Foreign Office, this time at the shocking conditions which were being allowed to continue in Vienna, where the people were still on the verge of starvation.

But in the dishonest muddle which was made of the business of Re-parations the British must be held equally guilty with the French. On this point, hatred of the Germans and the desire to 'make the brutes pay' submerged not only all decent feeling, but all common sense. The basis of the claim was to be found, fairly enough, in the Fourteen Points, and was specifically reiterated in the Armistice terms. The Allied governments, it was there said, felt 'that no doubt ought to exist' as to what was meant when the Germans were required to restore as well as evacuate all occupied territory: Germany would be required to compensate 'all damage done to the civilian population of the Allies and to their property by the aggression of Germany by land, by sea, and by the air'. This was understood to include all air-raid damage and all merchant shipping losses; and beyond this, the President's speeches had promised, there would be 'no contributions' and 'no punitive damages'. This was clearly something very different from the impression given, even by Lloyd George, to an electorate wholly ignorant of economic fact, that Germany would be held liable to the Allies for the total cost of the war and would meet it 'up to the limit of her capacity'. French politicians had gone even further in extravagant promises to their voters, and both governments were clearly pledged to two irreconcilable theses.

The first disastrous emendation of the Armistice Reparation claim seems to have sprung from a well-intentioned accident. For General Smuts, angered that Britain, who for the past two years had borne the major burden of the war and had suffered by far the greatest economic loss, should be able to claim for so much less material damage than the French, suggested that separation allowances paid to dependants of soldiers and all pensions to widows and to disabled men could properly be classed as 'damage done to the civilian population'. It was a very specious argument, and one which Lloyd George seized on eagerly enough, since it gave him the chance to make the sort of claim which would alone satisfy the electorate. Both assumed in the first place that they were in no way increasing Germany's liability. That, they thought, could be worked out on the basis of what Germany could reasonably be asked to pay; and the various claims of the Allies would then be scaled down in proportion to this total. All that he was trying to get was a bigger share of the total for Britain.

But by the time that President Wilson reluctantly accepted pensions and allowances as justifiable damage on April 1st, three months of intensive and competitive debate by various committees on Germany's capacity to pay had produced a bewildering mass of conflicting estimates among which the original principles laid down in the Armistice had almost disappeared from sight. To a generation which has had perforce to grasp the basic economic principles governing foreign trade and foreign exchange, a detailed account of these discussions among responsible public men, experts as well as politicians, is scarcely credible; and no summary can do justice to the fantasia of the reality.

When Lloyd George went to Paris he had in his pocket three different estimates of what Germany might reasonably be expected to pay, as an overall sum, in Reparations. The first, whose reasoning and conclusions have never been successfully challenged, was the work of a Treasury committee on which Keynes was the dominating influence. A reasonable claim for the total Allied bill of damages under the Armistice terms seemed to them to be about £4,000 million. But, after a careful analysis of Germany's pre-war industrial and commercial position and having regard to the facts that she would be deprived of her most profitable iron-fields in Alsace-Lorraine and of some of her best coalfields in Silesia, of all her colonies, of the bulk of her mercantile marine and much of her railway rolling stock, and that all her equipment and plant was out of repair and obsolete, the Treasury view was that £3,000 million was the most that could be exacted, and that it would be safer to count on no more than £2,000 million. It had been generally agreed that Germany should not be asked for more than could be paid off in a generation, which was reckoned in practice as thirty years, and on that basis this was already a huge figure, nearly ten times what France had been asked to pay in 1870, and representing, at 5% interest, an annual charge of £100 million until the principal could be paid off. Some idea of the effort and sacrifice to be demanded of a generation of Germans may be gained by comparison with the £35 million a year which Great Britain in 1931 found it impossible to go on paying as debt settlement to the United States, though she suffered at that time from none of the major handicaps laid on Germany in 1918. But an estimate separately prepared by the Board of Trade reached roughly the same conclusion, and the figure was not, at any rate, chimerical.

The third estimate in Lloyd George's possession had resulted from the intense dissatisfaction of Mr. W. M. Hughes, the Australian Prime Minister and a member of the War Cabinet, with the Treasury report. Though entirely unqualified, he ridiculed these figures and so consistently maintained that Germany could be made to pay the whole cost of the war that Lloyd George appointed him to preside over yet another committee, on which politics, banking, political economy, and the City were all represented, the most influential member being Lord Cunliffe, the recently retired Governor of the Bank of England. On what basis this committee calculated nobody knows. But it put the cost of the war to the Allies at £24,000 million, and saw no reason why Germany should not pay £1,200 million a year, which would mean finding in all £40,000 million to discharge both principal and interest within a generation. Apparently sublimely unaware of the conditions governing payments between nations, the committee blandly reported that 'the fear of economic ill effects on the Allied countries from the repayment of the costs of the war is not well-founded'. Still more surprising, *The Economist*, in articles on December 7th, 1918, and April 5th, 1919, confirmed this view, though Keynes easily demonstrated that, to create the surplus of exports over imports needed to pay the interest alone, Germany would have to capture more than half the English export market and the whole of the French.

Hughes clearly never grasped the basic conditions of foreign exchange, and his arguments when he was challenged were puerile. How Cunliffe, with his banking experience, can have been brought to approve these figures nobody has ever explained: the family legend states merely that it was his habit to think things like that out in Church, during the sermon. Lloyd George, it would appear from his own accounts, was downright dishonest. In his 1932 book, *The Truth about Reparations and War Debts*, he shelters behind the experts and points out that the bankers, not 'the fire-eating politicians', boosted the figures to these absurd heights. But in 1939, in his *Memoirs of the Peace Conference*, he wrote that both he and Bonar Law regarded the Hughes-Cunliffe Report 'as a wild and fantastic chimera'.[1] This is certainly the truth, and it makes it inexcusable that he used their figures, of which he had advance information, for electioneering purposes and six weeks later nominated Hughes and Cunliffe, together with Lord Sumner, a judge of impeccable probity but no financial experience, to represent Britain on the Reparations Commission in Paris.

It is unnecessary to follow in any detail the four months of futile discussion which followed on the Reparations Commission and between the Commission and the Council of Four—Clemenceau, Wilson, Lloyd George, and the Italian, Orlando—who in March took over direction of the conference and thereafter debated in secret. The French Finance Minister, M. Klotz, the only Jew he had ever met, Clemenceau said, who knew nothing of finance, was prepared to meet Lord Cunliffe with figures for French war damage even more astronomically inflated. He put the cost of restoring the devastated areas alone at £5,360 million; and though M. Loucheur, the French representative on the Commission, scaled this down to £3,000 million even that figure was nearly four times what it actually cost in the end to re-equip the devastated territories on a far more luxurious scale than that of 1914. Even Loucheur and the 'Heavenly Twins', Cunliffe and Sumner, could not produce

---

[1] This is taken from the American Edn. of 1939. The earlier version, published in England in 1938, was entitled *The Truth about the Peace Treaties*.

figures high enough to satisfy statesmen anxious to placate hysterical constituents and supporters. Indeed, feeling in the House of Commons ran so high that at the beginning of April Bonar Law felt that, as Leader of the House, he was losing control. A certain Colonel Charles Lowther, who had distinguished himself in 1901 by demanding that the Boers should be made to pay in full for that war, led off with a fighting speech demanding £25,000 million from Germany and Reparations payments to last until 1969. 'If we allow Germany the chance of recuperating,' he ended up, 'if we allow pity and sentiment to run riot, as sure as I stand here, that country will never rest until it has ground us underfoot. Let us never give her the chance.' A few days later Mr. Kennedy Jones, Northcliffe's henchman in the Commons, sent a telegram to Lloyd George, as from 370 Conservative members, urging him to stand firm for payment in full.[1]

Lloyd George slipped over from Paris and dealt with the revolt in one of his happiest speeches. But even before this, under the pressure of this public opinion at home, ceaselessly exercised through Cunliffe and Sumner, the strong men who were going to make Germany pay, he had reached the conclusion that it would be best in the end to name no figure at all in the Treaty, but to stake a claim for payment in full and leave it to a Reparations Committee to work out details later; and Norman Davis, the American Treasury representative, agreed. 'If we can quiet down the Heavenly Twins', he said, 'by agreeing any fool report for the Three, and then get rid of them by winding up the Commission, we can get around with some human beings and start quite afresh.'[2] Already in February the first step had been taken towards manœuvring the President out of his absolute insistence on the Armistice Reparations clauses, which all concerned had perfectly understood when they had signed them. The Americans persuaded the French to abate their claim for the whole cost of the war on the grounds that they would actually get a bigger share of what Germany could finally pay by limiting all claims to damage actually suffered. But, to make things easier for the French ministers *vis-à-vis* their own public, Wilson was persuaded to allow a clause to appear in the Treaty in which Germany accepted liability for the full cost of the war, though it was understood

[1] The mood of this period has been very well studied in R. B. McCallum, *Public Opinion and the last Peace*, 1944.
[2] R. F. Harrod, *op. cit.*, p. 236.

that she would not be asked to pay more than what had been agreed in the Armistice terms. So, without anyone, even Keynes, realising what its ideological and practical consequences would be, the famous War Guilt clause was slipped into the Treaty as Article 231:

> Germany accepts responsibility for causing all the loss and damage to which the Allied and Associated Powers and their nationals have been subjected in consequence of the war imposed on them by the aggression of Germany and her allies.

This by itself, though wounding to German self-esteem, need have done no practical harm so long as the total claim eventually made was limited to damage actually suffered. But Smuts's memorandum, accepted by Wilson on April 1st, drove a second breach into the American position by persuading the President that it was reasonable to include pensions and separation allowances as actual damage suffered. This was much more dangerous. It laid the Allies open to an accusation of breach of faith and it also opened the field to the swollen estimates of Cunliffe and Sumner and the exaggerated clamour of Colonel Lowther. But there was still the safeguard that Germany was not to be asked for more than could reasonably be paid off in a single generation, so that the German grievance would still be only theoretical. On April 5th this last bastion fell. Although Davis told the Council of Four quite clearly that the President had conceded pensions only on the understanding that they 'would not materially increase the actual amount Germany would have to pay', the clause defining the thirty-year limit, the only remaining safeguard for this condition, was that day dropped from the Treaty. Wilson was ill and was represented at the discussion by House, and he probably did not realise until much later the real effect of this decision. Most of the others concerned had reached the same weary conclusion as Lloyd George. Despairing of any immediate agreement on actual figures, they preferred to leave the detailed claim to be settled by experts when public opinion in France and Britain had cooled down and it would be possible to talk sense.

But the floodgates had been opened. The war-guilt clause stood, laying on Germany unlimited liability, while the claims piled up unrestrainedly in Annexe I to the Treaty, condemning Germany to incalculable forfeitures and, if she seriously sought to meet the claims, permanent economic enslavement. The confiscations thereupon enforced deprived her of the means both of making any immediate payment of reparation and of recovering economically sufficiently to make any payment in the future. She forfeited her merchant shipping, a large proportion of her railway rolling-stock, all her holdings of foreign investment, whether publicly or privately owned, and all her gold, the sources of 75% of her pre-war iron ore and 75% of her zinc. She forfeited her colonies, but remained liable for the capital debts incurred in developing them, in the building of railways and so forth. For much damage she was to pay twice over. In compensation for the ruin of their own coal mines the French were, quite reasonably, given the Saar coalfield for fifteen years. But the Germans had then to make up to France as well the difference between her pre- and post-war coal output to the amount of 20 million tons a year for five years and of 8 million tons for a further five years. With additional forfeitures to Italy, Belgium, and Luxembourg, the loss of the Saar and of minefields in Silesia, Germany was in fact condemned to lose half her pre-war coal output. She was to run her industry, which alone could create the exports to pay for Reparations, on half the amount of coal which in 1914 had barely sufficed, and that only if her exhausted, starving and demoralised miners could maintain the 1914 level of production, which they clearly could not.

A full catalogue of the stupidity and self-defeating greed embodied in Annexe I would make dreary reading. Keynes's blistering analysis of it in *The Economic Consequences of the Peace*, written in the white heat of passion in 1919, has never on its economic side been seriously challenged,[1] and all subsequent investigation has tended to confirm both his facts and figures and his conclusions. This book by what M. Tardieu called 'the pro-German scribe from Cambridge' whose estimates 'overstep the limits of permissible foolery' and 'only make fun of Germany's victims', shaped the opinions on Versailles of a whole generation of Englishmen. It made them aware of the downright dishonesty and injustice of the economic clauses of the Treaty and so permanently clouded their judgement of legitimate French fears and difficulties and blinded them altogether to the menace which lay behind the German complaints. They came to share the German resentment that

[1] Except, perhaps, in M. Mantoux's book already quoted, and his economic arguments are effectively disposed of by Sir Roy Harrod, *Life of John Maynard Keynes*, pp. 275–8.

one nation alone should be saddled with the responsibility for the war. They forgot the terms in which even Keynes had condemned the Germans' 'reckless self-regard' and remembered only that the Allies had cheated on the Armistice terms, had given the Germans no chance to negotiate, but faced them with what they called a 'Diktat', and had excluded them as pariahs from the League at a moment when it was necessary above all things to rehabiliate them and reincorporate them in the brotherhood of nations.

Moreover this lasting sense of guilt towards the Germans has tended to obscure the fact that the French emerged from the Versailles settlement with grievances which proved in the long run to be better founded than those of the Germans. It gets forgotten that within five years the experts were at work scaling down German liabilities even beyond what Keynes had thought reasonable and American bankers were stepping in to give Germany that generous help in industrial capital for which he had pleaded in vain to Wilson. In the end the Germans paid only £1,000 million in Reparations, or half Keynes's lowest reasonable estimate, while they drew from America and private investors elsewhere loans which were never repaid totalling £3,000 million—three times what Wilson had been asked to lend them in 1918. But France was cheated altogether of the security guarantees she had asked for. She was induced to surrender her permanent claim to the left bank of the Rhine, by the offer of a joint guarantee by Britain and America against German aggression. But the American Senate refused to underwrite the President's commitment; and the British thereupon withdrew theirs, so that France was left exposed to a rapidly recovering Germany with nothing but the hesitating goodwill of her sometime allies to depend on. French fears and grievances, and the truculence which resulted from them, were never understood in England and came to be merely resented as a prolongation of the injustice and hypocrisy of Versailles. So the Treaty achieved the worst of all available worlds: festering and legitimate grievances both in Germany and France; guilt and uncertainty in Britain which would prevent the use of the harsh sanctions of the Treaty, when they legitimately and properly ought to have been used, to prevent German rearmament, because they had already been misused by the French to enforce Reparations. In the upshot the Allies lost both the goodwill which might have resulted from a generous treaty and the safety which might have been ensured by a severe one intelligently enforced. They had, indeed, in the words of a French friend of Keynes, laid the foundations 'd'une guerre juste et durable'.

The last act of the tragedy was played out, of course, not at Versailles but in Washington. Already, in the spring of 1918, when he was hammering out the first plans for a League of Nations, Wilson had been made aware of the difficulties which a traditional American isolationism would make for the project. He had been forced to drop from his plan the idea of an armed force permanently at the League's disposal—the idea which the French had sought in vain to revive at Paris. Since then Wilson had lost still more ground. An ill-judged election manifesto which seemed to claim war and victory as exclusively Democratic achievements had done more harm than good, and he was faced by 1919 with a Republic majority in the Senate. Disgust with the actual terms of the Treaty grew throughout 1919, and there was increasing reluctance to accept the surrender of sovereign initiative involved in the Covenant. Wilson himself broke down half-way through a great propaganda tour of the Middle West which might just have saved the day, and he was unable from his sick-bed to rally the forces which he needed. Even with a conciliatory Democratic amendment which would have preserved to Congress entire freedom of action on any League recommendation, the Treaty, and with it the Covenant of the League, failed to get the two-thirds majority vote needed in the Senate on March 19th, 1920.

So the League of Nations started its life under the grave handicap that three of the potentially most powerful nations in the world, the United States, Germany, and Russia, were not members. It had been designed as a machine for the peaceable revision and adjustment of discrepancies and injustices in international affairs. But, thanks to a closely woven system of alliances among the new small powers of Central Europe, the French were able to use it largely to preserve the Versailles Treaty at all costs, injustices and all, and to use it as a substitute for the guarantees of which they had been disappointed. This in turn undermined the faith of many Englishmen in the efficacy of the League and created a certain reluctance to entrust it with the power to be effective in a crisis. But these trends lay in the future; and for the moment, truncated as it was, the League appeared to most thinking Englishmen the only post-war institution which might eventually, in spite of critical set-backs, bring Smuts's new world to birth.

A lesser, but none the less very important consequence of the American refusal to ratify the Treaty, was their withdrawal from the Reparations Commission. All those who opposed the punitive demands of the French had pinned their hopes to this body which, in a cooler atmosphere than that of 1919 Paris, would be able to moderate the grotesquely inflated claims of Versailles. With an American Treasury representative in the chair, this would undoubtedly have occurred. Without him, the chairmanship went to France and with it the absolute control of the Commission. For the Belgian representative always voted with the French for the maximum demands on Germany, and, even if Great Britain and Italy stood out for sanity, the French had the chairman's casting vote and so always prevailed. So the Reparations Commission became merely a machine for prolonging the worst follies of Annexe I.

The remaining treaties, St. Germain with the Republic of Austria, in September, 1919; Trianon which established a new and much shrunken Kingdom of Hungary, though without a king; Neuilly with Bulgaria, and Sèvres which purported to settle the new frontiers of Turkey, though disastrous in their general effect of Balkanising the whole of Central Europe, were not of intimate concern to Great Britain. It was found impossible along those wavering racial frontiers to apply the principle of self-determination with any precision, and all the 'succession states' were left with racial minorities, most of which were treated very badly. This was particularly true of the German frontier of Poland and the Polish corridor to the sea at Danzig, which became a free city under international jurisdiction. There were the seeds here of many possible wars, and one overwhelming danger. Germany was surrounded with small powers too weak to defend themselves should she ever recover her strength, and too aggressively nationalist and quarrelsome to stand together effectively for safety. Out of them France wove her Little Entente whom she helped with arms and munitions as a desperate remedy for the insecurity which obsessed her. For the moment they represented only one more problem of reconstruction for overworked European statesmen, very remote from the preoccupations of the Englishman of 1920.

The Treaty of Versailles

On June 28th, 1919, the Germans, after a moment of terrifying hesitation in which they threatened to call what was by then a gigantic Allied bluff, protestingly signed the Treaty in the Hall of the Mirrors at Versailles where the German Empire itself had come into being in 1871. The next day King George went in person to the station to meet Lloyd George and drive him back to Buckingham Palace amid scenes of great enthusiasm. It was a summer of parades and reviews, culminating in the great Victory Parade on July 19th—'the most impressive sight', the King wrote, 'I have ever seen'; and slowly, with a good deal of discomfort and disorganisation, England settled back to peace.

CHAPTER 3

Peace, Boom, and Slump

The Versailles negotiations had kept Mr. Lloyd George abroad almost continuously until the summer, and even after that he was not much in England. He appeared in the House of Commons for occasional forays, such as the crushing of the Lowther revolt, but it was November, 1919, before he was present, for the first time since the Armistice, to answer questions in the House. Moreover Versailles had given him a taste for conducting foreign affairs at what would nowadays be called the summit, so that in the following years he was constantly preoccupied with continental conferences, travelling about Europe with the swollen secretariat housed, when in England, in the hutment area behind 10 Downing Street which earned it the nickname of 'the Garden Suburb'. This not only infuriated his Foreign Secretary, Lord Curzon, who had succeeded Balfour in October, and who quite rightly protested that it introduced an element of great confusion into British foreign policy; it also meant that the Prime Minister's interest in the problems of reconstruction at home was intermittent and perfunctory. The energy which had galvanised into activity first the Ministry of Munitions, and then the whole British war effort from 1916–18, was diverted elsewhere.

The justification for the election of 1918 and the preparation of the Coalition had been the cry that the men—and more especially the man —who had won the war should win the peace; and that meant not merely settling Europe, but resettling Britain. He had promised the electors of Wolverhampton in November, 1918, that slums should be swept away, agriculture revitalised, and the people brought back to the land, and that 'inhuman conditions and wretchedness must surrender like the German fleet'. But he brought to these tasks none of the administrative bustle and zeal of his wartime days; and oracular, metaphorical pronouncements, such as the speech with which he closed the first session of Parliament in August, were no substitute. 'Navigation is difficult and dangerous,' he said. 'Some seek to help; some lie prostrate and weary. Some try to upset the boat, either because they dislike the steersman, or want to steer themselves, or because they prefer some crazy craft of their own. With a clear eye and steady hand we will row through into calmer and bluer waters, but we must know where we are rowing. The Government have done their best to give a direction. Let all who will man the boat and save the nation.' But most of the steering was in point of fact left to Mr. Bonar Law who, honest, straightforward and admirable as he was as Leader of the House, himself confessed that the only two subjects which ever stirred him to real passion were Ulster Unionism and Tariff Reform. Nor was there any impulse to reform—any discernible intention to jump in and 'man the boat'—in that very second-rate House of Commons.

The result was that, although the war system of a small, inner cabinet had been perpetuated for the very purpose of directing the work of reconstruction, the government in fact did very little to give a lead, and the colleagues left to cope at home had a difficult time of it. The first department to run into trouble was the War Office, where Churchill had hurriedly to be transferred from dismantling the munitions industry to salvage his predecessor's far too intelligent demobilisation scheme. Priorities had been worked out during the last year of the war so that key men should come out first to make the reabsorption of the rank and file into industry as smooth as possible. But since the key men had often been the last to be spared for active service, the scheme ran up against the basic British sense of justice. Sickened by years of mud and misery, and still more by the spit-and-polish atmosphere of peace-time soldiering and by the continuation of poor food and uncomfortable billets which only the emergency of war had made tolerable, the ordinary 'temporary' soldier was merely longing for home. The sight of slick types, only combed out of industry to meet the crisis of 1918, getting instant priority for demobilisation was too much for him. There were serious disturbances and some actual mutinies: at Calais the R.A.S.C. and R.A.O.C. struck and 2,000 infantrymen formed a soviet; and only brilliant handling by Lord Byng retrieved the situation without blood-shed. Five battalions of Guardsmen marched from Shoreham to present a list of grievances to the Mayor of Brighton, and there were demobilisa-tion riots at Luton. The government weathered the crisis. Demobili-sation was speeded up to a rate of 50,000 a month, selected on the principle of 'first in, first out', and an entirely new army of 900,000 men was raised for the tedious business of garrisoning the Rhineland.

This was not an auspicious start, but the government had one stroke of unexpected luck. Instead of the slump confidently predicted, there was a wild trade boom. High wartime wages and the shortage of goods had produced a good deal of enforced saving which, with demobilisa-tion gratuities, gave men a false sense of prosperity, so that for eighteen months there was a wild spending spree during which manufacturers could sell any kind of goods as fast as they could produce them. In con-sequence the returning troops and the now redundant munition workers were absorbed into industry with unexpected ease. The number of unemployed remained about 300,000, which mostly repre-sented the norm of seasonal and temporary unemployment, and their difficulties were solved by extending to all manual workers save agricultural labourers and domestic servants the benefits of the Un-employment Insurance scheme of 1911. Unfortunately the respite thus granted was not used for the formulation of any constructive policy. A beginning was made by Dr. Addison to implement the promise of 'homes fit for heroes' with a plan for building 350,000 houses, to be subsidised partly by the central, partly by local government. This was, in fact, far too few houses, and they proved extremely expensive, but they were at least built. There the creative contribution of the govern-ment came to an end. It faced in fact a dilemma which, given the type of supporter it had to rely on in the Commons, it could not solve.

On the one hand there was, in spite of the boom, an almost universal discontent among the working population of the country. Of a number of factors causing this, two were probably of major importance. One was the mood of the returning troops, resentful of any form of discipline and feeling strongly that the nation owed them a cushy job and a high rate of pay as some compensation for the mud, vermin, discomfort, danger, and relative poverty which they had endured, some of them for years. It did not, of course, work out like that. By and large the service man was less valuable in any industry than the man who had seen no service; and the longer and harder a man's service had been, the more likely he was to be suffering from the cumulative effects of shell-shock, wound disabilities, or an addiction to drinking spirits, all unfitting him for the more responsible and better-paid jobs. There was also a strong feeling that the state which had with apparent ease found £7 million a day to run the war could very well afford to spend some similar sum to ensure a decent living for those who, while the emergency lasted, had been taught to regard themselves as national heroes.

A different, but equally sour spirit pervaded those who had stayed at home in reserved occupations and essential industries, such as munition workers, miners, and railwaymen. All these had been employed, directly or indirectly, by the government for the duration of the war, and they were not prepared without a struggle to surrender the high level of guaranteed wages and the improved working conditions which they had been enjoying. The miners, in particular, had every reason to fear a return to pre-war conditions in an industry which had begun to feel the effects of foreign competition before the turn of the century. There was infinite variation in standards of wages and conditions between good and bad pits, between long-established, almost worked-out coalfields and areas of recent development like South Yorkshire, and between collieries where the management was prosperous or intelligent enough to install modern equipment, and those which took what profit there was without regard to the welfare of the industry or of the workers. War had given the miners guaranteed national wage rates, and they were determined to preserve them if they could by insisting on nationalisation. They, perhaps, more than any other body of workers, justified the claim made by Arthur Henderson and G. D. H. Cole in a report to the Labour Research Society in 1919 that the many small grievances and troubles in industry were really part of a much larger discontent with 'the whole existing structure of capitalist industry'. The railwaymen, under the lively and spectacular leadership of J. H. Thomas, were equally determined to keep if they could the benefits of wartime nationalisation.

There were, of course, all sorts of other causes of grievance and discontent, one being the fact that the rush to buy in the boom sent prices up more steeply even than during the war, and wages never quite caught up with them. The result, in any event, was an unparalleled wave of strikes. There were over 2,000 separate stoppages in 1919 and 1920; and in 1919 32 million days' work were lost, which meant that an average of 100,000 men had been out on strike every day throughout the year. In August, 1919, there was even a police strike, not very serious in London, but in Liverpool bringing half the force out without notice and causing a good deal of rioting and disorder until the army was called in to restore the situation. In this case the government acted with a proper firmness: and strikers were dismissed and forfeited their pensions. Otherwise its handling of the situation was fumbling and uncertain. When, also in July, there occurred one of the periodical stoppages in the Yorkshire coalfield, 1,500 naval ratings were rushed north to replace the safety men in the pits, while a temporary settlement of the vexed question of hours and wages was reached with commendable speed. But the negotiations with the railwaymen were grossly mishandled by Sir Auckland Geddes, the Minister of Reconstruction. The engineers and firemen secured an entirely satisfactory agreement as to the rates they were to get when the government's wartime bonus was withdrawn at the beginning of 1920. Thomas presented similarly reasonable demands for the N.U.R., designed to leave the unskilled men roughly at the same rate relative to the skilled as they had received in 1914. After long and unnecessary delay, Geddes retorted in September with an offer, which he described as 'definitive', which would leave them some 15% worse off; and Thomas, losing patience, brought the railways to a standstill for nine days, thereby forcing a resumption of negotiations and a settlement based on a sliding scale related to the cost of living which proved to have solved the problem for the next 20 years. The public was vastly inconvenienced. Lloyd George denounced the strike as 'an anarchist conspiracy', and Thomas may have acted somewhat hastily. But he was concerned to keep the confidence of the men he represented, and the entire blame for the breakdown of the negotiations undoubtedly lay with Geddes.

All this led to a strong, though quite unjustified feeling among the propertied classes that the country was moving rapidly towards revolution. Mr. Cole and some of his friends, with their eyes on events in Russia, were talking in a sinister way of the inevitability of a class war. There had been a remarkable—to many an alarming—rise in the total

Trade Union membership, from two and a half million in 1910 to six and a half in 1918 and eight and a quarter million in 1920; and a group in the Trade Union Congress, calling themselves the Council of Action, were claiming that they, 'sprung from the loins of the common people', were far more genuinely representative of the nation than the House of Commons. There was indeed a wavering in the direction of non-parliamentary, revolutionary action, but it only represented a serious threat while the Labour movement remained divided within itself. Sylvia Pankhurst who, in search of further excitement, had joined the Communist Party, was, somewhat illogically after suffering so much to get women the vote, clamouring for non-co-operation with Parliament. But Lenin, who knew a revolutionary situation when he saw one, damped her down. 'To renounce participation in parliamentary elections is a mistake,' he wrote.[1]

It was not surprising that Conservatives, and even Liberals, should develop an obsessive fear of the spread of Russian Communism. The news of the murder of the Tsar and his family, the fact that British troops were still engaged in 1919 round Leningrad helping one of the many White Russian armies which sought to displace Lenin, and the knowledge that the Comintern was specifically organised to control the spread of the revolution throughout the world naturally drove the propertied classes to see sinister and far-reaching designs behind the wave of strikes, which were only in fact a symptom of post-war malaise. Even in Labour circles there was a fear that the unions might transfer their allegiance from their own increasingly sober moderation to something headier, infected by what William Paul called 'a breath from Moscow, a breath from the east, where there is wisdom'.[2] They were quite right, of course, to treat offers of Communist support as very Greek gifts indeed. 'Support Henderson', ran Lenin's instruction to the Communist Convention at the Cannon Street Hotel in July, 1920, 'as a rope supports the hanged.' But where they were all wrong was in underestimating the insularity, the conservatism, and the patience of the English worker. Only on the Celtic fringe, among the Clydeside and Liverpool Irish and in the coalfields of Fife and South Wales, did the Communist Party get any permanent hold; and even then the membership never rose beyond

[1] Pelling, *The British Communist Party*, p. 6.
[2] Speech to the Leeds convention, 1922, Pelling, p. 4.

10,000 at any time before 1931. It is perhaps significant that their solitary Member of Parliament was called Saklatvala, and there was a slight element of farce in their solemn conventions: the Cannon Street meeting of 1920, which was gravely assured by a gentleman named Macmanus that it was 'the lesson of history that it is never the revolutionary who is responsible for the shedding of blood; it is invariably the counter-revolutionary'; or the Convention which formally founded the Communist Party of Great Britain in 1922 at the Victory Hotel in Leeds, conspiratorially booked for a conference of the National Fruiterers' Association.

All the same, there were real dangers lurking in the situation of the coal industry, and some realisation of this penetrated even to the House of Commons. The strikes of 1920 were mainly concerned with technical formulae too recondite for the average layman to understand. The miners had been granted an hour off the working day, and the difficulty was to decide the percentage increase of piece-rate wages which would fairly compensate their loss of earnings. Some idea of the complexity of the issue may be gathered from the formula finally agreed in July, 1919, that: where $11 \cdot 1\% =$ the reduction in output over the whole country, $47 =$ the average loss of minutes in working time, $Q =$ the percentage reduction in time for any given class of workmen, and $X =$ the percentage amount of advance in wages, then $X = \dfrac{11 \cdot 1 \times Q}{47}$. The figure 47 became the crux of most of the argument, and came to be known as *the constant*. The miners stood out for $46 \cdot 8$ and the colliery owners for $47 \cdot 5$ and the intransigence of both involved Sir Richard Redmayne, the government's expert negotiator, in endless tortuous discussion.[1]

The difficulties encountered in returning the mines to a peace-time basis induced the government to appoint a Royal Commission under Lord Justice Sankey in January, 1919, to enquire into the whole issue of nationalisation. It had been curiously selected, the miners and the owners having nominated three members each, to whom the government added three known socialists and three industrialists. All therefore turned on the chairman. Lloyd George was certainly aware that Sankey had strong socialist sympathies, and so were the miners' leaders, the veteran Smillie, and Frank Hodges, both extremists. Thus, in promising

[1] For an excellent account of all this see Redmayne, *Men, Mines, and Memories*.

in advance to implement whatever scheme the Sankey Commission might recommend, Lloyd George had apparently committed himself in advance to nationalisation of the coal industry without much thought for the difficulties in which he might be involved with his own followers.

The Sankey Commission met in an atmosphere of industrial crisis. For behind the miners there stood what was known as the Triple Alliance, between miners, railwaymen and the transport and general workers. It amounted in fact to little more than a general agreement to concert policy between the three unions, since a strike without warning by any one of them might cause widespread unemployment and hardship for the members of the other two. Though it was a fact that a simultaneous strike by all three would bring the nation's industrial life to a standstill, thus engineering in effect a general strike, only perhaps the more extremist of the miners had thought of using it in this way. But when all three unions simultaneously issued ultimatums in January, 1919, it looked very like the beginning of a move towards that General Strike which had haunted the imaginations of pre-war revolutionaries and was still a haunting fear in the Conservative mind. The three unions did not, in the event, carry their concerted action any further. The railway dispute dragged on to its settlement by the strike in September. Legislation was introduced to improve conditions for the transport workers. And the mining industry, after a great crisis in March, firmly and brilliantly handled by Bonar Law, settled in a welter of only minor disturbance to await the Sankey Commission's report, an interim award on wages having met the main, immediate grievance.

1919 was thus a year of trade union aggressiveness: the year in which the rank and file sought to bring home to government and Parliament the sort of new deal they believed, though in a very muddled and hesitant fashion, they had fought for and earned. But they struck little response from the serried ranks of the government's supporters in the House of Commons. There are odd jottings in Neville Chamberlain's diary and letters which give a clue as to what might have been achieved in the twenties and had in fact to be postponed to 1947, had there been a few more men who were trying to build a new world rather than struggle back to an old one. For that restless Mayor of Birmingham, as a true son of his father, was ceaselessly preoccupied with the reorganisation of public utilities and bringing them into some more rational relationship with local authorities. He judged Addison's housing plans to be not only financially unsound, but totally inadequate; and he longed to see the state spend £100 million on houses which local authorities should administer, and which working men should be encouraged by all means to buy for themselves. When the majority report of the Sankey Commission duly recommended nationalisation, he thought the case well made out, though he would have moved cautiously towards achieving it. 'Many people', he wrote, 'have been sceptical about the suggestion that there was to be a new England, and many others have never intended that it should be very different from the old, if they could help it.'[1]

Such views as these struck little response from either leaders or rank and file in the Coalition. Bonar Law had indeed the imagination to see something more than indiscipline and truculence in labour unrest. When his hostess, after a big political meeting, asked him what the strikers 'really wanted', he glanced reflectively down her luxuriously appointed dinner table and murmured: 'Perhaps they want a little of all this.' But he was ageing and tiring and he lacked Chamberlain's restless energy. Neville's ambitious views on housing merely brought down on him a severe rebuke from his brother Austen, the Chancellor of the Exchequer. The Sankey report, in spite of Lloyd George's promises, was not implemented, though Bonar Law had gone even further and pledged the government in advance to carry it out 'in the spirit and in the letter'. Of its three main recommendations, only one, the reduction of the working day to seven hours, was made effective. The suggestion of an all-round wage increase of 2/- a shift was met in part only; and nationalisation was rejected altogether, the government putting forward a scheme of its own, modelled on the minority report of Sir Arthur Duckham, which was entirely unacceptable to both owners and miners. The plain fact was that Conservative members were not thinking at all in terms of increased expenditure which might mean some measure of self-sacrifice. They were preoccupied with the fact that taxation still stood at wartime levels; that the national deficit for 1920 was £473 million; and that the budget of 1921 envisaged an expenditure of £1,300 million, a large portion of which would go in subsidies—£23 million for the railways, £15 million for coal, £45 million on bread, and, strangely

[1] Feiling, *Life of Neville Chamberlain*, p. 83.

enough, £65 million for a munitions industry which had not yet wound itself up. They wanted no further adventures in subsidy, but the good, old-fashioned remedy of retrenchment.

The Lloyd George of 1911 would have responded eagerly to the ideas which preoccupied Neville Chamberlain. By 1921 it seems that an obsession with international affairs had closed his mind and imagination to all other issues save, occasionally, the problem of keeping himself in office. There had been tentative talk between him and Bonar Law of a capital levy, at any rate on war profits, to meet some of these swollen commitments, but the project was let slide until it was too late. The mood of the leaders came to match that of the majority of their followers, and Neville Chamberlain's sceptics who had doubted the possibility of a 'new England' were triumphantly vindicated. As far as the miners were concerned, no immediate penalty was exacted for the government's betrayal. The Yorkshire strikes of the summer of 1920 concerned the application of the new wage rates, not the nationalisation issue, and the industry as a whole was prosperous as never before, though at the expense of Europe's, and especially France's misery. Coal which cost 37/6d. a ton at the pithead commanded an export price of 115/-, and there were large profits to be shared between owners, miners, and the home consumer. But in September a slight fall in the index of wholesale prices gave warning of the end of the boom, and by the end of October most mines found themselves with three weeks' stock of unsold coal. In December the Governor of the Federal Reserve Bank of America, voicing the triumph of orthodox finance, telegraphed from London to New York, 'World deflation has been started.'

Writing in 1952 about his own book on *Inequality of Incomes*, Hugh Dalton says: 'I find it remarkable, looking back to this book, that I had then no apprehension of mass unemployment.'[1] Not only the London School of Economics, but the whole business and political world seems to have been taken equally by surprise by the slump which struck British industry in the winter of 1920–1, and from which there was to be no complete recovery for the next twenty years. The total number of unemployed, down to 200,000 in the summer of 1920, rose by December to 700,000 to 1,300,000 by March, 1921, and touched its peak of over 2 million in June, thereafter gradually declining until it settled by the

[1] Hugh Dalton, *Call Back Yesterday*, p. 107.

end of 1922 at the more or less permanent figure of 1,400,000. The newly launched scheme for contributory unemployment insurance was made bankrupt before it had fairly started; and the government was brought face to face with problems with which most of its members were singularly unfitted to deal.

Lloyd George's Unemployment Insurance arrangements were quite inadequate to deal with such a situation. To make the scheme actuarially sound there had to be a time limit for the drawing of benefits. If for some reason a worker remained unemployed beyond that limit, he must then turn to the old Poor Law machinery, and fall on to Parish Relief. The Act, of course, had been framed on the assumption that unemployment would remain an infrequent and transitory phenomenon; it had even been assumed that the old Poor Law machinery would fall entirely into disuse and the Guardians disappear. A large, permanent body of unemployed, whose period of 'covenanted benefit' quickly ran out, in many areas actually reversed this expectation. In East London, in Durham, and in South Wales the Poor Law Guardians found themselves burdened as never before. It was no longer humanly possible to apply the 'Workhouse Test' of 1834; and there were areas where one-third of the population was on outdoor relief. Inevitably, too, these areas were those where there was little property of high rateable value: the burden fell on the Boroughs which were least able to carry it.

This unforeseen effect of the last relic of Tudor welfare arrangements, which threw the able-bodied poor on to local rates instead of national taxation, created a situation which could only be remedied by large-scale legislation. But Conservative governments, still haunted by the spectre of Speenhamland, and still imbued with the Victorian conviction that a man out of work was discreditable and less deserving than one who was employed, obstinately refused to face the facts. In consequence in some boroughs where Labour ruled, and especially in Poplar, the Guardians took the law into their own hands, abandoned all attempt at solvency, and ran up huge debts which they left to be settled out of Metropolitan Common Fund. Poplar and West Ham were both owing £2 million by 1925. Unfortunately the Socialist Guardians in such areas were tempted to carry the war into enemy country. Forced by circumstance to break the law, they defied it altogether, providing benefits and amenities for the unemployed which, however desirable, were not allowed for in the Acts. Some, like that simple-minded, passionate, generous idealist, George Lansbury, turned relief into a crusade, and went to gaol for their defiant bankruptcy. Others, in South Wales and in Durham, turned it into a racket. Both kinds of extremism did as much harm as good by giving reactionaries some grounds for saying that in Poplar and West Ham life was more comfortable for the workless than for the worker, and the clamour of popular sympathy for Lansbury and his friends met a more obstinate resistance from the government than it need have. 'Poplarism' became the Speenhamland of the 1920s and vitiated all industrial and political relations, until Neville Chamberlain at last grasped the nettle in 1929.

Not unnaturally in this general disaster it was the coal industry which was first and hardest hit and in which the main crisis occurred. The export price of coal dropped from 115/- a ton, first to 85/-, and then, in the spring of 1921, rapidly down to 24/-, while the cost at pit-head had gone slightly up, to 39/- a ton. The government was still in control of the industry and was not due to hand the mines back to their individual owners until August of 1921; and it found itself spending £5 million a month to balance the coal budget alone. Under this pressure it was decided, at only three weeks' notice, to bring the date of decontrol forward to March 31st, thereby provoking, though with unnecessary violence, a dispute which was probably inevitable anyway. The miners, though foiled of nationalisation, were determined to stand out for a wages' pool which would give them an even rate throughout the industry and compel the more prosperous coalfields to subsidise the less economic. The owners insisted on district settlements and made it clear that there would have to be an all-round reduction in wages whatever happened. On March 31st, when control ended, the mine-owners announced their new and lower wage rates, lock-out notices terminating all existing contracts went up at every colliery, and the crisis was on.

It threatened to be a battle on a very wide front, for this time the miners had taken steps to make sure that the Triple Alliance should actually function effectively, and both railwaymen and transport workers were pledged to come out in what would be, in effect, a sympathetic strike. It was conceivable that this would produce something like a national stoppage and a complete breakdown of the economy, since the government was without plans to meet the threat when, on April 8th, the Triple Alliance announced a strike of all three unions to begin in four days' time if no settlement had been reached with the miners. Neither railwaymen nor transport workers were keen to strike. Thomas was working hard for conciliation, and so was Ernest Bevin, who was rapidly becoming the dominating force in the Transport Union, and since negotiations were still going on, they postponed their strike on the 12th to midnight on the 15th. It seems likely that they would then have been driven to honour their promises, but for an almost incredible blunder by Frank Hodges, who was conducting negotiations for the miners. At a meeting with Conservative M.P.s he stated that in certain circumstances he would be prepared to negotiate district settlements, and everybody concerned except the miners seized eagerly on a concession which would let them all out. The miners at once repudiated Hodges, but they were too late. The other unions, lukewarm anyway, made the apparent fluctuation in the miners' demands and their final intransigence an excuse for backing down; and at 3 p.m. on April 15th, which was to go down in Trade Union history as 'Black Friday', Thomas appeared on the steps of Unity House to announce that the triple strike was off.

So the miners were left to go it alone with very little chance of success. Though the government had called out reservists and concentrated troops at likely centres, there was no serious disturbance. But the strike dragged obstinately on until June, when the government stepped in with the offer of a £10 million subsidy to tide over the transition period if the strike were settled immediately, and the miners gave way, accepting district settlements everywhere at substantially lower rates. Mr. Hodges lost his job, and promptly went into management, where he did very well for himself, becoming a director of steel and colliery concerns, and dying in 1947 worth £100,000. Jimmy Thomas, though he kept his hold on his railwaymen, became for many trade unionists 'Traitor Thomas'; and although he won a libel action against a left-wing newspaper which had portrayed him as Judas Iscariot, a reputation for slipperiness clung to him for the rest of his days. The 'Cripple Alliance' became a theme of scorn, and the cry of 'Who sold us on Black Friday?' was liable to disrupt the unity of labour meetings for many years to come.

Sir Richard Redmayne, whose evidence before the Sankey Commission had been in favour of nationalising coal royalties, but not the industry as a whole, hailed the settlement as 'a great experiment in profit sharing',[1] since the basis of the new agreement was a division of the profits in each district, 83% to go to the workers, 17% to the owners.[2] Few others, except the owners, were pleased with this return to a system of individual ownership which had been almost universally condemned as 'extravagant, inefficient, and unprogressive'. Moreover the mining lock-out was only the opening campaign of what has come down in socialist history as 'the employers' offensive'. In one industry after another, in engineering, in shipbuilding, and in cotton, the workers were forced to accept lower rates. The Agriculture Act, ushered in in 1920 by one of Lloyd George's greater speeches which the *Spectator* had rather oddly hailed as a 'milestone', was now repealed as regarded guaranteed wages, though not as to prices; and unemployment benefits which had been increased in the spring were reduced again in the autumn. The general wage level, which had stood at 177% above the pre-war figure in January, 1921, had fallen by October, 1922, to 80% above.

It is only fair to add that the level of retail prices fell even further, and the man who was in full-time employment was, in terms of real wages, generally better off. But a very high proportion were working short time and felt the pinch severely; and prices did not fall nearly far enough to make the lot of the unemployed tolerable. 'It is impossible to expect people to subsist upon the unemployment benefit of 15/- for men and 12/- for women', King George wrote to Sir Maurice Hankey in the autumn of 1921, for onward transmission to the Cabinet. 'The King appeals to the government to meet this grave, but he believes temporary difficulty with the same liberality as they displayed in dealing with the enormous cost of the war.'[3] But the government was not thinking at all in terms of liberality. It was applying the classic remedy of economy in public expenditure; and a committee of business men under the chairmanship of Sir Eric Geddes, a rigidly unimaginative puritan, was engaged in cutting down departmental estimates 'with an axe'. Already the sacking of Dr. Addison and the drastic curtailment of his housing scheme, combined with the withdrawal of the agricultural wage subsidy,

---

[1] Redmayne, *op. cit.*, p. 237.
[2] This was later altered to 85% and 15%.
[3] Nicolson, *op. cit.*, p. 342.

had saved £75 million. The 'Geddes Axe' shore away another £60 million, mainly on the defence estimates, but partly at the expense of education. There was no move to meet the King's plea for 'work and not doles' for the unemployed. 'Emergency works', His Majesty had suggested, 'such as road-making, land reclamation, light railways, forestation, although unremunerative, will nevertheless be doing some good and meet the claim of those who demand work and not charity.'[1] But the King showed himself to be both more humane and a sounder economist than his ministers, who were not thinking along such constructive lines at all. They did, indeed, make some attempt to create extra purchasing power which might slow up the recession; but it went where it was least needed and could do least good, in a reduction of the standard rate of income-tax from 6/- to 5/-, which the quarterly *Round Table* likened to a man taking his wife to the opera instead of paying his gas bill.[2]

This negative approach to the internal problems of Great Britain which throughout characterised the Coalition government was certainly one reason why it declined so rapidly in popular esteem. By-elections had gone badly as early as 1919, and in the spring of 1920 the opposition was strengthened by the return of Sir John Simon and of Asquith who, at Paisley, not only won a three-cornered fight, but caused his Conservative Coalitionist opponent to forfeit his deposit. But Asquith, great parliamentarian though he remained, was losing his effectiveness. He dined too well and had little zest for debate after 10 at night. The real difficulties of the Coalition were internal: too large a majority to handle easily, and the rebelliousness of the Conservative Party machine when it was required to assist Coalition Liberals. There had been a move towards fusion of the whole into a single centre party, which was the dream of all the most intelligent members of the government, Birkenhead, Austen Chamberlain, and Churchill among them. It would also have suited Lloyd George very well by giving him the only two things he lacked: an organised party behind him, and a party fund. But at the moment when the Conservatives, some of them very reluctantly, were prepared to take the plunge he failed to carry with him the Liberal members of his government, who set much store on retaining the appellation of Liberal. So Lloyd George was left as before, with nothing but

[1] Nicolson, *op. cit.*, p. 342.
[2] Somervell, *The Reign of George V*, p. 229.

his personal prestige to sustain him, permanently exposed to the danger of Conservative revolt; a danger which considerably increased when exhaustion and ill health forced Bonar Law to withdraw from the government, though not from Parliament, in May, 1921.

Without the cushioning skill of Bonar Law and under the impact of mounting economic crisis, relations between the Prime Minister and his Cabinet began to deteriorate rapidly. He had, as Beaverbrook put it, 'become something of a dictator without a dictator's apparatus of power and terror'.[1] He was not often enough present to hold his Cabinet together, and peevish notes from abroad, such as this to Curzon from Genoa in April, 1922, did not help matters:

> The strain of the conference is great enough without further complications of that sort, and you will recognise that I cannot be expected to accept any variation of my instructions, however desirable they may seem to my colleagues in London, while I am doing my utmost to give effect to the agreed policy of the Cabinet under circumstances of extreme difficulty out here in Genoa.[2]

The fluctuations in government policy on agriculture and housing and the failure to enforce a war profits tax drew a long and reasoned protest from Churchill in October of 1921, at the end of which he put his finger on the root cause of the government's ineffectiveness: that the Prime Minister's thought, so clear and 'searching' on the economic difficulties, always 'stopped short of reaching any conclusion of a definite character on which a policy, or even a provisional policy could be based'.[3] Moreover there were no triumphs outside Britain to offset the government's decline in prestige at home.

Some of the difficulties were pure bad luck. No real blame, for example, can be attached to the government for the disastrous worsening of relations in India which resulted from the Amritsar massacre of April, 1919. General Dyer, the responsible officer, openly admitted that he had given his troops the order to fire on a crowd when the danger of riot was in fact over in order to strike terror into the hearts of all who might be tempted to riot elsewhere. He was removed from his command, and the action of the Commander-in-Chief was approved by Montagu, the Secretary for India. But the Conservatives scented victimisation of an

---

[1] *Men and Power*, p. 338.
[2] *Ib.*, p. 389.
[3] Correspondence from Appendix IV, Beaverbrook, *op. cit.*, p. 406.

honest soldier by a minister whom they disliked as a Jew and a Liberal and far too pro-Indian, and Bonar Law had the greatest difficulty in saving his colleague, whom he personally disliked, from the wrath of his followers.

It would be equally unfair to blame the Coalition for the disastrous events of 1919–22 in Ireland. No English government has come really well out of the Irish Question, and the post-war difficulties were in any case the inevitable legacy of the postponement of Home Rule in 1914 and the Easter Rebellion of 1916. Events in Ireland none the less played a large part in lowering the government's prestige and in weakening the cohesion of Lloyd George's following. After endless mismanagement, the Irish Question had reached that phase which carelessly handled political problems sometimes do reach, of total insolubility. A cast-iron case, on one ground or another, could be made out against any solution anyone could propose, and England was back where she had been in the XVI century when a weary and bewildered Francis Walsingham had told Elizabeth I that the only hope was for Ireland to disappear beneath the sea.

After ten years of negotiation and fighting, the basic, intractable facts of the Irish situation in 1919 were fairly clear. In three-quarters of the island Sinn Fein, emerging from an innocuous past as a society chiefly devoted to the propagation of the Gaelic language, had, by a mixture of enthusiasm and terrorism, carried all before it. Its 73 elected members of the British Parliament sat in Dublin as the self-constituted Dail Eireann of a new Irish Republic. In that part of Ireland the Unionist minority, mostly Protestant and of English descent, had already by implication been abandoned to its fate. But in six of the nine counties which made up the Province of Ulster, Protestant Unionism was equally triumphant, and had since 1914 made it clear that it would fight rather than submit to any form of rule by an Irish Parliament in Dublin. Equally in the North there were enclaves of Catholic Nationalists who, if the Unionists had their way, were also doomed to become a permanent political minority. As a final complication, there were two disputed counties of Ulster where the result of a plebiscite would depend entirely on how the boundaries were drawn. As Churchill said in one of his more famous speeches in 1922: 'The mode and thought of men, the whole outlook on affairs, the grouping of parties, have all encountered violent and tremendous changes in the deluge of the world, but as the deluge subsides and the waters fall we see the dreary steeples of Fermanagh and Tyrone emerging once again.'

The whole presented a neat *reductio ad absurdum* of the principle of self-determination; and when the two Irish delegates who wished to present their case to the Peace Conference secured an interview with President Wilson, that harassed man told them that they had touched 'on the great metaphysical tragedy' of the day. When he had raised the hopes of millions of peoples by proclaiming self-determination he had done so 'without the knowledge that nationalities existed which are coming to us day by day'. For him the necessary rejection of the Irish case meant the loss of valuable Irish-American votes which may well have helped to turn the scale when the Peace Treaty came to be debated in the Senate. For the English government it meant that every single feasible solution of the Irish Question had now been rejected with passionate conviction by one or other of the parties concerned. Sinn Fein launched a campaign of arson and murder against the Royal Irish Constabulary and such landowners as were brave enough to stay in the country, and 15,000 armed police, though supported by 60,000 regular troops, could not halt the mounting tide of murders, chiefly of police, by a terrorist force which can scarcely have numbered more than 3,000. When murderers were caught, it was impossible to find prosecution witnesses or juries willing to convict; and when the King anxiously enquired what the government's policy was, Bonar Law drily replied that it remained that of 'supporting the Irish Government in taking whatever measures they think necessary to secure orderly government in Ireland'. Field Marshal Lord Ypres had already been installed as Viceroy. Hamar Greenwood, who was reckoned a strong man, was sent out as Chief Secretary; and a special force of police was recruited from demobilised officers and N.C.O.s of the British army, the Black and Tans, who were to break the rebellion by main force. Meanwhile a new Home Rule Bill, the Government of Ireland Act, was passed through the Westminster Parliament, granting far wider autonomy than anything dreamed of in 1914, but granting it to two separate Parliaments: one in Belfast for the six Ulster counties and one in Dublin for the rest of Ireland, with a provision for a Council of All Ireland to which both Parliaments were invited to send delegates as soon as they felt prepared to accept Dominion status for a united Ireland.

Too much political passion still runs on these issues for any objective history of events in Ireland in these years to be written yet. Partition remains a burning issue and Irish historians waste much ink in proving that it was never a demand of either Unionists or Nationalists, but was obtruded into the situation in desperation by the British government, as it undoubtedly was.[1] Nevertheless the Parliament which King George V opened in Belfast on June 22nd, 1921, though it was not what the northern Unionists really wanted, has safeguarded them from being engulfed in a united Ireland; and until they are outvoted by Nationalists in their own six counties they are unlikely willingly to give it up. Equally the last word has still to be said on the Black and Tans, whose reputation for unrestrained ferocity in terrorist reprisals has perhaps been too easily accepted in England, as in Ireland. Certainly they were in a fair way to crushing the rebellion when a truce was announced on July 11th. The King's statesmanlike speech at Belfast, inspired largely by Smuts, with its plea for 'forbearance and conciliation', had borne fruit; and though the negotiations dragged on for another six months, a treaty giving an Irish Free State virtually Dominion status was signed on December 6th and ratified in the Dail by the narrow margin of seven votes.

Since the treaty safeguarded the independence of Ulster, it was carried through the House of Commons by a comfortable majority—407 to 58. But the whole course of the struggle had put a severe strain on Coalition unity, and extreme Unionists were still suspicious even at the end that Ulster would somehow be betrayed. Moreover the question had brought Bonar Law back into active politics much refreshed after a rest in the south of France, making Lloyd George wonder if he was out to supplant him as Prime Minister and Austen Chamberlain, who had taken over the leadership of the Conservative Party, write, rather over-dramatically, that he was 'fighting for his political life'. Nor did these stresses end with the signature of the treaty. Ireland became divided between Free Staters and die-hard Republicans, and on April 13th, 1922, Rory O'Connor seized the Four Courts in the centre of Dublin, proclaimed an Irish Republic, and launched from there a fresh campaign of murder and outrage throughout Ireland, while the Irish government stood by, too fearful to eject him.

[1] See, for example, Stephen Gwynne, *The History of Partition*.

The climax of this phase came with the murder of Field Marshal Sir Henry Wilson, an avowed and fanatical Unionist, on the steps of his London house by two Irish gunmen as he returned, in uniform, from opening a war memorial. Nothing could have been more calculated to outrage Tory feeling, or to strengthen the views of those who had all along mistrusted the Irish settlement. Lady Wilson greeted Austen Chamberlain, when he called to condole, as 'Murderer', and tried to exclude all members of the government from the funeral. Churchill, as Colonial Secretary, at once announced that firm steps would be taken to compel the Irish government to do its duty and clear the Four Courts; and this was in fact done, plunging Ireland into civil war, but putting an end to the terrorist campaign. Tempers, however, had worn dangerously thin, and the last words of Bonar Law's speech in answer to Churchill had been that, if the government did not see the matter through, 'I will be against them and I hope the House of Commons will be against them too.'

There were other forces working that summer to disrupt the unity of the Coalition. There had been a good deal of unpleasant talk for some time of the cynical, and even corrupt way in which Lloyd George and the Coalition Liberal Whips handled the distribution of honours. He had been in trouble with the King for promising a peerage without getting His Majesty's previous consent as early as 1916, and had half promised, though only verbally, to be more careful in future. In fact from 1919 onwards he cast care to the winds. It was widely felt that the Honours List was too large and numbered far too many unsuitable persons whose sole claim to public service was a substantial contribution to Lloyd George's election fund. Whether, as it was rumoured, the Coalition Liberal Whips actually sold titles on a definite tariff cannot be proved. But it is said that one of them openly boasted in the Reform Club that he was the only man living who had actually sold an earldom;[1] and the background activities of a strange creature called Maundy Gregory, who was subsequently convicted for 'touting for honours', lend colour to the accusation.[2] The Birthday Honours List of 1922 precipitated the crisis. Three wealthy men, none of impeccable reputation, were awarded peerages; and the case of one of them, a South African

---

[1] The evidence for this is anecdotal, but first-hand.
[2] See Gerald Macmillan's book, *Honours for Sale*.

financier named Sir Joseph Robinson, provoked a sharp debate in the House of Lords and an immediate announcement from the South African Prime Minister that he had not been consulted. 'It must be regarded', the King wrote in a long, angry letter to Lloyd George, 'as little less than an insult to the Crown and to the House of Lords.'

Lloyd George showed himself more or less unrepentant. He deplored chiefly in his letter of apology to the King the 'unfortunate publicity' which had illumined the recent cases, and rode off the Tory fury in the Commons with the promise of a Royal Commission. Sir Joseph Robinson was ultimately persuaded to refuse his peerage, and the storm died down. But it left the gap between the Conservative rank and file and the Coalition government wider than ever. The Conservative ministers, including all the best and most experienced brains in the Party except Curzon, were still under the little man's spell, believed him indispensable and would still have preferred fusion with the Coalition Liberals into a strong party of the centre. But the die-hard wing of the Party, led by Lord Salisbury, was in almost open revolt; and their mistrust, not only of Lloyd George, but of his policies, was shared by many of the junior ministers and by a powerful group of back-benchers led by Sir Samuel Hoare. Meanwhile, brooding in the background and about to re-enter active politics, though with no intention of challenging the leadership of either Lloyd George or of Austen Chamberlain, there was Bonar Law, far from happy about Ireland, and deeply suspicious of the acrobatic adventurousness of the Prime Minister's foreign policy. It was an explosive situation, but Lloyd George was not unduly worried. It was unlikely that the Tory masses, without any of their most effective leaders, could do more than grumble ineffectually; and, ironically enough, considering how far Lloyd George sacrificed the control of domestic policy to his new-found interests and excitements in international affairs, it was a series of blunders in the handling of Middle Eastern affairs which precipitated the crisis and his own political ruin.

CHAPTER 4

A New Political Pattern

'The Prime Minister', Beaverbrook had written to Bonar Law during his retirement, 'is active, and his interest in his own situation never falters. Evidently he never gets bored with power.'[1] In fact Lloyd George does seem to have had very little idea of the forces which were working against him. Too many people had told him in 1918 that he was indispensable, and his Cabinet colleagues, especially the Conservatives, were still saying so. Even the King, who had long regretted Mr. Asquith, had come to value his Prime Minister, wrote sympathetically to him of the additional burdens cast on him by Bonar Law's withdrawal, and as late as October, 1922, when the Coalition was on the brink of dissolution, was still expressing the hope 'that you will be able to remain my Prime Minister'. Moreover, Lloyd George alone of the big three of Paris still survived in power, for Clemenceau too had fallen a victim to the Versailles Treaty, rejected by the French, ironically enough, for having been too lenient with the Germans. The Prime Minister's prestige was thus at its highest abroad just when, in England, it was beginning to decline.

Yet, in spite of all the rushing round—to a conference at Spa in July of 1920, to talks in Paris to prepare the ground for the London Conference of May, 1921, and further conferences at Cannes and Genoa in January and July of 1922—very little was achieved. 'Fantastic gatherings,' Curzon called them, 'which are really only designed as a stage on which he is to perform.'[2] It was easy enough in the opening stages to relieve Germany of her immediately disposable assets; but these were rapidly absorbed in the occupation costs of the Allies in the Rhineland,

[1] Blake, *op. cit.*, p. 427.   [2] Ronaldshay, Vol. II, p. 297.

and the really difficult question which had baffled the Paris negotiators was left untouched: the fixing of the precise sums payable as Reparations and the method of payment, all of which had to be settled by May, 1922. Here Lloyd George had undoubtedly counted on a change in the climate of public opinion which would enable him, in conjunction with the Americans, to force more reasonable figures on the French. In England by the end of 1920 that change had undoubtedly begun. War hysteria was dying away, and the views set forth by Keynes in *The Economic Consequence of the Peace* were having a profound effect on thinking opinion both in England and America. But the withdrawal of the United States from European affairs had left the Reparations Commission at the mercy of the French and Belgians, who had suffered no change of heart.

The meeting at Spa did little but allot the proportions of any final payment to the various allies. At the Paris discussions France was represented by the new Prime Minister, M. Briand, and the Finance Minister, M. Doumer, whose understanding of international exchange procedure was as negligible as that of M. Klotz, and Lloyd George found himself involved in the most embittered argument. He used with great force and clarity, now that it was too late, the Keynsian arguments, and was met only by a stubborn refusal to face facts. He could not bring the total demand on Germany down below £10,000 million, which was to be paid off in 42 annual instalments of £600 million.[1] To this demand, when he was presented with it in March, the German representative replied in an insolent speech with an offer of approximately a tenth of that sum. Since there was indisputable evidence that the Germans were at the same time evading the disarmament clauses of the Treaty, on this occasion Lloyd George gave his full support to the French decision to extend their occupation to Düsseldorf, Ruhrort, and Duisberg, which may have facilitated disarmament control, but certainly reduced still further German industry's capacity to meet the Allied demands.

By the time the final terms came to be fixed in London in May, 1921, Lloyd George had managed to hammer the French estimate of German indebtedness down by half, to £6,850 million, which was almost

---

[1] Lloyd George printed some large extracts from these discussions in *The Truth about Reparations and War Debts*, 1932.

exactly the figure forecast by Keynes. This the Germans, reluctantly and under the threat of further occupations in the Ruhr, accepted; and that summer they actually made their first payment, buying foreign currency for the purpose. Immediately the whole weakness of the Allied position was revealed. The value of the Mark on foreign exchange, already depreciated, abruptly fell another 50%, and there began that flight from the Mark which was to plunge Germany into the chaos of the inflation and make any immediate payment of Reparations quite impossible. By the autumn it was clear that Germany would be unable to meet the sums due in January and February, and Rathenau, one of the most courageous and independent of the German leaders, and the most anxious to see Germany regain her international standing by fulfilling the Treaty, put up a powerful case for a moratorium. The Reparations Commission could reach no agreement on this—'one of the occasions', as Lloyd George remarks, 'when the absence of an American delegate on the Commission proved fatal to wise action'. So the stage was set for the last two conferences of the Lloyd George era, Cannes in January and Genoa in April, from which the Prime Minister was to emerge with irretrievably damaged prestige.

The Cannes débâcle was really bad luck. It started off more promisingly than any of its predecessors, and Lloyd George, strongly supporting Rathenau's plea for a moratorium and for more reasonable practical arrangements to enable Germany to pay, was not without hope of talking Briand round. As he said himself, 'M. Briand was amenable to the appeals of reason.' He set himself to charm and win over the French Premier by every art at his command, and their ripening friendship was symbolised by photographs in all the newspapers of Briand taking a lesson in golf from Lloyd George on the Cannes links. But this was just what the French public and deputies most feared: that Briand would succumb, as Clemenceau had before him, to the wiles of the Welsh wizard and France would be talked out of her just penalties. Half-way through Rathenau's impassioned final plea to the Conference the proceedings were interrupted by a telegram from Paris announcing the fall of the government. Briand was replaced by Poincaré; and as Lloyd George sadly observed, 'arguments reinforced with irrefutable facts and figures were as fruitless with M. Poincaré as a shower on the Sahara.' Poincaré's whole being was eaten up with hatred of Germany, and he did not cherish the happiest memories of wartime collaboration with the British. He had no manners, and opposition would make him behave, as Curzon put it later, 'like a demented schoolmaster screaming at a guilty schoolboy'. Lloyd George may have been right to attribute much of his unreason and bombast to the humiliating memory of his secret flight, as President, from Paris to Bordeaux at the time of the first Battle of the Marne, which had left him looking very ridiculous. Germany got her moratorium, but on conditions of Allied control over her internal finances which were quite unacceptable. Her rejection of these terms was received in Paris on the very day of the opening meeting at Genoa of what had been hopefully named the World Reconstruction Conference.

This time Lloyd George had invited not only Germany, but Russia and the United States to be represented, in the hope of directing the effort of world diplomacy towards revision of treaties and a general lessening of tension and grievance. The U.S. government, still pursuing the dream of isolation and resentful of the confusion into which Versailles had plunged Europe, declined the invitation. The Russians eagerly accepted. Poincaré made it a condition of French acceptance that there should be no modification of Reparations, and though he did not attend himself, he is alleged to have sent M. Barthou, the French representative, no less than 1,000 telegrams in his frenzied determination to avoid concessions. The French demanded that the Allies should take over the German Customs, expropriate the German State forests and mines, themselves raise the taxes in the occupied provinces, and seize a majority of the shares in such German firms as were doing well in spite of the economic blight. They still insisted that payment could be made in Marks regardless of the German trade balance, and that Allied control of the Reichsbank would easily restore the exchange value of the Mark. Failing agreement on this, if Germany defaulted on her May Reparations instalment France would not wait for the Reparations Commission to declare the default, but would occupy the Ruhr, in flagrant defiance of the Treaty of Versailles.

Since there was no chance of convincing M. Poincaré that economic facts were facts, deadlock was reached within a week. But that was long enough to enable Rathenau and Chicherin, the Russian representative, to get on terms, and the final blow to Lloyd George's hopes was the

Treaty of Rapallo, which the two of them slipped away to sign, re-establishing diplomatic relations, waiving all reparations demands between themselves, and, as it later turned out, with secret clauses opening to Germany the chance of training the nucleus of an air force under the guise of helping Russia with technical advice and assistance. Lloyd George loudly denounced this as 'the intimacy of two pariahs'. But English opinion was strongly inclined to blame him personally for this serious worsening of the European situation as a result of the Genoa Conference, and to demand an end of this restless meddling in international affairs.

The futility of this series of European conferences and discussions was thrown further into relief by the comparative success of the Washington Naval Conference of November, 1921, which did at least make a tentative beginning towards the general disarmament half promised in the clause of the Versailles Treaty which had imposed limitation of all arms on Germany 'in order to render possible the initiation of a general limitation of the armaments of all nations'. The motives of the various participants were not perhaps quite as simple as that. Great Britain which had just spent £1,000 million on a war could no longer dream in terms of the two-power standard in fleet building, and the Admiralty estimates had been particularly hard hit by the Geddes Axe, as all the admirals very noisily complained. On the other hand it was not very clear against whom we should be building a great battle fleet now that the German High Seas Fleet, having duly surrendered, had scuttled itself in Scapa Flow. The Americans had started to build against Britain in the early days of the war with the idea of forcing on her the doctrine of the freedom of the seas. They had broken off in 1916 to put all their effort into merchant shipping, but had resumed building super-dreadnoughts after the war, and could clearly outbuild Great Britain any time they liked.

The crux of the matter, both for the United States and for Great Britain, was the as yet undeclared intention of Japan. The recent closing of the United States to Japanese immigration had greatly strengthened the hand of the imperialist and militarist group in Japan's governing class who already cherished dreams of dominating Asia and challenged the hold of the more liberal party who thought still in terms of peaceful progress in harmony with the western powers. They viewed Manchuria and Korea as obvious outlets for their teeming population, and China as an area to be exploited exclusively by themselves. These ambitions roused hostile suspicions both in America and Britain; and the Japs, too, were laying down a battle fleet of super-dreadnoughts. Finally, to make the whole problem acute and urgent, there was the Anglo-Japanese Treaty, dating from 1905 and due for renewal in 1921, which had been invaluable to Britain during the war in enabling her to leave the protection of the Pacific trade routes to the Japanese fleet. If it was renewed, the Americans, already faced with the possibility of a Pacific war, would be forced to build against Britain and Japan combined. An unthinkable situation would develop for the two great English-speaking powers, which it was a prime interest for both to avoid. Finally there was a strong desire among American statesmen to show that, though they had rejected the League of Nations, they were prepared to work constructively for peace.

These were the circumstances which led the new American President, Harding, to invite the leading naval powers to Washington in 1921; and the discussions resulted in three treaties, all severely limited in scope, but all perfectly in harmony with the general principles of the League, and all representing some small initial progress towards a more peaceful world. The Five Power Treaty was concerned exclusively with battle-ship strength. Great Britain and the United States were to limit their battle fleets to 500,000 tons each, Japan hers to 300,000 tons, while France and Italy were allowed 175,000 tons apiece. No restrictions were imposed on any other class of vessel since the needs of the powers in cruisers and submarines were so diverse that clear, mathematical limitations seemed impossible. Alongside this there was a Four Power Treaty which was designed to temper the blow of the non-renewal of the English alliance to the Japanese by including them in a general agreement which bound them, the British, the Americans, and the French all to respect each other's territorial possessions in the Pacific. The Japs persuaded the Americans to demilitarise the Philippines and the British to dismantle the fortifications of Hong Kong, but failed to prevent the building of a great British naval base at Singapore. Finally—and this was the greatest step towards paralysing Japan's ambitions by entangling her in alliances and common policies—there was a Nine Power Treaty, in which Italy, the Netherlands, Belgium and Portugal were included, by which all subscribed to the policy of the 'open door' for trade with China and guaranteed to respect her territory and sovereign independence.

All in all, these treaties represented a very adequate plan for containing Japanese ambitions, always provided, of course, that the powers were prepared to take action to enforce them if any one of them should violate the terms laid down. But that did not lie within the control of the Washington negotiators. What diplomacy could do to keep the peace in the Pacific diplomacy had done. Balfour had well earned the Garter with which he was rewarded on his return from leading the British delegation; it was not to be his fault that his countrymen weakened on their commitments when the crisis came.

For the final discredit of his whole foreign policy with the British public Lloyd George was himself directly and personally responsible, and it arose out of the dismemberment of the Turkish Empire which, by the end of the war, was more or less a *fait accompli*. The Sultan was left with only a small hinterland of European territory surrounding Constantinople. Allied forces occupied both shores of the Dardanelles pending the internationalisation of the Straits. Egypt and all the Arab lands had broken away. Turkey was beaten, exhausted, and apparently powerless, and the Greeks saw a splendid opportunity of carving out an empire for themselves in Asia Minor, where there were already well over a million Greek immigrants. They were in high favour with the Allies, having driven out their pro-German King, Constantine, substituting his son, Alexander, and installed as Prime Minister M. Venizelos, who had consistently supported the western powers. They could make out a case on self-determination for Wilson; and Lloyd George was for some reason madly pro-Hellene. They were therefore allowed by the Supreme Council in Paris in May, 1919, to launch an an army of 200,000 forward from Smyrna towards the borders of Anatolia.

What nobody had allowed for was the quite unexpected and vigorous national revival which this provoked among the Turks. By the time the Allies, in August, 1920, had imposed the Treaty of Sèvres on the Sultan, Mustapha Kemal had already established himself as President at Ankara and had summoned a National Assembly which repudiated both the Treaty and the Sultan who had signed it. The young King of Greece was bitten by a pet monkey and died in October. King Constantine returned, Venizelos was defeated in a general election, and the Allies promptly withdrew their support from the Greek venture, France going even further and concluding a secret treaty with Kemal. Only Lloyd George, in the teeth of the advice of his generals, who had no opinion of the Greek army, continued to dream of a powerful Greece safeguarding British interests in the Eastern Mediterranean, thereby making great difficulties for Lord Curzon with the French and very great difficulties for the government of India, where his support for Greece deeply offended 80 million Moslems.

For nearly a year of tension the armies faced each other in central Asia Minor while the western powers argued. Then, in August, 1922, Lloyd George provoked the probably inevitable crisis by making a speech in the House of Commons which was so pro-Greek that King Constantine had extracts from it published as a Greek Army Order. Expecting this encouragement to precipitate a Greek attack, Kemal promptly attacked himself on August 10th, with overwhelming success. The Greek army was annihilated, Smyrna taken and burnt, and the Greeks were left with no foot of land in Asia Minor and the further problem of resettling the million or so refugees who had escaped massacre by the Turks. By mid-September Kemal's victorious troops were halted hurling insults across the barbed wire which covered the Allied neutral zone south of the Dardanelles at Chanak. The French and Italian contingents of the international force had been prudently withdrawn, and there remained only six battalions of English troops under General Harington. There was a very real danger, as Bonar Law said later in a letter to *The Times*, that the Turks, flushed with victory, would carry their massacre across the Straits into Thrace, and by attacking Constantinople touch off another Balkan war. There was also the obvious danger that Britain might find herself fighting the Turks single-handed.

All these dangers were averted, mainly by the skill, courage and tact of General Sir Charles Harington and Sir Horace Rumbold, the High Commissioner on the spot. The French, after an exceptionally stormy scene in Paris between Lord Curzon and M. Poincaré, were induced to see reason, and Kemal at last consented to an armistice, signed at Mudania on October 11th, under the terms of which yet another international conference was to be summoned to replace the now irrelevant Treaty of Sèvres. What could not be averted was the political crisis at home which ended in the break-up of the Coalition and the political ruin of Lloyd George.

The rumblings of discontent had been growing steadily within the Tory Party throughout the year, and the Honours scandal, coming on top of the murder of Sir Henry Wilson, had brought much of it into the open. What was more, there was evidence that mistrust and disillusionment with the government were spreading throughout the country. In normal times the English electorate is suspicious of too much cleverness in its political leaders. In a great crisis it will fall back on a man of erratic genius and follow him with almost blind devotion. At other times it prefers something less spectacular, more sober, commonsensical and predictable. The khaki election had caught them while Lloyd George's spell was still working, but by 1922 the wizardry was beginning to wear thin, and the Tory Whips, much more sensitively in touch with public opinion than the leaders, were aware that the little man was ceasing to be an electoral asset—was indeed in a fair way to becoming a liability. An adventurous foreign policy which alienated the French and at the same time threw Germany and Russia into each other's arms inspired the deepest mistrust. The communiqué of September, for which Churchill was mainly responsible, and which suddenly revealed that war with Turkey was not only possible, but almost unavoidable, that we had no allies but the defeated Greeks, and that the Dominions were being asked for military assistance, came as a severe shock. Moved to indignation though it had been by the wholesale massacre of Christians in Asia Minor, the British public cared not a straw for Greek ambitions; and the three weeks of acute anxiety which followed while Harington saved the situation completed the disillusionment of the country with Lloyd-Georgian methods of conducting foreign policy.

The Coalition Cabinet had become something of a mutual admiration society, more than usually infected with that occupational disease of politicians—the illusion of their own indispensability. When, in July, a group of Conservative junior ministers informed their leaders that it was time to break up the Coalition, they were merely snubbed. Birkenhead, generous, affectionate and well loved though he was in the circle of his own intimates, was becoming increasingly intolerant of brains less clear than his own, and increasingly arrogant in his dealings with them. The hectoring rudeness with which he rebuffed his junior colleagues on this occasion only increased their dissatisfaction with their own leaders. Austen Chamberlain's acquiescence in Lloyd George's decision to hold a quick general election before the Conservative Party's annual conference in November could reach any awkward decisions brought the discontent to a head. The Tory Whips reported that they would no longer be able to hold the Party together and that there would be non-Coalition Conservative candidates in at least 184 constituencies; and when on October 10th the Cabinet, Baldwin alone dissenting, confirmed the decision to hold an immediate election, both the Chairman of the Conservative Party and its Chief Whip informed Austen Chamberlain that they would be forced publicly to repudiate his leadership.

Chamberlain, still convinced that the Coalition, and Lloyd Goerge himself, must be preserved, thought he could ride the storm. He did not believe that the Tory Party could get along at all without himself, Birkenhead, Balfour, Walter Long, and Sir Robert Horne. As he put it in a letter to Birkenhead, 'they would be in a d——d fix'. But he decided that he must call a meeting of the Party at the Carlton Club on October 19th to force the issue, and so rushed upon his own doom. For he had reckoned without two vital factors. One was Bonar Law's devotion to the Party he had served all his political life. He had meant his retirement to be permanent, and, though both Ireland and Chanak had brought him out into the open again, his pronouncements had been the oracular warnings of an elder statesman with no personal axe to grind, delivered firmly from the back benches. He had scrupulously refrained from challenging Chamberlain's leadership; had firmly refused appeal after appeal from friends and colleagues to 'come forward and lead us'; and to the very last minute his friends and his family, all working on him at top pressure, were uncertain whether they would get him to the Carlton Club meeting at all.

In fact by October 18th Bonar Law had become convinced that if Chamberlain had his way they would split the Party and would condemn it to years in the wilderness, as Peel and Disraeli had done between them in 1846. When on that day Sir Arthur Salvidge called on him in a last attempt to rally his support for the Coalition, he found him weary and very reluctant, but convinced. He also found that Lord Curzon was waiting for an interview in another room. That nobleman, goaded at last beyond endurance by the ceaseless interference of Lloyd George and the Garden Suburb in the proper conduct of foreign affairs, had placed his resignation in Lloyd George's hands and was joining the malcontents. The last straw for him had been a wildly irresponsible speech on the coming negotiations with Turkey which the Prime Minister, 'in the highest spirits and the most bellicose mood',[1] delivered at Manchester on October 14th. The eve of a peace conference in which a victorious and self-assertive Turkish government had to be coaxed to a reasonable settlement, to which the French must also be a party, was an ill-chosen moment to denounce the barbarous excesses of the Turks and the perfidy of the French government. Curzon had had enough. He had made his views plain to Lloyd George and Chamberlain; and though his colleagues later bitterly denounced what Churchill called a 'sudden and nimble' change of sides, there was truth in Curzon's own claim that it had in fact been 'slow, and perhaps even belated'.[2]

This was the second factor which disrupted Chamberlain's calculations. 'So our punctilious Pro-Consul has ratted,' someone said gloomily, when Salvidge rushed back to the Cabinet with the news; and Curzon's desertion of his Cabinet colleagues was in the event decisive. Chamberlain may have been right in thinking that Bonar Law would have great difficulty in forming a government with nobody but himself, the very inexperienced Baldwin, and a handful of junior ministers to draw on, though he would certainly have had a try. With Curzon's vast experience, skill, and prestige available for the key post at the Foreign Office, the thing became instantly far more feasible and the vote at the Carlton Club almost a certainty, however hard Balfour might bang the table with his fist and shout: 'Fight them, fight them, fight them.' The news the next morning that an independent Conservative had won a by-election at Newport with a Coalition Liberal at the bottom of a three-cornered poll more or less settled the issue. Unrepresentative though they might be, the Conservative rank and file were reflecting at that moment the movement of opinion in the country.

Plenty of dramatic accounts of the Carlton Club meeting have been written, but really, by the time the 275 members gathered at 11 in the

[1] Ronaldshay, p. 314.   [2] Letter to the *Morning Post*, Nov. 10th, 1922.

morning on October 19th, the drama was already over. The three speeches which mattered were Austen Chamberlain's, coldly repressive and unconciliating, a very able plea to put an end to the Coalition from Stanley Baldwin, and Bonar Law's decisive statement that in the immediate crisis he attached more importance to keeping the Party united than to winning the next election. Privately he thought they might very well do both, having calculated that in a straight fight the Conservatives would gain an overall majority of 25. In the immediately important vote the Party decided to leave the Coalition by 187 votes to 87. The strength of the vote alone disposes of the legend that Lloyd George had been made the victim of a reactionary clique. Salisbury's die-hards mustered at the most 50. Chamberlain felt bitter to the end of his life at having been deprived of the leadership of the Party for the second time by Bonar Law; but there is no doubt that he had lost its confidence, and that Bonar Law's action had saved the Party from disruption, as it had indeed on the earlier occasion in 1911.

Lloyd George waited for no more, but called immediately on the King with his resignation; and as soon as he had been re-elected to the leadership of his Party, Bonar Law accepted the King's invitation to form what Churchill and the Tory intellectual stars contemptuously referred to as 'a government of the 2nd XI'. The Foreign Office went as a matter of course to Curzon, the Exchequer, after it had been turned down by McKenna, who preferred being Chairman of the Midland Bank, to the highly inexperienced Baldwin. Seven peers in the Cabinet emphasised the shortage of able men, but there were some names in the list which would soon be better known: Amery, Edward Wood who was to become successively Lord Irwin and Lord Halifax, and Sir Philip Lloyd-Graeme, later Lord Swinton. Outside the Cabinet still more talent was to show itself. Neville Chamberlain, the Postmaster General, the Attorney General, Sir Douglas Hogg, and Sir Samuel Hoare who had led the back bench revolt and now became Secretary for Air, were all to show themselves unexpectedly able in office. At least the election which followed justified Bonar Law's decision and the Carlton Club vote. Not all Birkenhead's contemptuous references to 'second-class intellects' nor Lloyd George's gibes at 'Mayfair and Belgravia' intrigues would stir the country from its settled conviction that, as Lord Robert Cecil put it, second-class intellects were preferable to second-class characters.

When Lloyd George described Bonar Law as 'honest to the point of simplicity', he provided him with the best slogan of the campaign. The Conservatives emerged with a majority of 77 over all other parties combined, which was almost exactly what Wickham Steed, the editor of *The Times*, had prophesied to Bonar Law before the crisis.

It was not a triumph which owed anything to imaginative, constructive political ideas. The only thing of that sort offered to the electorate in 1922 was the Labour plea for a Capital Levy to extinguish the bulk of the national debt—an idea largely developed for them by Hugh Dalton, a newcomer from the London School of Economics. To this fact they may have owed the doubling of their Party strength in the new Parliament, where Ramsay MacDonald became official leader of the Opposition with a following of 142.[1] Bonar Law offered the country nothing but 'tranquillity and economy', and that, after four years of Lloyd-Georgian 'meddle and muddle', was just what it wanted: no more adventures and no excitement, but time to nurse its wounds and recover its nervous tone. That election marked the end of wartime political organisation and the extinction of Lloyd George—he returned with only 59 followers. Otherwise it opened no new age, but merely a pause while the impossible dreams of 1918—the utopias of the idealists and the golden age fantasies of the conservatives—were scaled down to the practical realities of 1923.

The short period of Bonar Law's administration—it had only been going for 209 days when his health again collapsed, irrevocably—was thus principally a period of tidying up. It was both a return to a party government and to Cabinet government. The Garden Suburb was disbanded, the responsibility for departmental administration was thrust firmly on to the appropriate ministers, who were henceforth free from the wayward, sudden interferences of the Lloyd George epoch. The inexperience of his colleagues, who shone, as Curzon put it, 'more in silence than in speech', threw a heavy Parliamentary burden on the Prime Minister; but responsibility was firmly devolved, and the men soon rose to it. The breach with France was by now too wide to be bridged and in January, 1923, after a series of ineffectual conferences, Poincaré sent the French troops into the Ruhr to occupy Essen. This

[1] Throughout this book the figures for Party strengths are taken from *Whitaker's Almanack*.

was not technically a breach of the Treaty, since he had obtained in advance an official pronouncement from the Reparations Commission that Germany was in default. It was nevertheless in all its consequences a disastrous move, which could have no real object but to sabotage any possible German recovery. Even Poincaré cannot have believed that, in the teeth of the passive resistance of German industry, he could screw an extra penny in Reparations out of such a policy. What he did achieve was a permanent, and in the eyes of most thinking men a justified German grievance against Versailles and all that flowed from it, and an almost equally permanent estrangement of English opinion—what some wag called the 'rupture cordiale'. So ended the first phase of the Reparations question.

Fortunately Curzon was more successful with the Turks. The Congress of Lausanne, over the first phase of which he presided himself with great energy and masterly skill, reached in the end an entirely satisfactory settlement to replace the Treaty of Sèvres and restored that Anglo-Turkish friendship which the Conservative Party had inherited as a Disraelian tradition. The other great international question still outstanding and so far not seriously tackled by anybody, was that of inter-allied indebtedness, and more particularly the problem of the British debt to America of about £900 million. The settlement of this issue was left, with less happy results, to Mr. Baldwin.

Just as Reparations had destroyed Anglo-French collaboration, this question of allied debts was to bedevil relations with the United States for the better part of a generation. The legal position was perfectly clear. Though her late allies owed her four times as much, and though even a large portion of the British debt to America was in respect of munitions supplied to those same allies, the obligation had been incurred by Britain and was inescapable. On the other hand a strong case could be made out for cancelling all these debts; and Keynes's last act before he shook the dust of Paris off his feet had been to present for Wilson's consideration a scheme which not only provided for cancellation, but also for a gigantic further loan from America to finance the rehabilitation of Central Europe. What was called the Keynes plan—'a sort of Marshall Plan, albeit on a smaller scale'[1]—was taken up by Lloyd George with Wilson and urgently argued. In a war in which every

[1] Harrod, *op. cit.*, p. 246.

one of the allied nations had sacrificed men, money, and materials un-
stintingly in the common cause, it was legal enough, but not strictly just
that the money debts alone should be computed at the end. In casualties
the U.S.A. had suffered one-fiftieth of the British loss, a hundredth of
the French. The European allies had all but ruined themselves in the
common cause, throwing in every asset they possessed, whereas the
United States had emerged not only relatively, but actually and
materially richer from the war. Lloyd George wrote to Wilson:

> Britain has already bled itself white for the sake of the Allies. It asks
> nothing which is impossible, but it does claim that it has the right
> to ask its colleagues of the Peace Conference both to compel
> Germany to pay whatever she is capable of paying, and to place
> their own credit at the disposal of the nations for the regeneration
> of the world as Great Britain placed hers unreservedly at the service
> of the Allies in order to save the freedom of the world.[1]

The moment was badly chosen. Wilson was not happy with the way
his treaty was working out and very conscious that he had already a very
difficult case to present when he got back to America. There was also
logic in his retort: 'How can your experts or ours be expected to work
out a *new* plan to furnish working capital to Germany when we deliberately start by taking away all Germany's present capital?' Keynes
had to admit that there was 'substantial truth in the President's stand-
point', though he found the spirit of his letter 'far too harsh for the
human situation facing us'.[2] The truth is that Americans of that generation lived at two extremes in such matters. The distinction between
business transactions and the exercise of benevolence was clear-cut and
absolute, and for them the two worlds did not mix. Their business ethic
was hard and ruthless; their capacity for charitable, disinterested
generosity unbounded. But they were two distinct codes of rules. To
obtrude arguments based on generosity into a business transaction was
to whine—an attempt to play on the other man's weakness or senti-
mentality. To obtrude business considerations into a charitable transaction was equally offensive. The British, in this particular series of
transactions, offended both ways. By arguing that moral justice might
be something different from the written letter of a contract into which

---

[1] Lloyd George, *The Truth about Reparations and War Debts*, p. 107.
[2] Quoted Harrod, pp. 247–8.

they had freely entered, they brought to the surface the hard, business streak in every American politician: that streak which made even a great liberal and anglophile like Walter Page write with unconcealed satisfaction to Wilson on August 2nd, 1914, when he knew that Britain was committed to war: 'Our shipping and foreign commerce will gain immensely,'[1] and which was to elicit later from that 'insignificant, sourfaced little man', President Coolidge, the celebrated sneer: 'They hired the money, didn't they?' It was equally offensive when the British urged the interest of the United States themselves in handling these matters generously, intruding huckstering considerations upon charity and robbing a noble and generous gesture of its proper reward in self-satisfaction by suggesting that there was also self-advantage. Keynes put his finger on the truth in his second book, *A Revision of the Treaty*, in 1922:

> The average American, I fancy, would like to see the European nations approaching him with a pathetic light in their eyes and the cash in their hands, saying, 'America, we owe to you our liberty and our life; here we bring what we can in grateful thanks, money not wrung by grievous taxation from the widow and the orphan, but saved, the best fruits of victory, out of the abolition of armaments, militarism, Empire, and internal strife, made possible by the help you freely gave us.' And then the average American would reply: 'I honour you for your integrity. It is what I expected. But I did not enter the war for profit or to invest my money well. I have had my reward in the words you have just uttered. The loans are forgiven. Return to your homes and use the resources I release to uplift the poor and the unfortunate.' And it would be an essential part of the little scene that his reply should come as a complete and overwhelming surprise.

But this was not how the British government approached the matter, and Baldwin set out in January, 1923, with all the cards stacked against him. What was worse, the Balfour Note, issued by the Foreign Office in August, 1922, had informed Britain's European debtors that they would only be expected to pay enough to cover the British debt to America. This was common sense, but it infringed the American monopoly of generosity and it seemed to hold a pistol to the American head. Did they refuse to compromise they would be branded as the Shylock of the world, insisting on their pound of flesh, while the British generously

---

[1] *Life and Letters of Walter H. Page*, Vol. III, p. 130.

waived their claim. American opinion hardened at once, and there was a prompt demand for the immediate funding of the British debt.

What Baldwin had been commissioned to achieve was a lowering of the interest on the loan from the original exorbitant 5 % to 2½ %, so that the whole could be settled at the rate of £25 million a year. Even this, moreover, was to be conditional on Britain reaching a satisfactory settlement with her European creditors. Failing such terms, Bonar Law would have preferred to default, and both McKenna and Keynes agreed with him, though no one else of any importance did. As Keynes pointed out, 'it is the debtor who has the last word in these cases'. But Baldwin, meeting an inflexible demand for 3½ % without any conditions about European debts attached, harassed by the American government and by the British Embassy to reach a settlement before Congress rose, concluded that this would be the best offer he could get and closed with it, without reservation. He had slightly improved the terms originally offered. But he had committed Britain to paying £34 million a year for ten years, and thereafter £40 million for a further fifty-two years. What was worse, he then proceeded to make it almost impossible for the Cabinet to repudiate his settlement by disclosing its terms in detail to journalists at a press conference when he disembarked from the *Olympic* at Southampton, before he had even met his colleagues. On top of that, he justified his admittedly regrettable decision to the English papers by a reference to the ignorance of the American public which started off a major row on both sides of the Atlantic. When King George protested at this, Bonar Law drily replied that he 'was sorry Your Majesty should have noticed that paragraph'.[1] But he himself was in despair. He felt that acceptance of such onerous terms would in the long run do more damage to Anglo-American relations than an immediate repudiation. 'I should be the most cursed Prime Minister that ever held office in England', he said, 'if I accepted those terms.'

Nevertheless in the end he did accept them. The whole Cabinet, while agreeing with him in deploring them, felt bound in the circumstances to stand by them, and he all but resigned, thereby precipitating a first-class political crisis. It took a week-end of wrestling with his conscience to accept what was in effect the worst of both worlds and condemn Great Britain for the next few years to pay the Americans on

[1] 'And why should I not notice it?' the King retorted. 'I read the papers.'

the nail and collect nothing from Europe. What was even more galling, as American opinion softened all sorts of European debts were cancelled and the loans for reconstruction became available in even greater profusion than Keynes had dared to contemplate. But there was no softening towards Britain. Feeling itself to have been manœuvred into an attitude which was less than generous, the government of the United States maintained it with all the pride of obstinacy.

Oddly enough, Baldwin emerged from the whole episode with a stature not diminished, but enhanced. He had to spend what he described as the most miserable two hours of his life listening to Bonar Law debating the terms with the American Ambassador. But, while frankly admitting that he ought to have cut out his tongue rather than say what he did to the journalists, he stood equally by his conviction that his were the best terms available at that time, which was probably true, and continued to insist in his public speeches on the importance for the regeneration of the world of upholding the 'sanctity of contract'. His speech on the Address a fortnight later, after emphasising this, ended on a peroration castigating all creeds based on hatred which struck a new note in English politics:

> It is no good trying to cure the world by spreading out oceans of bloodshed. It is no good trying to cure the world by repeating that pentasyllabic French derivative 'Proletariat'. The English language is the richest in the world in monosyllables. Four words, of one syllable each, are words which contain salvation for this country and for the whole world, and they are 'Faith', 'Hope', 'Love', and 'Work'. No government in this country today which has not faith in the people, hope in the future, love for its fellow men, and which will not work and work and work, will ever bring this country through to better times, or will ever bring Europe through, or the world through.[1]

It was easy for opponents to denounce this sort of thing as rhetorical clap-trap. But it appealed to an audience far wider than the House of Commons; and it seemed to suggest an escape from the crass and selfish materialism of the 'hard-faced men' of 1918—something more ambitious and exciting than Bonar Law's modest 'tranquillity and economy'.

It was as well for the Conservatives, and for the nation, that Baldwin

[1] See A. W. Baldwin, *My Father: the True Story*, p. 120.

survived the crisis as he did, and that he further strengthened his position with a sound, orthodox budget and a first-class budget speech in
April. For the Cabinet crisis averted in January recurred, and unavoidably, in May. Bonar Law's health gave way finally, though only his
intimate friends knew that he had incurable cancer of the throat; and on
May 20th he tendered his resignation to the King, thereby provoking
the second great drama of the year within the Tory Party. The obvious
successor, in his own and almost everybody else's eyes, was Lord Curzon. He had lived his whole public life in the expectation of this, and it
had been a life full of distinguished achievement. In the absence of the
still sulking Coalitionists he towered in experience and prestige over all
his colleagues. Baldwin, the only conceivable alternative, had hardly
been heard of before that year, and had shown his own inexperience all
too plainly only a few months before. Yet Bonar Law personally had
grave doubts of Curzon. If first-class character mattered more than
first-class intellect, then beyond all doubt Baldwin was the man. Curzon
was pompous and touchy and an indigestible colleague, constantly
complaining of slights, real or fancied, and of infringements of the prerogatives of his office and dignity. He had also shown himself once or
twice to be a slippery customer, apt to run with the hare and hunt with
the hounds. Finally he was a peer, which might prove a serious handicap
to a Prime Minister in a self-consciously democratic age. He had been
plaguing Bonar Law with testy, often downright rude letters, even during the past month when he knew how sick and tired his leader was; and
it was with thankfulness that Bonar Law learnt from Lord Crewe that
he need not suggest a successor to the King. For he felt that he could
not conscientiously recommend Lord Curzon as a leader of men, but
yet that he could not pass him over.

The dénouement for Curzon was as cruel and disillusioning as his
worst enemy could have wished. He had remained for the critical weekend among the feudal splendours of Montacute in Somerset, where
there was not even a telephone, awaiting the summons which, after a
lifetime of expectation, he believed must come. A telegram on the
Monday night summoning him to meet Lord Stamfordham in London
the next day brought him up, full of happy plans for the government he
would form, only to be told that, out of consideration for his feelings,
the King had wished him to be told privately and in advance that he

was sending for Mr. Baldwin, 'a man', as Curzon burst out in his first rage and disappointment, 'of the utmost insignificance'. Pride and a very real magnanimity for which his enemies had never given him credit saw him through. He consented to keep the Foreign Office for the time being, if only to preserve the unity of the Party, and he himself, in a felicitous speech, proposed the election of Baldwin as leader four days later, but his heart was broken and he did not long survive the disappointment.[1]

Bonar Law lived only a few months longer, enjoying then, perhaps, a higher place in public esteem than he had during the whole of a stormy and distinguished career. His name comes down in history associated neither with any great achievement nor yet with any great failure. The only public cause he had triumphantly championed had been the somewhat negative one of Irish partition. But at the end men began to see him as symbolic of certain solid qualities and permanent values all too rare in wartime and post-war England. There was a belated sense of gratitude, which caused, for example, the diners in a Brighton restaurant during his retirement to rise to their feet as he walked out as a gesture of respect; and which, more surprisingly, resulted in his being buried in Westminster Abbey—the first Prime Minister since Gladstone to be accorded this posthumous distinction. It was as he left that funeral that Asquith made his famous comment: 'It is fitting that we should have buried the Unknown Prime Minister beside the Unknown Soldier.' But the many thousands who filed past his grave during the following afternoon and evening suggest that he deserved a less contemptuous epitaph.

The advent of Baldwin, much more than the break-up of the Coalition, marked an era. It opened that fourteen-year period which Churchill has called the 'Baldwin-MacDonald Régime',[2] in which the minds and temperaments of these two men influenced the course of events to a quite unusual degree, and which shaped the first awkward beginnings of what might one day be a new Britain. Smuts had been all too right when he had said in 1918 that the new world was not ready to be born. Utopian dreams of sudden and spectacular changes had been dis-

[1] The clearest analysis of the intrigues which contributed towards making Lord Stamfordham advise the King as he eventually did is in Blake, *The Unknown Prime Minister*, pp. 517 et seq.
[2] *The Second World War*, Vol. I, p. 17.

appointed. The dead weight of the past had been too heavy. Now there was to begin a more sober spade-work: a slow and quite unspectacular progress which, in a series of crises and difficulties, passed almost unnoticed, but which, it can perhaps be claimed, created the conditions out of which a new and healthier social structure might be built.

CHAPTER 5

The Baldwin-MacDonald Régime

T he four years which followed the Armistice had done little to improve either the industrial or the political situation in Great Britain. Englishmen are apt to forget, except when they contemplate American politics, what a very difficult and dangerous experiment a mass democracy, based on direct election and universal suffrage, still is. It is a method which more than half the world has rejected as inefficient and whose dangers are only too apparent when inexperienced men seek to apply it among peoples new to self-government. Ever since the Reform Bill of 1832 had committed Great Britain by implication to universal suffrage successive new blocks of new voters had been enfranchised, while the Parliamentary machine continued to function on oligarchic, XVIII-century assumptions which created a perpetual danger that the social needs of the people would find little response in the remote minds of their legislators. In a century of British industrial near-monopoly and continuously expanding trade, full employment could be achieved and social progress maintained with the minimum of Parliamentary interference, as it were by accident, until they seemed as inevitable as the evolutionary processes of natural selection.

By the time the pinch came, at the turn of the XIX century, there was a real danger that politics would become, as French politics so often have in the past 150 years, a game as artificial and remote from social needs and realities as first-class cricket: an entertaining spectacle with meaning only for its enthusiasts. Lloyd George's radical budgets and the payment of Members of Parliament had done something to bring the House of Commons back into contact with reality; but the war had precipitated all the crises which still seemed comfortably remote in 1914 and left no time for leisurely adjustment. And it brought the radical leaders face to face with a problem which had perplexed them off and on since the days of the Chartists: whether essential reforms could be achieved by political action through the existing constitutional machinery, or whether the urgency of the situation demanded new machinery and speedier methods.

This was really the position of the advocate of 'direct action' in 1920. They were the political heirs of the men who had turned in despair from Parliament in the 1840s and 1850s to the organisation and development of Trade Unionism: not Communists necessarily, though they were lumped together with them by the inflamed imaginations and uneasy consciences of their Conservative opponents, but revolutionaries in the sense that they despaired of the existing political machinery and sought eagerly after any method, syndicalist or otherwise, which would achieve what Parliament could not or would not do.

The facts that a violent explosion of such discontent was avoided and that the Parliamentary machine, however creakingly and protestingly, did prove itself capable of meeting the new demands which were made on it lead people today to take that particular triumph for granted. We forget that to have carried through a social revolution without a political upheaval is an almost unique achievement, and that in 1920 it was by no means a foregone conclusion that we should do so. Revolution, it is true, was still a long way off. But both in the rank and file of industrial workers and among their leaders there was a wide and growing sense of frustration which must have grown very fast to the point of explosion had there not been opened to it some reasonable hope of betterment by working in and through Parliament. In 1923 that hope seemed to be receding. Bonar Law personified, in a negative way, an equal despair. He was not unaware of or unsympathetic to the hunger and misery of the unemployed. He merely thought that there was nothing his, or any other government could do about it. 'I am convinced, as of course you know,' he told a T.U.C. deputation that January, 'that the scheme which is recommended by so many members of the House of Commons, involving a complete upsetting of our present social conditions, would not make things better but worse.'[1] He would not even meet a deputation of hunger marchers who, he thought, were merely wasting money

---

[1] Quoted Blake, *op. cit.*, p. 499.

and shoe-leather; and he openly admitted that the policy of all post-war governments, of concentrating every effort on balancing the budget and deflating the currency, made unemployment a great deal worse. Entrenched in the government, in the Court of the Bank of England, and in the board rooms, the Old Guard freely confessed that they had no new answers: only the old ones which were already proving failures. However sincere and honest, such an attitude was an open invitation to revolution. That it was avoided was very largely the personal achievement of the two men whose names, for Churchill, stamped the Régime: Baldwin and MacDonald.

It was the fate of both these men to become, at the end of their lives, centres of the most embittered controversy. MacDonald was to die with the curses of those in whose service he had spent his life ringing in his ears for the 'great betrayal' of 1931. Baldwin's declining years were poisoned by thousands of bitter, reproachful letters from those who laid all the disasters of 1940 and the sufferings of London under bombing at the door of his political cowardice. It is possible that this witch-hunting mania, particularly in Baldwin's case, has still not died down sufficiently for the historian to penetrate to the real contribution of these men whose personalities Churchill rightly saw as the dominating factors in English public life for over a decade. Most of the published memoirs still reek of contemporary prejudice, contemporary ignorance, and a partisan blindness to facts. The historian, seeking some truer perspective, must remember how different the problems of 1925 were from those of 1945; and must in fairness record that both men succeeded abundantly in certain tasks for which their abilities remarkably fitted them, and failed sadly in others for which they were quite unfitted. It is also wise to remember that a democracy does on the whole get the leaders it deserves; that very few of those who lived through the years between the wars have any right to say 'I told you so'; and that it is not a right in any case which the generous care to exercise.

To his colleagues and contemporaries Stanley Baldwin appeared always as something of an enigma—often a maddening enigma. Certainly there was none of that simplicity of character which Englishmen love to simulate and so rarely possess. For the cartoonists and the public at large there was the bowler hat and the pipe, the Sunday walks in Worcestershire which ended in the contemplation of his pigs: Squire

Baldwin, simple, straightforward, homely and above all trustworthy. But he could be caught in front of a looking-glass practising suitable angles for the pipe, and his agricultural interests were entirely amateurish: the pigs were just the object for a walk through the sort of countryside which he deeply loved. It would have been nice for his Socialist opponents to be able to bill him as the wealthy and selfish capitalist, comfortably descended from generations of iron-masters and cushioned against social privation. But the reality eluded them, not so much because of the fifth of his fortune which he gave to the Exchequer in a forlorn attempt to set an example in 1919, as because of the evident sincerity with which he could speak of the workers of his factory as being 'of his family'. Much of the rest of that fortune was lost because he scorned to sell out at a profit and leave so many others whose welfare was inescapably pinned to the fortunes of the family firm in the lurch; and there were few Socialists who could excel his savage contempt for 'the vulgar luxury' of those who constituted themselves 'the best propagandists of revolutionary doctrine'.

Many of the accusations which have been levelled at him were, of of course, true. By the standards of either Winston Churchill or Neville Chamberlain he was indolent. In his Cabinets there would be none of that restless interference in departmental administration by which Churchill was to galvanise a wartime government into prodigies of effort. That ceaseless stream of minutes from Prime Minister to Secretary of State beginning 'Please report at once', or 'Let me see immediately', or 'I am much concerned', would not have seemed to Baldwin to be part of a Prime Minister's job at all. It was his business to formulate the general principles of policy, to preserve harmony and coherence at Cabinet meetings, to direct Party strategy, and to leave it to ministers to run their own departments. He did not lead Cabinet meetings through a prepared agenda, as Bonar Law did. He let discussion range until it reached a conclusion. Austen Chamberlain said that he could only once remember Baldwin influencing a Cabinet decision. To colleagues his detachment—often even his patent boredom with schemes on which they had lavished hours of hard work—was maddening. 'I am almost in despair', Curzon wrote to him in 1923, 'as to the way foreign policy is carried on in this Cabinet. Any member may make any suggestion he pleases and the discussion wanders off into helpless irrelevancies. No decision is ever arrived at and no policy prepared.'[1] And the testiness with which Neville Chamberlain records the 'deplorable impression' made on him by a trivial incident in 1925 throws a vivid light on both characters: he had become aware as he developed a complicated case that Baldwin was not listening, and was enraged when the Prime Minister passed an open note across him to Churchill: 'MATCHES. Lent at 10.30 a.m. Returned?'[2]

Chamberlain's mind, restlessly preoccupied with complicated plans for housing and derating and public transport, was indeed very remote from the leisurely, philosophical and contemplative habit of his leader. Soaked in the English classics and in a paternalistic tradition of public responsibility, Baldwin moved towards different objectives and in a different way. He set himself to bring back into Conservative politics an element of high principle, to restore the confidence of the workers in the goodwill of employers and of the people in their leaders, and some respect among politicians for the integrity of opponents. A Conservatism which was merely 'an appeal to the rights of property and the fear of Socialism' filled him with distaste. Yet there was a disconcerting efficiency behind the leisureliness and the philosophy. Churchill called him 'an astute and relentless politician', and considered that he was 'the greatest party manager the Conservatives ever had';[3] and those who complained so bitterly of 'a leader who sits in the smoking-room reading the *Strand Magazine*'[4] had also to admit that when it came to Parliamentary tactics Baldwin had them all 'stone cold'.

In attempting, quite consciously, to remedy the existing state of affairs, Baldwin had thus set himself a double task. In the first place he had to lead Conservatives to some imaginative understanding of the situation which had called a Labour Party into being and to convince them that their survival depended on finding a better practical answer to the problem than Labour's. Secondly he sought to convince Labour that all Conservatives were not blood-sucking capitalists, that humanity and idealism were not the exclusive prerogatives of left-wing thinkers, and that tolerance of opponents and discrimination in opposition were essential virtues if Parliamentary government was to survive and party

[1] Quoted G. M. Young, *Stanley Baldwin*, p. 50.
[2] Feiling, *op. cit.*, p. 184.
[3] *Second World War*, Vol. I, p. 26.
[4] G. M. Young, *op. cit.*, p. 72.

not to degenerate into mere faction. MacDonald had the same task in reverse. He had to convince the nation that Labour was a responsible Party, perfectly competent to take over the government, and resolved to achieve its programme of reform within the framework of the constitution. He had also to persuade Labour itself that it was in and through Parliament that social progress could best be achieved: that the existing constitutional machinery was not designed to shore up capitalism and preserve privilege, but was available to any party which could secure a democratically elected majority; and that, even in opposition, a Labour Party could exercise a steady pressure which could force some measure of constructive reform even out of a Conservative government.

Ever since what they have called 'the Great Betrayal' of 1931, MacDonald's former colleagues have sought to present him to posterity as a shallow snob of second-rate intellect and indecisive character, boundlessly ambitious and wholly without principle or loyalty. The picture which they have sought to paint does not bear critical analysis; nor does it accord with what they said, wrote, and thought about him a few years earlier when he accomplished what then seemed the all but miraculous feat of leading an all-Labour government to kiss hands and assume office. The thirty-year struggle which had led from his first job, as a penniless lad from Lossiemouth addressing envelopes at 10/- a week for the Cyclists' Touring Club, to No. 10 Downing Street, and Chequers does not read like the career of a man exclusively, or even passionately concerned with personal advancement. The rigid and unfashionable pacifism which clouded his political career both during the Boer War and from 1914–18 proves him not only high-principled, but extremely courageous. And if, at the crisis of his life, he recognised loyalties which overrode the claims of his colleagues and his Parliamentary supporters, an overwhelming majority of his countrymen at the time approved his action and thanked God for it.

A certain snobbery, a weakness, at which he himself smiled, for duchesses, may be conceded. But even here the reader of Hugh Dalton's gibes and anecdotes illustrating it is apt to be more struck with the snobbery of the writer than that of his target. Sir Samuel Hoare described MacDonald's essential quality as romanticism; and certainly he loved to contemplate his career in a setting of historical background and savoured to the full the sensation of a confidential relationship with the King, as well as deriving great support from it. Hoare goes out of his way to say that there was 'nothing snobbish in his attitude', which was, indeed, 'less incongruous than Chatham's obsequiousness to George II'. There was, too, a certain confusion of thought, a cloudiness of mind, introspective and hesitant, which made it hard for him to make up his mind; and even when his thought was clear to himself, he was apt to wrap it up in rambling, complicated sentences which often obscured it to his hearers. Lenin said that his speeches and articles were 'the best example that could be given of that smooth, melodious, banal and Socialist-seeming phraseology' under which British Labour concealed its bourgeois origins. When one reads the argument which MacDonald at this time put forward for dropping the name of Socialist in favour of Labour—'and then you will have a heart and spirit that in some sort of mystical way associates yourself with the great, simple heart of the common people, with all its failures, yet with all its divine potentialities and possibilities'—one sees what Lenin meant.

Yet his very defects enhanced rather than reduced his qualifications as the only possible Parliamentary leader. The cloudiness of his thought, the unquenchable optimism of his tone, and his rather simple faith in the fundamental goodwill of all men gave him a capacity for adjustment and compromise essential in all parliamentary politics and almost entirely lacking among his followers. For his party derived from two quite separate sources, each rigidly uncompromising in its intellectual habit. The real Socialists were the academics of the Party, the product of the Fabian Society or the Independent Labour Party, grounded in the theory of the Movement, apt to ask first of any proposal whether it was sound Socialism, and scarcely interested in whether it was sound policy or good politics. The other element, in sharp and conscious contrast to these men 'who had never done a day's manual work in their life', was the Trade Unionist: men like Clynes and Arthur Henderson, the iron-moulder, for whom the standards of living of the industrial worker were the only touchstone of policy, and who spent their lives fighting not so much capitalism as capitalists. It is significant that the wartime conscientious objectors were drawn exclusively from the intellectuals. Henderson and Clynes both served with distinction on Coalition governments, Clynes in particular making a name for himself as Lloyd George's Food Controller.

For the first essential task of fusing these discordant elements into a single effective Party Ramsay MacDonald was almost irreplaceable. Tall, strikingly good-looking and leonine, with a seductive charm of voice, he had an impressive manner which combined well with that acrobatic imprecision of thought which once made Churchill describe him as 'the boneless wonder', and which could obscure differences of opinion in a smoke screen of comforting, blanketing phraseology. It enabled him, too, to become a first-class Parliamentary tactician, which neither Clynes nor Snowden ever was, and a smooth, elusive debater, so that the leadership of the Party in the House fell naturally to him the moment he got back to it in 1922. He set himself, successfully, to forge out of his discordant and grumbling following a Party which was not Socialist, nor Trade Unionist, but rather an extension of XIX-century radicalism: an eligible successor as the Party of progress to Lloyd George's Liberalism, which indeed it became.

For his secondary task of convincing the old governing classes and the electorate that a Labour victory would mean nothing so very terrible after all, and at the same time coaxing his followers to make the social compromises on inessentials which would ease their passage to ultimate triumph, he was also uniquely well equipped. Here again his defects of character helped rather than hindered. He would enjoy assuring an anxious Lord Stamfordham that 'of course', if invited to dine at the Palace, he would accept and would be properly dressed; to know that Stamfordham had found him 'quite a gentleman', which would have reduced most of his colleagues to truculent rage, would for him only emphasise pleasurably the gulf which stretched back to Lossiemouth and the C.T.C. King George's fussy preoccupation with correctness of dress and Labour touchiness and fear of ridicule made all ceremonial questions potentially explosive; but MacDonald was surely right in insisting that it was worth while to meet the King over what was, after all, a harmless if irritating foible, if thereby his often very valuable help could be secured on more important matters.

It was not long before he was required to put all these techniques into action, for Baldwin opened his first period as Conservative leader with a grave electoral miscalculation. From the Party point of view he seemed to be sitting pretty in the summer of 1923 and there was no need, on the face of it, for any dramatic or decisive action from him at all. The European climate, it is true, was unpleasant. The French sat obstinately in the Ruhr without wringing an extra penny out of Germany, and there was nothing Britain could do save advise the establishment of an international control of German finances to restore the Mark and make some feasible arrangements for resuming Reparations payments, and wait for the logic of events to bring the French round. Moreover the first tentative attempts of the League to establish its procedures and authority were not encouraging. It had so far failed to make the Poles give up Vilna, which was earmarked as the capital of the new state of Lithuania; and when a major dispute between Italy and Greece developed in the autumn, though the Assembly was actually sitting, it funked the issue and delegated the whole question to a Conference of Ambassadors at Paris. The whole episode was, indeed, far from reassuring: an early example of what a later generation was to call 'appeasement'. The advent of Mussolini and his Fascists had given a fresh impetus to what Orlando at Paris had called Italy's 'sacro egoismo'. The assassination of an Italian general on a boundary commission in Greece was made the excuse for sending the Italian fleet to bombard Corfu citadel, which contained only refugees from Asia Minor of whom a great many were killed. The bluster worked. Though the Greek government was in no way proved blameworthy, Mussolini was induced to withdraw only at the price of humiliating Greece and fining her £500,000.

The Ruhr occupation had its compensations for Britain, since it reopened some of the export markets lost to Germany by her coal industry and enabled the miners to regain some of the ground lost in 1921. They achieved a settlement which gave them a wage ranging from £2 to £4 a week, which at least brought the lowest-paid men up to a subsistence level. Unemployment at last fell from round about the two-million mark to 1,300,000, though below that the figure obstinately refused to go; and it was that figure which made Baldwin disturb this apparently placid political situation. His whole mind and temperament indignantly rejected Bonar Law's passive acceptance of unemployment as a phenomenon as uncontrollable by the government as the weather. For him, 1,300,000 was not just a figure. It represented a mass of wholly deserving fellow men condemned to soul-destroying idleness, and queues of drawn, hopeless faces waiting every week at the Labour Exchanges to be told that there was nothing for them but to go on feeling hungry on an inadequate dole until a turn in the trade cycle gave them back their jobs. Governments must either deal with such situations or perish: that was what governments were for.

The financial techniques for maintaining a community in full employment are still an economic battlefield on which experts fight even over fundamentals. In the 1920s even the fundamentals of the problem had scarcely been grasped. In the long run Maynard Keynes was to do humanity the inestimable benefit of discovering and indicating the lines on which a solution might be found. Already he had begun to see some of the truth and had raised his voice against orthodox banking and Treasury practices which met a crisis by restrictive action which further reduced purchasing power and so contributed to a still more severe stagnation of industry and trade. But Keynes was still a voice crying in the wilderness. The bitterness of his criticisms in his book on Versailles had ostracised him from the official world, and his pronouncements were greeted by the Chairmen of the great banks in their annual speeches with the sneer of the practical man for the theorist.

It is probably only fair to add that Keynes himself was still only groping his way through this highly complex problem. The Athenaeum jest that, in any gathering of five economists, there would be six differing opinions, two of them held by Keynes, was not entirely unfounded, and would remain so until he had hammered his way to the complex conclusions of the *Treatise on Money*. It was to take him five years of Cambridge semi-seclusion to write that, and another five before its more practical analysis reached the world with *The General Theory of Employment, Interest, and Money*. He had gone far enough already to know that King George V's demand for large-scale public works was economically sounder than Bonar Law's orthodox policy of 'balance the budget and pay our way'. But he himself was still as orthodox a Free Trade Liberal as Mr. Philip Snowden, the Labour Party's financial pundit. Not until after 1930 would Keynes come round to the view that in certain situations 'a measure of protection' might be helpful in creating, rather than restricting employment.

Baldwin reached this last conclusion in 1923, though certainly without any understanding of the complicated reasoning which would lead Keynes to it, nor of the reservations with which Keynes would have hedged about his tentative suggestion. Viewing the contrast between the conditions of labour in 'sheltered' industries like building, and the 'unsheltered' which had to find an export market in an increasingly competitive world, he concluded that the manufacturer must have his home market protected for him if he was to compete on fair terms abroad. On the evidence available, he was probably wrong in thinking that Protection would in 1923 have served to reduce unemployment. That summer the Bank of England, 'acting under the influence of a narrow and obsolete doctrine',[1] raised the Bank Rate from 3% to 4%, thereby intensifying a deflationary drive which made higher unemployment inevitable, whatever happened about Protection. But Baldwin's decision was that only tariffs could in the long run cure unemployment; and when he announced this in a speech at Plymouth in October, 1923, he brought about his ears the whole of the ancient Tariff Reform quarrel which had torn his Party in two twenty years before and which roused the deepest of English political convictions and passions. He also committed himself to holding an immediate general election. For Bonar Law, just to avoid this very row within the Party, had given a public pledge not to open the issue of tariffs without first consulting the electorate.

Many incidental explanations have been advanced of what turned out to be a suicidal decision: among them, that Baldwin was anxious to win back the support of the Coalitionist Conservatives, thinking that an election, even if it led to defeat, would pull the Party together. It is true that he did win 'the whole and entire support' of Austen Chamberlain and Birkenhead and he did consolidate his position in the Conservative Party. But this is not a convincing explanation. The plain truth is that he thought it was the right thing to do and that, having gone through all the constituencies with the Party managers, he thought he would win. In the event he lost disastrously. The threat to Free Trade, even though there were to be no taxes on food, reunited the Liberals, though it did not genuinely reconcile Asquith to Lloyd George. It brought the Socialists into line with orthodox Liberalism; and it roused a lot of forgotten passions and misconceptions. The result, declared on

[1] Keynes. Quoted Harrod, p. 338.

December 8th, was a deadlock: Conservatives 258, Labour 191, Liberals 157. In view of what has since been said and written about Baldwin, it is worth recalling *The Times* Leader of December 10th: 'He will be remembered as the Prime Minister who risked his own career because he thought that by doing so he would make life easier for thousands of his fellow-countrymen.'

For the next move in the game Baldwin shares the credit with Asquith and the King. These three set their faces against the clamour for an alliance of the older parties to avert the unthinkable disaster of a Labour government, which would, indeed, have left Socialists and Trade Unionists with an irremovable and justified grievance. The proper constitutional forms were scrupulously observed. Baldwin met the new Parliament, was almost immediately defeated on a motion on the Address, and resigned. The King sent for Ramsay MacDonald as the leader of the next largest Party in the Commons, and he with some difficulty formed an administration from among his inexperienced colleagues; and on January 22nd, 1924, they kissed hands as the first Labour government.

Partly because he was faced with a genuine dearth of talent and experience, partly because he had always fancied himself as an expert on foreign affairs, MacDonald took over the Foreign Office as well as the premiership—a double burden which has seldom been carried successfully, and which was in fact to be too much for him. He eased the burden by making the lovable, efficient, but guileless Clynes, who had led the Party in his absence after the war, Lord Privy Seal and Deputy Leader of the House of Commons. There was never any doubt that the key job at the Exchequer would go to Philip Snowden, a sharp, embittered fighter of the old-guard intellectual wing, warped perhaps a little by infirmity, invincibly certain always of his own rightness, and not easily tolerant of those whose minds moved more slowly than his, or along lines less impeccably orthodox. Henderson, the Party's veteran Secretary, represented the Trade Union wing at the Home Office, and Mr. Sidney Webb, its supreme pontiff, crowned a long career of academic Socialism by taking over the Board of Trade. Of the younger, more militant, post-war element in the Party only John Wheatley was in the Cabinet. Finally—the only one of them, probably, who relished the situation as thoroughly as did the Prime Minister—there was Jimmy

Thomas, the N.U.R.'s beloved Secretary, who took the Colonial Office. Cheerful, shamelessly vulgar and unaffected, Thomas entered completely into the spirit of the thing, delighted to find himself top-hatted or in evening dress, smoking his cigars with relish, treating big-wigs with the same cheerful familiarity as he did the railwaymen, and hugely delighted when he told the messenger at the door of the Colonial Office that he was the new Secretary of State, to hear the man murmur to his assistant: 'Another shell-shock case, I'm afraid.'

This then was the team, surprised to find themselves a little over-awed, and still more so to be put so quickly at their ease, when they listened to the King's final appeal to them on January 23rd: 'The immediate future of my people and their whole happiness is in your hands, Gentlemen. They depend upon your prudence and sagacity.' As a matter of fact a good many people were comforting themselves with the thought that what the King said was not strictly true. The die-hards reflected that a minority government could not get into too much mischief, and trusted rather to the 'prudence and sagacity' of Mr. Asquith, on whose Liberal votes the survival of the new government depended. The older and wiser heads could rejoice to see Labour given some experience of the responsibility of office before they acquired the untrammelled power conferred by a clear majority. And for the ministers themselves there was some advantage in this limited tenure of power which allowed them to find their feet in circumstances where the Liberals could always be blamed for any unadventurousness or failure to implement election promises.

The government lasted for less than a year. Inevitably in the circumstances there could be no attempt to realise the dream of 'socialism in our time', and ministers could only hope to demonstrate that they could administer a capitalist society more efficiently than their rivals. The only one to establish any serious claim to have done so was the Clydesider, Wheatley, whose Housing Bill was a masterpiece, greatly enlarging the scope of Chamberlain's measure of a year before by more generous subsidies to local authorities, and adding a further half-million houses to the post-war building achievement. The unemployed were given a few extra shillings on the dole, and Snowden's budget, of Gladstonian orthodoxy, devoted most of its surplus to 'the great radical idea of the free breakfast table', reducing duties on tea, coffee, cocoa and sugar. The rest went to the abolition of the so-called McKenna duties levied for the past eight years on various manufactured articles, which created still further difficulties for the export trade, particularly in motor-cars, and caused a good deal of grumbling in Trade Union circles. Apart from this, Labour proved as barren of ideas for reducing unemployment as were the Conservatives.

The real success of the government was in the sphere of foreign affairs, where MacDonald showed himself outstandingly able. Admittedly he took over at a fortunate moment. The palpable failure of the Ruhr occupation and the fall of M. Poincaré gave him a more docile French public opinion and a much easier Prime Minister—M. Herriot —to deal with. The Germans, rendered miserable by the frustrations and hardships of the great inflation—the Mark sank finally to a rate of 22,300 million to the £ by the end of 1923—were prepared to back their new foreign minister, Stresemann, in a policy of 'fulfilment' of the Treaty. The Americans were emerging from their isolationist cave in a mood to reconsider loans for the reconstruction of Europe, and a committee under their General Dawes had worked out a scheme for combining that with a satisfactory regulation of the Reparations situation. But when all has been said, clearly MacDonald handled these favourable factors with great skill. His talent had always lain in negotiating—in reconciling the apparently irreconcilable and finding formulas to bridge gulfs. That was why he was Leader of the Labour Party. He now coaxed all the parties concerned to London, and on August 30th triumphantly produced the London Agreement. The French were to evacuate the Ruhr. The Germans, with their new currency already stabilised, accepted, along with an American loan of £40 million, the Dawes Plan for a gradual resumption of Reparations payments.

To have reached a negotiated settlement in place of the much resented 'Diktat' of Versailles was a notable triumph for MacDonald, though his Party reacted rather sourly, suspecting him of enjoying the limelight too much and sacrificing affairs at home to his own vanity. There were other, less spectacular triumphs, including a treaty which ironed out some long-standing Italian grievances in Somaliland, and two treaties with Russia. But this attempt to bring Russia, as well as Germany, back into the fold, sensible though it was, was the beginning of the end for the Labour government. There was a certain irony in the circumstance that Arthur Ponsonby, MacDonald's Under Secretary at the Foreign Office, who had aroused grave displeasure in Court circles in 1908 by denouncing Edward VII's visit to the Tsar as 'hobnobbing with a bloodstained creature—a common murderer', was now in trouble with King George for hobnobbing in his turn with the murderers of the Tsar. The fruit of his activities was an innocuous commercial treaty, another by which Russia agreed to reimburse the British holders of Russian Imperial Bonds, and a project for a third arranging for a Russian Loan on the London market as soon as the Russians had paid off the sums due to the bondholders.

It was the third treaty which stuck in the Conservative gullet. Worse still, the Russians raised their terms at the last minute, demanding the promise of the loan when only half the bondholders' debt had been paid. MacDonald broke off the negotiation, but was compelled to resume it and sign on the Russian terms by powerful pressure from the Party Executive, an extra-Parliamentary body presided over by that veteran idealist, George Lansbury, which regarded itself as the keeper of the government's conscience and constantly interfered in policy with protests and advice. There was a considerable row when, right at the end of the session, with no time for a debate, the House was informed that the treaties, in an even less advantageous form than that which had been reluctantly agreed, had already been signed. Worse still, to the Conservative mind, was the nature of the pressure from an irresponsible body uncontrollable by Parliament which had forced the Prime Minister to change his mind.

The rumblings of discontent over the Russian Treaty did not, as MacDonald had hoped, die away during the summer recess. They represented a deep and genuine mistrust of the government's foreign policy which was proving much harder to keep under the control of the House of Commons than its activities at home. Unfortunately these suspicions were not confined to the one slightly questionable transaction, but were extended to the Geneva Protocol, the one really statesmanlike attempt ever made to transform the Covenant of the League into an effective weapon against war. That project, worked out by the Prime Minister with the help of Lord Parmoor and Arthur Henderson and in close consultation with M. Herriot, was, broadly, a scheme by which the nations should bind themselves to submit all irreconcilable disputes to arbitration and to accept the resultant verdict. They were further to agree to go to war collectively, if necessary, to enforce such verdicts against any nation which broke that pledge. It was adopted unanimously by the Assembly of the League that September, and actually signed then and there by nine nations, including France. But by then it was already clear that the government was doomed, and the British ratification of the Protocol had to be postponed to another Parliament.

The actual cause of the government's fall was the mismanagement of the prosecution of Mr. J. R. Campbell, acting editor of the Communist *Workers' Weekly*, for a seditious article inciting the armed forces of the Crown to mutiny. MacDonald, informed after the event of the initiation of proceedings by the Attorney General, entirely approved them; he also agreed later that the prosecution should be dropped in view of the facts that Campbell was only acting editor and had a good personal war record, provided that he wrote a letter of apology. Campbell, however, wrote no such letter. Instead, on the sound Communist principle of making as much trouble as possible for everybody, he published a statement that the prosecution had been withdrawn because of pressure on the government from left-wing extremists in the Party—in fact from the already suspect Party Executive. All the deepest suspicions both of Conservatives and Liberals seemed confirmed, and both Parties tabled motions amounting to votes of censure, accusing the government of 'interfering with the course of justice'.

The real causes for the ending of the experiment of a Labour government on Liberal sufferance went, of course, much deeper. One was that there was a real rift in the Labour ranks which made it difficult to formulate policy or conduct government. MacDonald and most of his colleagues were preoccupied chiefly, as he put it in his final report to the King, with showing that they had 'the capacity to govern in an equal degree with the other parties in the House', and that patriotism was 'not the monopoly of any class or party'.[1] Lansbury and the Webbs and the Party purists were revolted by the resulting compromises, which seemed to them a dabbling with unclean things. They would have challenged the other parties with a programme of militant Socialism, capital levy and all, regardless of the Parliamentary consequences. The

[1] See Nicolson, *op. cit.*, p. 401.

Tories were becoming similarly restive under the restraining hand oı Baldwin, who was determined to give the minority government a fair run for its money and to suppress if possible all merely factious opposition, so long as there was no aggressively Socialist legislation. The Campbell case, on top of the Russian treaties, combined with misgivings about the Geneva Protocol, made his right wing very hard to hold. But the decision rested in the end with the Liberals, who had seen too late that support for a Labour government had led them into a trap. It had looked to many of them as though their 151 seats placed them in an arbitral position, from which they would hold the balance between the parties of the extremes, perhaps even force another coalition, or even take over government themselves. In practice their support for a Labour policy watered down to Radical Liberalism meant that Labour took the credit for any achievement, while they were blamed for its inability to achieve more. They were thus steadily losing support on both wings. Some of their constituents were turning Conservative because they tolerated Socialism: others went Labour because they did not tolerate enough of it. So they decided to end the disastrous experiment.

MacDonald had made it clear that, if defeated, he would ask the King for a dissolution; and on October 10th, since he could not persuade either Baldwin or Asquith to form a coalition or a minority government, very reluctantly the King agreed to the third general election in three years. The results justified the restiveness of the Conservatives and confirmed Liberal fears: the Conservatives won 414 seats, Labour 150, and the Liberals were reduced to 39. A great deal was made at the time of the effects of the publication by the Foreign Office, a week before polling day, of a letter purporting to be written by M. Zinoviev in the name of the Third International, urging English Communists to undermine the loyalty of the army. The Russian government denounced it as a clumsy forgery, which it well may have been, though it was entirely typical of the instructions periodically sent from Moscow to the British Communist Party. Conservative candidates seized on it gleefully and made the most of it. Socialist opinion has always hankered after the view that it was a Tory forgery foisted on the Foreign Office and deliberately released when there was no time to challenge its authenticity effectively before polling day. No shadow of proof for this has ever been found, nor is there any indication that it had a serious effect on the election result. Labour in fact polled more votes than it had the time before. The relatively small number of votes which gave the Conservatives this startling turnover were Liberal votes; and the main consequence of the political transactions of 1923 was the almost total eclipse of the Liberal Party.

It was not only the size of his majority which put Baldwin now in a much stronger position than a year before. The Protection election had cut off the Coalition Conservatives from their Liberal allies and they were all back in the fold, so that the government this time was very much a Conservative 1st XI. What was more, by a stroke of political genius Baldwin caught Winston Churchill stranded between two parties for the second time in his life and brought him in too with a well-timed offer of the Exchequer. With Austen Chamberlain as Foreign Secretary and his brother, Neville, at the Ministry of Health, Curzon, soon to be replaced by Balfour, as Lord President, and Birkenhead at the India Office, together with the younger talent revealed under Bonar Law he had what looked like a very formidable and experienced team. Their only weakness was that they had not anything very constructive in the way of a programme.

One thing which it was quite clear the government would not do was to stand by the Geneva Protocol. There had been wild talk of Lord Parmoor 'selling the British fleet', of the impossibility of 'indefinite commitments' and of Britain 'becoming the world's policeman'; but a mere rejection of the Protocol, already ratified by the French, would leave the nation without policy or prestige. The Foreign Office, when consulted, talked wistfully of the time when the Concert of Europe, 'with its admirable balance of power', had kept the peace, and Austen Chamberlain fell back on the idea of some more regional pact to reassure both Germany and France: working, as he put it, 'for some date like 1950 or 1960, when German strength will have returned, and when the prospect of war will again cloud the horizon'. Churchill and his Treasury advisers had nothing more progressive to propose than a further pursuit of an already suicidal deflation and the re-establishment of the Gold Standard in all its 1914 glory. Only Neville Chamberlain had detailed plans for a complete overhaul of local government and its relations with the Ministry of Health which would consolidate the gains of the past and provide a firm platform for future progress. Baldwin, content with having, in Disraelian phrase, tamed the shrew of Socialism and put his Party back in power, hoped in the true Tory tradition that it would be enough if His Majesty's Government quietly carried on and governed. Unemployment was dropping for the first time below the million mark. The Reparations problem seemed solved at last. The King had begged him on taking office to 'restrain his followers from doing anything in the House of Commons to irritate their opponents' and to 'combat the idea of anything like class war'. In that Baldwin could whole-heartedly co-operate; and there is no evidence that his thought had gone much beyond that. 'What this government will not do', he said at Birmingham on March 3rd, 'is to attempt to control the industries of this country.'

Of the various departmental plans and achievements, only Neville Chamberlain's deserve unmixed praise. Reasonably secure in office for four years to come, he laid before the Cabinet a programme, unique in its range and detail, representing 'a connected series of reforms' in Poor Law, National Health Insurance, and Rating which involved projects for 25 separate Acts of Parliament, 11 in 1925, 10 more in 1926, and 4 in 1927. Many, of course, were merely prolongations of existing legislation, as part of a general administrative tidying up. Many were relatively trivial enactments—Smoke Abatement, Regulation of the Sale of Proprietary Medicines, Tithe Redemption, and the like— though all were carefully interlocked with the larger undertakings. These were a complete reform of the Poor Law, Contributory Widows' and Old Age Pensions, an extension of National Health Insurance, and a new scheme of rating and valuation for the whole of England and Wales. What, broadly, he aimed at was to remove the chaos and over-lapping between local authorities and voluntary bodies and the Ministry and to bring all the Health, Insurance, and Poor Law services into a single, coherent whole; and this, in spite of national crises, of the lethargy and frequent fears of Cabinet colleagues, and of deep-rooted local and national prejudices, he doggedly achieved step by step. Almost all the issues involved were controversial and there were many criti-cisms and many protests. But without his achievement the transition twenty years later to what has been called the welfare state might have have been very much slower and more difficult.

Apart from all the subsidiary legislation, Chamberlain's main con-tribution was embodied in three great statutes. The Pensions Act of 1925 was in principle only an extension of Lloyd George's Acts, though a valuable one, securing for widows and all men and women over 65 pensions of 10/- a week, with allowances for dependent children, for which all insured workers had to contribute an extra 2d. a week, their employers 4d., and the Treasury the balance, which was reckoned at over 1/-. A Rating Act at the end of that year consolidated rating power in the hands of County, Borough, and District Councils, and swept away a lot of antiquated Poor Law machinery, clearing the way for a new system, worked out in conjunction with Churchill, for block grants from ministries to Local Authorities so scaled that those areas poorest in highly rated property drew the largest sums. The seal of the whole of the three years' work was the Local Government Act which at last centralised all the Poor Law administration and put an end to Poplarism, and which he hammered through to its third reading in the spring of 1929, just before Parliament was dissolved. Inevitably he had, both in this Act and in all that he had been doing for the last four years, to deal firmly with abuses which, sentimentally exploited, became doubly destructive, and he was frequently accused of harshness, and even 'Fascism' by his Labour opponents, while Conservatives intrigued against what seemed to them State Socialism run riot.[1] There had to be Means Tests and a ruthless enforcement of law if the system was to work at all. It was Sidney Webb who silenced much hostile criticism by stating bluntly: 'Where the public purse comes to the assistance of any person we have a right to ask that the facts relating to his means should be known.' After his two hours' speech expounding his last bill Chamberlain had his brief reward. 'When I sat down', he wrote in his diary, 'the House cheered continuously for several minutes . . . what particularly struck and touched me was that Liberals and Labour men . . . joined with the greatest heartiness in paying their acknowledgements.'[2]

One other enactment of this government deserves mention as further illustrating the tentative progress towards a modified Socialism which was characteristic of the better sort of Conservative of those days—the Electricity Supply Act of 1926. The passionate XIX-century belief in free and private enterprise had left Britain far behind other nations in the efficient provision of electric light and power; and even in 1926

[1] See Feiling, *op. cit.*, pp. 132–3.   [2] Feiling, p. 147.

there could be no interference with the existing local organisations. But these now became 'authorised distributors' of current supplied over a nation-wide grid of a Central Electricity Board which was in turn, though very remotely, controlled by the Minister of Transport. Like so much else achieved in this period, it was a half-measure which would not be completed until after the next war. But it went as far as existing public opinion would allow, and the gain in efficiency within a very few years was remarkable.

While Neville toiled away in the background, it was his brother, Austen, who scooped the public laurels in the first year of the new government. Unhappily convinced that the Geneva Protocol would commit Britain to too many unforeseen and unforeseeable adventures, he felt compelled to offer the world some substitute. He was also anxious to bring Germany further back into the framework of freely negotiated security arrangements and to give France some compensation for the guarantees which had been snatched from her after Versailles. All this he seemed to have achieved by the Treaties of Locarno, signed on October 6th, 1925. Four of them were treaties of arbitration and mutual guarantee between various groups of European powers in which Britain had no part. The vital one, which seemed to enthusiasts at the time to herald a new age in international relations, was a guarantee of the frontiers between Germany, France, and Belgium, as laid down at Versailles, by those three powers with Great Britain and Italy as underwriters. All five powers pledged themselves to go to war against any one which violated them; and the perpetual demilitarisation of the Rhineland became subject to the same guarantee. The signature of this treaty was greeted with almost hysterical jubilation. 'I felt myself', Austen Chamberlain wrote, 'a little child again in spirit'; and his grateful Sovereign made him a Knight of the Garter. Its positive gains were that Germany had now freely and voluntarily accepted some more of the clauses of Versailles, and France had been given as good a guarantee of her eastern frontier as treaties could give her. Negatively it was a declaration of qualified isolationism by Great Britain. In accepting responsibility for the Rhine frontier she had specifically rejected it for Germany's eastern frontiers, or for any commitments further afield. Probably it is merely academic to argue that the Protocol would have been a lesser risk in the end and a far more statesmanlike undertaking. For, since, when the time came, Britain was to evade the commitments of Locarno, in all probability she would also have evaded those of the Protocol. Treaties, after all, are only scraps of paper, though only a German has ever had the bad taste to say so openly.

Churchill, too, hit the headlines in that first year of the new government, though with infinitely more disastrous consequences. With a little more luck and judgement the Locarno system might have been extended until it fulfilled most of the requirements of the Geneva Protocol. For the return to the Gold Standard in 1925 there was nothing to be said at all. It certainly reduced considerably the burden of the American debt on the British taxpayer and it was of advantage to the foreign investor generally. Even Mr. Asquith thought it a good move, and so did McKenna, though he visualised it as a roundabout way to a managed currency on which, alone among the big bankers, he saw eye to eye with Keynes. In fact only three authoritative voices were raised against it—those of Lord Beaverbrook, Vincent Vickers, who resigned in consequence from the Court of the Bank of England, and Keynes himself. Churchill himself claimed seven years later in conversation with Boothby to have gone 'the whole hog' against it and described it as 'a vile trap to destroy us'.[1] But he was in the hands of his experts in a field where the layman has no competent opinion at all. What seems so clear now, even to the layman, as Keynes pointed out at the time in a brilliant little pamphlet entitled *The Economic Consequences of Mr. Churchill*, was that the effect on export trade must be ruinous. A 10% rise in the value of the £ inevitably added 10% or near it to the price of every commodity Britain tried to sell abroad. There was no slack which could be taken up in the hard-pressed 'unsheltered' industries; and in two of the vital ones at least—coal and steel—there would be no compensating cheapening of imported raw materials. The basis of all heavy industry was coal, and by far the greatest item in the cost of its production was labour. If coal had to come down in price by 10%, miners' wages would have to do the same, or nearly; and there would have to be a similar fall in wages in all the export industries if the nation was not to starve. But few at the time understood that the relief to the taxpayer on the service of the American debt was in fact to be charged to the wage-earner, and that the first and heaviest impact must fall on

[1] Boothby, *I Fight to Live*, p. 40.

the miners. They, as Keynes put it, were 'the victims of the economic Juggernaut. They represent in the flesh the "fundamental adjustments" engineered by the Treasury and the Bank of England to satisfy the impatience of the City fathers to bridge the "moderate gap" between $4·40 and $4·86. They (and others to follow) are the "moderate sacrifice" still necessary to ensure the stability of the gold standard.'[1]

There seems to have been no inkling in Cabinet circles of the dangers which they were incurring. No very great damage need have been done had the return to gold been accompanied by a general policy for lowering all wages and salaries and raising income-tax. The cost of living might then have been brought down by the same percentage, so that the fall was in money wages only and not in real wages. But even this would have required a lot of careful explanation and propaganda. The psychological impact of a smaller pay packet is greater and more immediate than the gradual fall of commodity prices in the shops. It should have been a prerequisite of such a policy that the co-operation of the greater Trade Unions had been obtained in advance. In the explosive situation of industry generally in 1925, and especially in the coal industry, it was probably not a feasible policy at all. 'Whether the price of coal to the consumer is lowered or not,' so the last pronouncement of the Miners had run, 'the living wage of miners (together with hours and conditions) must be untouchable. . . . The present wage is not a living wage.'[2]

This then was the situation into which, in the spring of 1925, the government light-heartedly plunged—it cannot be said with their eyes open, since they were sublimely unaware that they had committed themselves to a vast social policy of lowering wages, with no weapon to enforce new wage rates save the bludgeon of mass unemployment, and no provision at all for sharing the burden in any equitable way among the different classes of the community. Even if they were successful they were likely to do irretrievable damage to export industries while prices and wages adjusted themselves, and they had given themselves no time for second thoughts. The impact of the budget on coal exports was immediate and decisive: on June 1st, 1925, the coal owners announced that they would have to terminate all existing wage agreements, and the crisis was on.

---

[1] Keynes, *The Economic Consequences of Mr. Churchill.*
[2] Julian Symons, *The General Strike*, p. 9.

CHAPTER 6

The General Strike

In the task which Baldwin had set himself of reconciliation all round, of eliminating bitterness, and of persuading both sides in industry and in politics that obstinacy in extremist courses was ruinous to all, he was nearly always to get a better response from his opponents than from his own supporters. Apart from the die-hards—the honest and out-of-date Tories led by Lord Salisbury—the Conservative Party had not wholly shaken off the hard-faced element which had disgusted so many of the responsible leaders in 1918. There was a block of men who regarded themselves as the mouthpieces of owners and managements alone; who spoke of 'discipline in industry' in terms reminiscent of the 1840s; who never talked of class war, but waged it unceasingly. Moreover in a crisis these men would often be able to carry with them a majority in the Cabinet. If a fight was on, normally generous and imaginative men like Churchill and Birkenhead would be unable to see anything beyond the need to win; and Neville Chamberlain's unimaginative impatience with anything which interfered with his clear-cut schemes for human betterment might make him equally pugnacious. Throughout 1925 and 1926 Baldwin's greatest problem, and his greatest triumph, was in the handling of his own Cabinet so as to keep it within the bounds of reason.

Outside Parliament the employers of labour presented the Prime Minister with the same formidable problem. They expected a Conservative government to represent them, and strongly resented any attempt to hold the balance even in an industrial dispute. And worst of all in this respect, with their minds obstinately closed to any kind of progressive idea or any interest but their own, were the coal owners, whom even the extremists in the Cabinet would find embarrassing allies. 'An unprepossessing lot', Neville Chamberlain called them; and Birkenhead remarked that he would have thought the miners' leaders the stupidest men in the kingdom had he not met their employers. Their one clearly defined ambition, so their political adviser, Austin Hopkinson, wrote in the *English Review*, was 'to make the position of interfering politicians so unpleasant that they will for the future think twice before they meddle with the basic industries of the country.'[1] They would not even collaborate in schemes for their own betterment, but persisted in a forlorn attempt to compete with the modernised, rationalised, newly equipped and highly integrated industry of the Ruhr with machinery and organisation which few of them were troubling to bring up to date. It is necessary to bear this constantly in mind, because it alone explains the miners' insistence on nationalisation as the only solution. Much of the suicidal inflexibility of their leaders sprang from a disillusioned scepticism about any promise of overhaul, reorganisation, or increased efficiency to which the owners were a party. They simply did not believe owners ever meant to carry them out, and they had abundant historical justification for their disbelief.

The leadership on the other side presented the industrial peacemaker with equally thorny problems. Ramsay MacDonald, who called *The Red Flag* 'the funeral dirge of our movement', intent on proving to the middle classes the fundamental respectability and reasonableness of Labour, could normally carry the Parliamentary leaders with him in meeting his opponents half-way. He could be much less sure of the Clydesiders and the intellectuals on his back benches, and to retain the leadership he often had to assume revolutionary attitudes which were highly distasteful. Still less could he be sure of commanding the leadership of the movement outside Parliament. Relations between the Parliamentary Party and the General Council of the T.U.C. were frequently strained; and the General Council itself exercised only the most precarious authority over its component unions. Ernest Bevin, of the newly formed Transport and General Workers' Union, was a powerful voice against a centralised body empowered to speak for so many diverse and divergent interests. He would have preferred a revival of the Triple Alliance, under the name of the Industrial Alliance, had

[1] Quoted Boothby, *op. cit.*, p. 43.

not the memory of Black Friday been too strong. Many other members of the Council, like Arthur Pugh, its chairman, were moderate and almost conservative in their Trade Unionism, and only embarked on adventurous policies with the greatest reluctance for fear of losing the leadership to the more irresponsible extremists. Like Ledru-Rollin, trailing behind the Paris mob of 1848, they would explain apologetically —'Je suis leur chef. Il faut que je les suive.'

Finally there were the miners themselves on whom almost everything else turned, and they were the most intractable of the lot; understandably so, for they had been having a very raw deal for a very long time. They were determined to stick to their seven-hour day, not only for their own comfort, but because longer hours would merely flood more coal on to the already glutted world market and would demonstrably lead to still lower prices and still more unemployment. As to wages, they wanted a national minimum wage which must certainly be no lower than what they were getting in the spring of 1925, which they did not regard as a subsistence wage. If there were to be economies they must come from the abolition of royalties and curtailment of 'the waste and parasitic growth of profits',[1] and by intelligent reorganisation and re-equipment. They regarded themselves as being already stripped to the bone.

Much time and patience were to be exhausted in 1925 and 1926 by the failure of everybody, except perhaps the owners, to grasp the fundamental logic of the miners' attitude. Over and over again they were to be invited to negotiate: to be offered concessions and to be asked what they could concede in return. Always the answer would be, with exasperating reiteration, 'Not a penny off the pay, not a second on the day.' They became, because of this intransigence, the villains of the piece, as much to the General Council as to the politicians. They appeared merely stupid and obstinately unwilling to face facts. But there was nothing unreasonable in such obstinacy in men who believed that they were already in the last ditch, which is by definition a place where negotiation and concession perforce cease. They put forward no positive demand which could be abated in give and take round the conference table. Their 'demand' was to be left as they were, which for most of them was near enough to starvation anyway. While their

[1] Julian Symons, *The General Strike*, p. 9.

Secretary, Arthur Cook, once a Welsh revivalist preacher and now an avowed Communist, charmed the pitmen and exasperated the bosses with dramatic, inflammatory speeches, it was the President of the Union, Herbert Smith, the Yorkshireman, who really embodied their attitude. Craggy, aggressively ill-mannered, and with a deep contempt for all who had not themselves worked at the coal face, he had only one answer to demands for concessions: 'Nowt doin'.'[1] Many hours were to be wasted round the conference table in attempts to negotiate with Herbert Smith.

Baldwin had opened the campaign of 1925 with a notable victory for the cause of industrial tolerance. On March 6th a private member's bill was brought before the House by a Mr. Macquisten seeking to compel Trade Unions to alter their subscription rules. As things stood, a voluntary contribution to the political levy for Labour Party funds was automatically included in Union subscriptions unless a man cared to risk the odium of 'contracting out' of it. It was a matter on which feeling ran very high, not only in Conservative circles, and it was widely felt that the onus should be thrown the other way: that men should contract 'in' and not 'out'. Macquisten's bill had the support of an overwhelming majority of the House of Commons, and probably of a majority of the Cabinet; and Baldwin himself thought it a just measure. But it would arouse intense bitterness on the other side and, in the greatest speech he ever made, Baldwin persuaded his Party to hold their hand, simply as a generous gesture, so as not further to embitter an already dangerous industrial situation. Every now and then he could, by sheer eloquence, raise the whole tone of politics above the norm of materialistic haggling, and when he did so he enchanted his opponents even more than his friends; so that Harold Laski would wonder wistfully why he was not a Socialist, and David Kirkwood would recall, fourteen years later, that evening when they had all been made to feel that 'the antagonism, the bitterness, the class rivalry were unworthy; and that understanding and amity were possible'.

They did not, unfortunately, seem nearly so possible to the men who were wearily conducting yet another Joint Enquiry into the mining industry. By June 1st they had reached a deadlock. With pit after pit

---

[1] Julian Symons in *The General Strike* has admirable portraits of Herbert Smith, one in prose, the other a photograph.

closing down the owners insisted that they could not carry on solvently without a return to the eight-hour day and wage cuts varying from 10% to 25%. Notices terminating the existing wage agreements were to go out on June 30th and expire on July 31st. The government announced that in no circumstances would it come to the rescue with a subsidy; and Smith flatly refused to offer any constructive suggestion. When W. C. Bridgeman, acting as government mediator, at last got him to a joint meeting he took his stand not unreasonably on Bonar Law's broken promise to implement the Sankey Report 'in the spirit and in the letter'. The miners' constructive suggestion had all along been nationalisation. 'Private enterprise', Smith said, 'is your baby, which you must supply with milk.' The government appointed another Court of Enquiry, and the miners simply refused to attend. They would confer no further until the lockout notices were withdrawn.

There was, however, one factor which the government had ignored when it took its stand on 'no subsidy'. The General Council of the T.U.C. had seen an opportunity of seizing the leadership of the movement and of showing itself more effective than the Cripple Alliance of 1921. The miners placed their case in their hands as 'the supreme trade union committee'. The co-operation of the T.G.W.U., the N.U.R., and the A.S.L.E.F. was assured; and, with perfect timing, the General Council announced on July 28th an embargo on all movement of coal with effect from July 31st unless the mine owners' notices were withdrawn. There followed three days of confusion and consultation. The second Court of Enquiry produced its findings, recommending a fixed minimum wage and uttering some cogent criticisms of the industry's management, and these were promptly and indignantly rejected by the owners. Meanwhile a delegate conference of Trade Union executives at Westminster voted whole-hearted support for the miners, so Baldwin was compelled at last to intervene personally. He found himself no more successful than anyone else at dealing with Smith. Having outlined the concessions he had wrung from the owners, he asked what the miners had to give in return. 'Nowt,' Smith said. 'We have nowt to give.'

When, as late as the afternoon of July 30th, Baldwin repeated to Smith his determination not to grant a subsidy, he probably thought he was calling a bluff. If so, he was grievously mistaken. By that evening orders had gone out which would bring all activity to a standstill at every railway station, dock and wharf in the land. It was, in effect, the long-dreamed-of general strike, and the government caught entirely unprepared, had no alternative but to surrender. A hastily summoned Cabinet agreed to a subsidy, which might cost anything from £7½ million to £24 million, to last until May 1st, 1926. After discussions lasting off and on through the night and most of the next day, Friday, the 31st, agreement was reached. There was, of course, to be another full enquiry into the mining industry, and lockout notices were to be withdrawn. The triumphant telegrams went out from the Union Secretaries, and another Friday—Red Friday this time—was added to the Trade Union calendar.

Actually it was a victory on which nobody had much cause for self-congratulation. Tory rage, naturally, knew no bounds, echoing the headlines in the *Express* and the *Mail*. 'Danegeld' it was, and 'A Victory for Violence'; and the Tory government had shown great weakness in categorically and repeatedly refusing any subsidy, and then capitulating when its bluff was called. The miners saw little cause for rejoicing in so negative an achievement, and Cook got very roughly handled at a delegate meeting for referring to it as a victory. Ramsay MacDonald voiced the misgivings of most of Parliamentary Labour when he referred to it as a victory for what a 'sane, well-considered, thoroughly well-examined Socialism feels to be probably its greatest enemy'. Even the General Council, the apparent victor, was uneasily aware that it had let loose forces which it might be unable to control, and was far from accepting the logical consequences of its own actions. For it was clear that the matter could not rest where it was. As Sir William Joynson-Hicks, mouthpiece of right-wing Conservatism, said, the question had been posed: 'Is England to be governed by Parliament and the Cabinet or by a handful of Trade Union leaders?' Even in the unlikely event of the new Commission under Sir Herbert Samuel finding a formula acceptable both to owners and miners, the challenge would come again in some other industry and a different crisis. Once challenged and warned, the government could not capitulate a second time: 'the response of the community', Baldwin said, 'will astonish the forces of anarchy throughout the world.' The relief which King George and Neville Chamberlain, and no doubt many others, confided to their diaries at being spared the 'incalculable and irreparable damage' of so great a stoppage was premature.

'Motor transport', that mild, non-partisan periodical, the *Round Table*, had remarked after the railway strike of 1919, 'is at present far too costly to compete with railway transport, but it has proved its capabilities as a substitute in emergency, and the railwaymen's claim that they could paralyse the community in 24 hours has lost its virtue.' Apostles of direct industrial action could retort to this that it was the solidarity of the Unions which would tip the scale. Add to the miners and railwaymen all the transport workers and dockers and the standstill would be complete. But there was a great deal more motor transport which was not under Union control in 1925 than there had been in 1919. A properly organised and self-confident government could face the threat; and the only reason it had not done so on Red Friday was, as Baldwin later frankly admitted, because it was not ready.[1] As Herbert Smith bluntly told the miners, it was not a victory, it was 'only an armistice'; and the course and fate of the General Strike of 1926 would in fact be decided by the use which both sides made of the nine months' respite provided by the subsidy.

The government already had in its pigeon-holes the outline of a plan for dealing with just such a situation as had arisen. Sir Eric Geddes had in 1919, laid the foundation with an emergency supply and transport organisation, never properly tried out because the railway strike ended so quickly. Churchill wanted to bring Geddes back to do it again in 1925; but the Geddes Axe was still so bitter a memory that this was rejected as too provocative. His plans, however, had been kept and tinkered with at intervals in the department of the Chancellor of the Duchy of Lancaster, so that the Labour leaders certainly knew of them, though they attached no importance to them: when Josiah Wedgwood handed them back to J. C. Davidson in 1923 he told him that he hadn't 'done a bloody thing about them'. Davidson had not done much either, and they were still too embryonic to save the government's face in the sudden crisis of 1925. Quietly and unobtrusively they were now brought out and furbished up in obscurity under the direction of a civil servant named Sir John Anderson. All the departments likely to be concerned in countering a general strike were got together weekly on an Emergency Committee on Supply and Transport. The island was divided up into regions, each under a Civil Commissioner, with officers responsible for

[1] G. M. Young, *Stanley Baldwin*, p. 99.

coal, finance, and food. The essence of the scheme was decentralisation not only of organisation, but of authority. Commissioners could enrol special constables, and their powers in an emergency, though ill-defined, were clearly intended to be almost unlimited. The assistance of the fighting services was provided for, and the key to the whole was an elaborate emergency transport system, basically dependent on the co-operation of the larger industrial firms in each area. It was all very unobtrusive and it was designed to be in a state of constant readiness, so that the government should never again be taken by surprise.

Far more stir was caused by the enrolling of volunteers from among 'well-disposed citizens' who would be prepared to make their labour, skilled or unskilled, available to the government in an emergency. This was designed to appear strictly unofficial and unpolitical. The Organisation for the Maintenance of Supplies—the O.M.S.—had official blessing, but no more. It was run by distinguished elder statesmen, ex-Viceroys and the like, on a strictly voluntary basis, and such finance as it required was provided by patriotically minded business men and firms. It claimed to have enrolled, by the end of six months, some 100,000 volunteers: drivers and special constables, some specialists such as electrical engineering students, and a mass of wholly unskilled folk to do duty as dustmen and railway porters, dockers, or whatever was wanted. It was all, from the outset, pretty light-hearted. What little training was done—teaching men to drive railway engines or drive buses—was sketchy and amateurish, and the activities of the O.M.S. excited nothing but derision from the professional workers who suffered, like everybody else, from the illusion of their own indispensability. In practice 'these jokers', as C.T. Cramp of the N.U.R. called them, were to do quite a good job, and it was probably invaluable to have enrolled in advance, and by districts, a nucleus of those on whom the government would have to rely in a crisis. But perhaps its most valuable function was to distract attention from the more serious preparations in the background. The palpable amateurishness of the O.M.S. made many Trade Unionists think that it would be easy to bring the nation's life to a standstill, and may have been one reason why the T.U.C. General Council did so little in the way of counter-preparation.

If there was to be a general strike at all in sympathy with the miners, it behoved the General Council to make similar preparations; the more so, since its action on Red Friday had forfeited the element of surprise which had, on that occasion, been decisive. For a number of reasons this proved entirely impossible. In the first place a general strike was a revolutionary weapon and could only succeed if handled as such by clear-headed men who knew exactly what they wanted to do. It is doubtful if anybody in the Trade Union hierarchy fulfilled this definition. They were not men who wished to subvert the constitution and substitute an alternative system of their own; they just wanted, in fact, to compel the government to see that the miners got a fair deal. They were reluctant to subject the community to the intolerable hardships which could alone give them victory and terrified by the thought of the violence to which such ruthlessness must eventually lead.

Then, behind this basic uncertainty of aim, there was still a struggle for leadership which effectively precluded decisive action. Red Friday's triumph had not settled this issue in the General Council's favour, but had roused the jealous hostility of some of the more powerful Unions who did not wish to see control of their own affairs slip into the hands of some superior authority which they would not always be able to manage. Some of the extremists demanded from the T.U.C. at Scarborough in September 'full powers to create the necessary machinery to combat every move by our opponents', but they did not get them. The General Council's leadership of the Trade Union movement as a whole remained precarious and uncertain, and this had two opposite, but equally disastrous effects on its actions. It would find itself moving forward against its own better judgement, for fear of losing the slender authority it did enjoy by seeming afraid; but at a crisis, when clear, firm leadership was needed, it would hesitate for fear of exceeding its powers. So, during the nine months' respite, while the government discreetly prepared, the Unions did nothing even to plan their campaign in proper detail.

On the other hand, humanly and very understandably, the less they acted, the more they talked. Cook, rampaging bombastically up and down the country, boasting of having already beaten 'the strongest government of modern times', may have alarmed the General Council as much as he did the middle-class electorate. But he was not the only one to make injudicious speeches, designed, no doubt, to keep up

Trade Union morale, but in fact raising hopes and expectations which would make it impossible for the leaders, when the time came, to draw back. Though, in view of the probable breakdown of communications, a highly decentralised organisation was essential, it was very difficult to delegate powers within a system so firmly established on a national basis. The leaders of the big Unions were reluctant to see any form of district authority interfere with their control over their own members, and the General Council was too unsure of itself to risk delegating any authority at all. When the time came there were no directives available to the hastily formed local Strike Committees on such vital matters as the action to be taken if peaceful picketing failed to immobilise transport and docks, on how to restrict traffic to essential food supplies, or for the provisioning of the strikers themselves and their families through the Co-operative Societies, which should have been easy enough to arrange. In fact most of the leaders, in Parliament and out of it, hoped against hope that the Samuel Commission would do the trick and that, if the worst came to the worst, the walls of Jericho would once again crumble at the mere blast of the trumpet.

Sir Herbert Samuel, called back from retirement after a distinguished career in the public service to study an industry of which he had very little knowledge, produced in March an extremely competent report, which immediately became a best-seller. On the organisation side it offered the miners almost everything they had asked for short of actual nationalisation. Royalties were to be bought out, the smaller, less solvent pits amalgamated, amenities such as pit-head baths were to become compulsory, and there were eventually to be beneficial schemes for profit-sharing and family allowances. There was, indeed, little in it which has not since been translated into law or fact. But it was comparatively easy to prescribe for a rosy future for the industry. What no Commission or Enquiry could alter was the basic and immediate problem. In February, 1926, out of a total of 808 colliery undertakings, 602, producing between them 72% of the national output, were only kept going by the government's subsidy.[1] Since these could not, without nationalisation, be run at a loss, either the subsidy must be continued, or the miners must accept a lower wage while the recommended improvements were carried through. So government and miners were left

[1] For a detailed account of all this, see Redmayne, *op. cit.*, pp. 241–2.

face to face with the same obstinate set of facts, and Herbert Smith's position remained what it had always been: that he could not offer concessions on what the miners already regarded as less than a decent living wage. 'We are going to demand', he said to the owners, 'a respectable day's wage for a respectable day's work; and that is not your intention.'

So once again the owners' notices went up to terminate the existing wage agreements on April 30th. MacDonald and Henderson were called in to help the T.U.C.'s Industrial Committee, and the discussions continued round the same futile circle. The government stood by its decision that there would be no more subsidy and that it would implement the Samuel Report if both sides would accept it. In the end both, in effect, rejected it. Smith would only consider wage reductions after the proposed reorganisation had been completed; and the owners' wage offer, transmitted by Baldwin to the General Council on April 30th, was substantially lower than Samuel's recommendation, involving a national minimum wage 13% below the existing minimum and an eight-hour day. The exhausted frustration of the last meeting can be felt in the account jotted into his diary by Neville Chamberlain:

> F.E. and I trying to pin them down to some statement of how they proposed to fill the gap between cost and price. . . . All that Herbert Smith would bind himself to was to discuss reductions of wages after we had put into operation the proposals for reorganisation. . . . As this would take years it was clear that it provided no solution of the immediate difficulty. Again and again Thomas declared that Smith had answered in the affirmative. . . . Each time he made this assertion there were angry and excited murmurs from Cook. . . . Time went on, 8, 9, 10 o'clock passed, and at 11 we broke off . . . having heard from Thomas one of his regular blood-curdlers, with his, 'My God, you don't know what this means; if we are alive this day week,' etc.

When he reported back to the Trade Union executives, who were in permanent session in Faringdon Hall, Thomas told them that he had spent the day 'almost grovelling'. He described the owners' offer, coming as it did five weeks after the government had accepted the Commission's report, and with 40,000 men already locked out, as 'involving such degrading terms that I refuse to believe there is any decent-minded man or woman who would tolerate it'. The next morning, May Day, a ballot of Union Secretaries showed a majority of over 3,600,000 in favour of investing the General Council with authority to speak for them all, and to call a National Strike for May 3rd. The coal stoppage had already begun, at midnight the night before.

Immediately both sides set their machinery in motion. Civil Commissioners mobilised their staffs, the O.M.S. was formally placed at the disposal of the government, and troops and warships were moved to strategic points. The Unions sent out their warning orders, and Bevin, a new and powerful force on the General Council, began to implement the plans on which he had been hectically working for less than a week for transferring authority to District Trades Councils. Yet there were still two more days of discussion to go before the General Council, almost inadvertently in the end, took the plunge into what Trade Unionists insisted was a National, not a General Strike. Though the Union Secretaries had understood their Faringdon Hall vote to be outright for a strike, the Council interpreted it as a mandate to strike or negotiate a settlement. More and more alarmed at the responsibilities they were shouldering, they approached Baldwin again, much to his surprise, and yet another *ad hoc* committee, representing the Cabinet and the General Council, sat down to the dreary business of contemplating the Samuel Commission's report which had already been rejected by both sides in the industry. It reached a formula, as it was almost always possible to do if the miners were not present; the lockout notices to be withdrawn, the subsidy continued for a fortnight, and the General Council to produce an agreed settlement 'on the lines of the Report' within that time; though by what magic the General Council proposed to transform the situation in the coalfields nobody knew.

This was the beginning of a series of embittered misunderstandings. The miners' leaders, except for Cook, had gone off, secure in the belief that the National Strike was already launched in their support, to arrange for collaboration with it. It naturally seemed to them the grossest treachery that the General Council, in their absence, should have accepted a formula which, as elaborated in further discussions on May 2nd, admitted the principle that a settlement might involve 'some reduction in wages'—the very point which the miners had all along refused to concede. Thomas, now that the issue was fairly upon them, had changed his coat and had infuriated Cook by saying that the miners must accept reductions as the railwaymen had. Even the acceptance of the 'formula' by the General Council was uncertain. Thomas said it was accepted, 'never mind what the miners or anybody else say'. Pugh said they could reach no decision without the miners.

It must be admitted that the 'formula's' chances of acceptance were slight. Possibly the full Cabinet, probably the owners, and certainly the miners would have rejected it out of hand. The point was never proved, for at this moment Baldwin seized on quite a trivial matter to precipitate what everybody had been working so hard to avoid. The Cabinet had already drafted a letter demanding the withdrawal of the strike notices as an essential prelude to further negotiations, and at midnight Birkenhead was still trying to get the 'formula', which he had sponsored, accepted by his colleagues. Joynson-Hicks, shamelessly reactionary, Neville Chamberlain, always rigidly unsympathetic to those who disagreed with him when he knew he was right, and Churchill who was apt in any critical situation to be too much aware of its dramatic values, led the argument against any further compromise. Birkenhead, Amery, and others would have negotiated to the last. Baldwin was apparently exhausted and exasperated. On all of them the news that the *Daily Mail*'s printing operatives had struck, rather than set up what they regarded as a wantonly provoking leading article, had a surprisingly decisive effect. Exhaustion, bad temper, and the feeling that it was time to bring things to a show-down which was sooner or later inevitable probably all played their parts in the abrupt Cabinet decision to break off negotiations. Pugh was summoned and handed a letter by a grave-faced Prime Minister which stated that, in view of the strike notices and this latest 'overt act', the government could negotiate no longer until the notices were withdrawn and the men back at work. The Cabinet dispersed, and when the General Council's representatives came to look for Baldwin to give him their answer they found he had gone to bed. 'I had done all I could', he said, 'and there was nowhere else to go.'

So there began a nine-day suspension of all normal activity which, for many who lived through it, was the most bizarre—and sometimes the most exciting—experience of their lives. A great silence descended on the country with the cessation of all but private transport; and the streets running into all the great cities were crowded with walking, bicycling, or hitch-hiking office workers who would seek to preserve throughout the standstill the illusion of 'business as usual'. The volunteers, a great number of them university students merely out for a lark, began to gather at the appointed depots to make their first attempts to drive buses or railway engines, or shift the cargoes which piled up on the docks under the contemptuous eyes of scornful strike pickets who still did not believe that the essential services could be maintained without them. Arrangements for fuel rationing and price control came smoothly into operation and Hyde Park became a vast food depot. The Navy moved unobtrusively into all the great ports. The Army, more obtrusively, with battalions in full battle order, marched through the streets to its concentration areas; and the dangerous energies of Mr. Churchill were canalised into the offices of the *Morning Post*, where he sat in the editor's chair and produced the government's official newspaper, the *British Gazette*, which by the end of the nine days had attained a circulation of over $2\frac{1}{2}$ million copies. The official publication of the other side, the *British Worker*, though much more efficiently produced by 'qualified Union men', never had anything like the same success. It dared not be aggressive and so became merely dull.

From the government's point of view the first 48 hours were the critical ones, for they opened the campaign with a first-class staff and administrative machine, but no army. The Ministries of Transport and Labour, the Home Office and the Board of Trade, had all worked out their plans for the emergency, and they were good plans. If they needed extra talent the executive heads of the great supply and distributing firms, such as Lyons, were at their disposal. But, in spite of the publicity given to the O.M.S., there were not nearly enough workers to keep the essential machinery going. All turned on the immediate response to the government's appeal for volunteers: in other words on the mysterious and unpredictable movement of public opinion. It is rarely safe to generalise about the nation's feeling on any particular issue, but at critical moments there are sometimes reasonable clues. It is fairly clear that in 1926 the overwhelming majority of those who thought at all about such things sympathised, either fervently, or guiltily and shamefacedly, with the miners. But, even allowing for the unthinking, cheerful adventurers from the universities, the tens of thousands of volunteers who queued up at once in answer to the appeal undoubtedly indicated a general feeling that a National Strike was an unfair attempt by a minority to coerce the whole community. In a muddled sort of way they agreed with Baldwin that constitutional government was being attacked, and that they were turning out 'to preserve the liberties and privileges of the people of these islands'.

Whether the General Strike—and, indeed, sympathetic strikes in general—were unconstitutional in the sense that they were illegal is a point on which distinguished lawyers, then and since, have differed. Mr. Justice Astbury, in a famous interlocutory judgement delivered on the eighth day of the strike, held it illegal under the Trade Disputes Act of 1906, and his view was strongly supported and even extended by Sir John Simon in the House of Commons. But Simon's conclusion, that any general strike ordered by the T.U.C. was an illegal conspiracy against the government, was disputed at the time by Sir Henry Slessor and afterwards by many more eminent jurists. It seems unlikely that the legal issue will ever be settled. The right of workmen to withhold their labour is universally conceded, and the law, on the other hand, will uphold any clearly defined contract. But the growth of unions into national organisations has meant that any modern strike is directed at inflicting hardship on the community as a whole and no longer at coercing a particular body of employers, and so has made it impossible to limit in any useful way the definition of a trade dispute. In plain truth the General Strike was a trial of strength: an attempt to compel a properly constituted government to take action which was distasteful to it; and in such a situation, as in a revolution, the niceties of the law are not important.

One reason why the strike failed so rapidly and conclusively was the uneasy unawareness of the General Council members that they were using a weapon basically revolutionary for purposes which were not revolutionary at all. Government speakers accused them of wanting to overthrow the constitution, but they had no wish to do anything of the kind. They just wanted reasonable terms for the miners. They were terrified of seeing control of their movement pass out of their hands into those of left-wing extremists who would push the strike to its logical conclusion, using all means, fair or foul, to force a government capitulation. But Jimmy Thomas's last tearful plea in the House of Commons had ended with the cry of 'God help Britain', if the government did not defeat any attack on the Constitution. That was what made Karl Radek, chatting that week with Robert Boothby in Moscow, say: 'Make no mistake. This is not a revolutionary movement. It is simply a wage dispute.' Thus from the very first there was a preference for half measures which weakened the impetus of the whole movement: the offer, curtly refused by Churchill, to help the government to organise food distribution; the confused instructions to the electrical engineers designed to cut off power but not light; and the order to call out all building workers 'except such as are employed definitely on housing and hospital work'.

It was only as the government began to develop its counter-measures that this infirmity of purpose made itself felt. At first all seemed to be going very well indeed. The response of the Unions called out was almost 100% and the stoppage as complete as had been intended. Only a very few of the 'pirate' buses were on the London streets on the first day; out of a normal 315 underground trains only 15 ran; and on the main railway lines throughout the country there were hardly any trains at all. The telegrams from District Strike Committees and the reports from despatch riders in the London area which poured into the General Council's Headquarters at Eccleston Square were uniformly triumphant. All union men were out. Pickets had successfully stopped all buses and unauthorised traffic. Spirits were high. This optimism and the impression of easy success lasted in general for another day. There were still very few buses, only a few trams, and hardly any more trains. In T.U.C. circles, though local organisers were worried by the lack of clear directives, there was still jubilation, in the London clubs gloom and a general expectation of violence. The Cabinet itself was divided, and Baldwin's view that any show or use of force was to be avoided only prevailed with difficulty over the clamour of Churchill and his friends for a dramatic display of strength.

Then, however, the thousands of volunteers began to make their presence felt, and there began a process of move and counter-move which inevitably produced mounting tension and an increase of violence on both sides, especially in the northern cities and on Tyneside. The volunteer-driven London General red buses were stoned and often immobilised, trams were overturned, and the drivers of lorries sent by private firms to pierce the dense crowds of strikers round the London docks were thrown into the river. The government provided policemen or soldiers to sit beside the drivers, and this in turn produced violent clashes between strikers and police, baton charges, and charges by mounted police. Reluctantly, as unobtrusively as possible, the government was in fact forced to use the armed forces in increasing numbers. When the Electricity workers came out, naval stokers provided the nucleus round which a heterogenous collection of volunteers, heavily guarded by the military, kept a limited service going from the power stations. Submarines moored alongside the wharves generated the current needed to save a quarter of a million carcasses and much other perishable food in the refrigerators of the London docks, and the tugs bringing the essential barge-loads of foodstuffs up the Thames were allowed by Lord Beatty to escape interference by flying the white ensign. And the strikers' siege of the London docks was only frustrated in the end by the sort of display of force dear to the heart of Winston Churchill: an armed column of lorries, with machine-guns trained on the silent crowds.

After a week of this sort of thing it seems fairly clear that, among those actively engaged in the thick of things on either side, both sides thought they were winning. On both sides violence was mounting: hooligan 'fascist' gangs seeking to break up local strike headquarters were meeting improvised 'defence forces' of strikers. In the cities like Newcastle and Glasgow where feeling ran high police baton charges were becoming more frequent; and where large numbers of hastily enrolled special constables were employed—irresponsible young men, mostly, very free with their truncheons—tempers were wearing very thin. But among the leaders on the two sides the feeling was very different.

On the government side the experiences of the week had produced a steady growth of confidence. Their organisation was working well and, if it was not violently interfered with, was likely to improve. They had got through the noticeably more riotous week-end without having to call out troops, and therefore sat with an immense reserve of power as yet unused. In consequence Cabinet opinion hardened against any compromise solution which might give the Unions the appearance of a partial victory. Even Baldwin had determined that he was in a position to insist on an unconditional withdrawal of the strike notices and that it was his duty to do so. The threat of coercion by means of a general strike must be killed for ever. So, though Sir Herbert Samuel, hurriedly recalled from Italy, continued to negotiate untiringly for the compromise which had already eluded him, the Prime Minister was careful to avoid committing himself to any promises whatever; and when the Archbishop of Canterbury, Randall Davidson, wished to broadcast an appeal on behalf of leading Churchmen for generous concessions to peace from both sides the government brought great pressure to bear on the B.B.C. to refuse him the opportunity. Sir Arthur Steel-Maitland summed up the government's feeling in a letter to Samuel: nothing could be done 'to procure the end of the General Strike by a process of bargaining'.[1]

The General Council, on the other hand, were now brought face to face with the decision they had so far managed to avoid. They had to face the fact that, magnificently though the Unions had responded, the mere strike, supported only by peaceful picketing, was not going to succeed. The armoured columns escorting the food trucks from the London docks could only be stopped by violence, risking a blood bath which the members of the Council could not even contemplate. It is true that the machine-gunning of large numbers of strikers might have swung public opinion violently over against the government and forced a settlement on them. But that would mean revolution and, even worse, a revolution which would immediately pass out of their control into that of irresponsible but far more determined local leaders. 'The General Council of the T.U.C.', so the Message to the Workers had run in the first issue of the *British Worker*, 'wishes to emphasise the fact that this is an industrial dispute. It expects every member taking part to be exemplary in his conduct and not to give any opportunity for police interference.' By the seventh day of the strike the bankruptcy of this policy was at last clear. They must either go forward to revolution, or back to surrender. Their attitude to the Archbishop's appeal contrasted sharply with that of the government. They would have welcomed any move to save their faces, and on the day the strike ended they sent a deputation to Lambeth to thank Dr. Davidson for his effort.[2]

Thus, by the evening of May 10th, after exactly a week during which, in the opinion of all the more competent local organisers, they had cer-

---

[1] Quoted Julian Symons, *op. cit.*, p. 188.
[2] See C. K. A. Bell, *Randall Davidson*, p. 1317.

tainly held their own, the members of the General Council were grasping eagerly at any excuse for a surrender which, in the circumstances, must be abject. Even to force conditions on the government for calling off the strike would involve an intensification of the struggle which they could not contemplate. They seized on reports, quite untrue and denied by their own intelligence organisation, that there was a general drift back to work among the railwaymen; that at Southampton tram drivers were going back and at Bridgwater the brick and tile workers; that the government was now in a position to run thousands of trains daily. They exaggerated the importance of Mr. Justice Astbury's judgement and Simon's speech which purported to have put them outside the law. Above all they seized on the Memorandum which they had hammered out with Samuel, who had no official standing whatever, and whose proposals were rejected outright by the miners when they eventually saw them, and by the coal owners, and would certainly have been rejected by the government. Perhaps genuinely convinced that the miners had entrusted the negotiation of their case to them by the vaguely worded resolution of May 2nd, they further persuaded themselves that the still firm refusal of Smith and Cook to accept wage reductions or longer hours was a rejection of a perfectly reasonable solution negotiated on their behalf. Thus, by a process of logic every stage of which was false and dishonest, they reached the conclusion that they would be justified in calling off the strike without even insisting on the preliminary withdrawal of the lockout notices in the mines. Thomas, who had throughout worked for surrender and without regard for truth, and his colleague, Bromley, representing the Drivers and Firemen, helped them to the conclusion by painting up the false picture of a breaking strike. 'We are busted,' Bromley said at the end of the meeting on May 10th, which was true only if the General Council was not prepared for more violent methods.

Throughout May 11th and in the early part of the morning of Wednesday, the 12th, the arguments with the miners went on. Ramsay MacDonald offered to intervene to convince Cook and Smith that their attitude was 'a tragic blunder', and was curtly warned off by Cook. The exasperation of the General Council with the miners is very understandable. Anybody who had to negotiate with Smith was reduced to phrenetic impotence. But the whole basis of their case was dishonest.

They were condemning the miners for rejecting the Samuel proposals as though these proposals had been accepted by the government. Not only had Baldwin carefully refrained from doing so; his knowledge, through Thomas and others, that the Council was weakening stiffened his determination to be bound by no conditions or offers, Samuel's or anybody else's. The miners were being thrown over, in fact, for rejecting what the General Council called offers which nobody had yet made or had any intention of making. At noon on May 12th, after hearing Smith's final and contemptuous rejection of their arguments, Pugh and his deputation called on the Prime Minister.

They found Baldwin in a mood far less mellow and reassuring than his recent broadcast utterances had led them to hope. He had appealed then to his reputation for honesty and to the vote of confidence the nation had given him at the last election. 'Cannot you trust me', he had asked, 'to ensure a square deal for all parties—to secure even justice between man and man?' It may be that he was more vividly aware, now that he actually confronted it, of the difficulty of applying this simple formula when he had no power to coerce employers some of whom were vindictively triumphant and all of whom were likely to be in great difficulties themselves as long as the coal stoppage continued. In any case, he had to speak now as the representative of a victorious government receiving an unconditional surrender, and his chief concern was to be certain that it was unconditional. Both Thomas and Bevin tried, with a rather pathetic dignity, to pin him to some definite promise that pressure would be brought to bear on employers to reinstate men on the same terms as before the strike. Both emphasised that they had taken a big risk and done a big thing in the interests of the national industry in calling off the strike. 'We felt sure', Thomas said, 'that the big thing would be responded to in a big way.' But Baldwin's phrases remained elusive. 'You know my record. You know the object of my policy.' His only practical suggestion was that they should get into touch with the employers as soon as possible; and with this cold comfort the Council deputation retired to send off the telegrams with the news, which many of the local Strike Committees at first refused to believe, that they had been not merely defeated, but routed.

CHAPTER 7

After the Strike

The normal English reaction to national calamity is one of self-congratulation. It was so with the General Strike. 'Our old country can well be proud of itself,' George V wrote in his diary when he got the news of the General Council's surrender, 'as during the last nine days there has been a strike in which 4 million men have been affected; not a shot has been fired and no one killed; it shows what a wonderful people we are.' The same note was struck in his message to his People issued that evening, calling on all to remember only 'how steady and orderly the country has remained', and it was echoed in countless speeches and newspaper articles. Even Mr. Attlee shared the same view: 'That it passed off with so little disturbance reflected immense credit on the British people.'[1] Foreigners took up the cry in wistful admiration of what is called on these occasions the 'political maturity' of the British people. The forbearance and patience which had made it possible for a police force armed with nothing more lethal than truncheons to keep control of the situation, the uninterrupted, stately progress of county cricket throughout what was supposed to be a revolution, above all that supreme example of English tolerance or English muddle-headedness, whichever way one chose to look at it, the football match at Plymouth between police and strikers for which the Chief Constable's wife kicked off, and which the strikers won by 2 goals to 1—these were the aspects high-lighted by American and Continental journalists and by the British themselves. The French who, if they had learnt no other political lesson in the past 150 years, at least knew how to conduct a revolution, were frankly puzzled. Why were not

[1] C. R. Attlee, *As It Happened*, p. 64.

more policemen killed, an audience of Paris Socialists asked Raymond
Postgate later, and what was the sense of advising strikers to dig their
gardens rather than haunt the streets annoying the police? The 1,760
prosecutions for seditious speeches and the 1,389 for actual violence, and
the severe sentences, almost always involving some months' imprisonment, imposed by the magistrates, were glossed over. The smashed glass
of every bus that ran was forgotten, and only the genial slogans with
which their undergraduate drivers decorated them were remembered—
'I have no more panes now, Mummy,' and, 'A stone in the hand is worth
two in the bus.'

This self-satisfaction was all the more remarkable in view of the fact
that the General Council's surrender entirely failed to stop the strike.
The reaction of the strikers when it gradually dawned on them that no
terms had been made for the miners, or even for their own return to
work, was one of bewildered rage. What Baldwin called a 'victory for
common sense' was for most of them black treachery. Individual
Unions, unprepared and without bargaining power, could for the
moment do little or nothing to fulfil the General Council's instruction
to negotiate fair terms with the employers; and almost all the large
employers of labour sought to use the opportunity for victimisation.
Admiralty dockyard workers were threatened with loss of pension
rights; railwaymen were only promised reinstatement as the situation
permitted, and often in much lower-grade jobs. Some ringleaders were
refused re-employment altogether, and all over the country there were
cases where only lowered wages were offered, and those often only on
the condition that men resigned from their union. If good humour and
tolerance had on the whole been the prevailing note of the strike,
bitterness and violence marked its ending. Abandoned by their leaders,
the men stood solid in their district groups, refusing to go back unless
all were reinstated without penalty; and those who had stayed at work
the previous week began to come out to join them. Three days after
Baldwin's triumphant announcement the number of strikers had
actually increased by 100,000, and feeling was running dangerously
high. It was not only the miners now who were shouting: 'Down with
Thomas.' Labour men in Parliament, mostly inarticulate and embarrassed throughout the previous week in face of a strike which they
could not approve and dared not oppose, began to talk of its being after

all justified;[1] and on the Tory back benches there was some unrepentant approval of employers who were seizing the chance to teach the Unions a lesson.

The exhausted Prime Minister was forced to make one final effort towards conciliation and to bring his own followers under control. His own unwise statement on the day the strike ended had been partly responsible for the damage. 'His Majesty's Government', it had said, 'have no power to compel employers to take back every man who has been on strike, nor have they entered into any obligation of any kind on this matter.' Events now forced him to change his tune. Speaking more to his own Party than to anyone else, he said, 'I will not countenance any attempt on the part of any employers to use this present occasion for trying to get reductions in wages below those in force before the strike, or any increase in hours.' His Parliamentary triumph was overwhelming, and it was easy enough for the government to bring the Admiralty and the Army Victualling Department to heel. But, since Baldwin was unalterably opposed to government intervention in industry, his words had only a moral significance, and it seems likely that the employers would have proceeded unperturbed by the loss of the Prime Minister's countenance, but for the solidarity and truculence of the strikers. Historians, echoing the complacency of the period, have boasted that 'the employers fully responded to Mr. Baldwin's plea for magnanimity';[2] and certainly the official terms finally offered the men mostly conformed in the letter to Baldwin's demand. But there were many loopholes left and there was in practice a great deal of victimisation especially on the railways, where the continuation of the coal stoppage gave good excuse for not restoring full employment. There were station masters who were dismissed and re-employed in low-grade jobs, ticket inspectors who were reduced to the status of signalmen or guards, and similar losses of status in all the transport industries. The best the N.U.R. could do after a week's negotiation was a promise to strikers of three days' employment a week until services returned to normal.

Meanwhile the coal strike dragged on miserably through the summer. At the very start the miners were offered the chance of accepting the

---

[1] Duff Cooper's diary, *Old Men Forget*, p. 153.
[2] e.g. Somervell, *op. cit.*, p. 364.

Samuel memorandum terms, and might have saved themselves much suffering by doing so, incidentally placing the government in a very embarrassing position, since they were much more generous terms than what the Cabinet was actually prepared to offer on May 14th. The miners' case was a much more reasonable one than their mere dogged refusal to make concessions suggests. Five separate enquiries into the industry had condemned the organisation and management under private ownership as inefficient and wasteful. If, therefore, a loss of income had to be borne while the necessary reforms were carried through, it was unfair that it should fall on the miners rather than on the owners or, if the government felt that way about it, on the state. There was, moreover, a brazen irresponsibility and intolerance of criticism and interference voiced for the mine owners by their Chairman, Evan Williams, which increased the public uneasiness. When some of the Church's leaders endeavoured to intervene on the miners' behalf and the Prince of Wales let it be known that he, like most of his better-informed contemporaries, sympathised with them, Evan Williams dismissed both with a sneer: 'We have never had any faith in princes or in governments—whether they are princes of the Church or princes of another kind—as far as industrial questions are concerned.' Even Churchill, with his feet back on the ground after the excitements of the General Strike week, and acting now for Baldwin who was taking his annual holiday at Aix-les-Bains, could not shake the complacent stupidity of Evan Williams. The fact that two Royal Commissions and three independent enquiries had branded him and his fellows as industrially wholly incompetent and selfish moved him not at all. A series of social, economic and political accidents had placed the miners at their mercy, and after six months of national disaster, having rejected every half-hearted attempt at mediation, the owners got the terms they wanted: district settlements instead of a national wage scale, lowered wages, and longer hours. Moreover the last clause, as had been foretold, produced a cut-throat international competition, and that in turn ensured a large number of permanently unemployed miners who were the best guarantee against any further trouble.

Many people have protested against the statement that the miners that summer were 'starved into submission'. 'If you substitute a longer working day for the wage reduction,' Neville Chamberlain wrote in his diary on June 13th, 'the women and children come out of the picture altogether. The whole burden then falls on the man, and he is not going to get a lot of sympathy if he is obliged to work as long as a railwayman'; and again, a week later, 'They are not within sight of starvation, hardly of under-nutrition, so well are they looked after by the guardians. . . . They are living not too uncomfortably at the expense of the rate-payer, while the nation is gradually overcome by creeping paralysis.'[1] This callous and unimaginative self-consolation was reflected in the righteous indignation of Conservative members who sought to denounce the Trade Agreement with Russia as a reprisal for the £1 million which the Soviet Council of Trade Unions subscribed for the miners—another matter on which the King showed himself both wiser and more humane than some of his ministers. 'It would be disastrous', he caused Lord Stamfordham to write to the Home Secretary, 'if the government's action could in any way justify a cry from the Socialist Party that the former were attempting to stop financial aid from Russia or from any other country to save the miners' women and children from starvation.'[2]

It was not only the Russians and the seriously impoverished other Trade Unions who subscribed to help the miners. Large sums came as a sort of conscience money from the general public; and anybody who visited mining areas in that period knew well enough the realities behind the soothing phrases. The gaunt despair which ultimately compelled the drift back to work in October and November, the pride which concealed behind the neat curtains of front windows in the mining villages the fact that all the furniture had been sold—these were facts no less real because they failed to pierce the armour of Mr. Chamberlain's complacency. More than half the candidates at army recruiting centres in the years following the General Strike had to be rejected as unfit, and those who were accepted gained on an average two stone of weight in their first six months on army rations.[3] All who visited 'distressed areas' got the same impression as Hugh Dalton when he first visited the Durham constituency of Bishop Auckland as Parliamentary candidate in 1928: children certified by the school doctors as 'suffering from malnutrition', shops shuttered, and 'men sitting silent in Workmen's Clubs, too poor to buy either a drink or a smoke', and charitable institu-

---

[1] Feiling, *op. cit.*, p. 158.   [2] Nicolson, *op. cit.*, p. 421.
[3] This statistic is derived from the study of the records of two regimental depots in the early thirties.

tions dispensing worn boots and clothes. If nobody actually starved to death, the threat was near enough to haunt most mining cottages for many years to come.[1]

Undoubtedly the permanent legacy of the General Strike and of the much more prolonged miners' stoppage was a grave one. Some of it could be measured easily enough in hard cash. During 1926, instead of exporting 50 million tons of coal, Britain imported as much as she exported. Imports fell by £70 million, exports by over £150 million. The direct cost of the nine days' stoppage itself was estimated at £30 million. The long-term indirect damage from loss of markets which were never wholly recovered is less easy to calculate, but the unemployment figures give a clue. Early in 1926, for the first time since 1921, unemployment had dropped below the million mark. By the end of that year it was 1 million, and it was not to fall so low again until the rearmament drive of the late thirties. Swollen demands for outdoor relief from the rates had unbalanced the budgets of many local authorities, and the Unions had squandered all but the essential reserves which backed their benefit and friendly funds. Thomas said that the railwaymen had spent over £1 million, and the T.G.W.U. was half a million in debt.

For the Trade Unions in general this was a severe, if temporary, set-back. Their membership, which had reached the record figure of 5½ million at the beginning of 1926, fell again by more than half a million in the following year, and a large number of Unions disaffiliated themselves from the T.U.C. The Communists, on the other hand, gained on balance. The expectation of direct and violent action raised their numbers from 6,000 at the start of the strike to over 10,000 in October, and though many fell away again there was some permanent gain.[2] Their increasing effectiveness can be measured by the rising note of exasperation in the denunciations of their infiltration tactics by Labour leaders, and especially Ernest Bevin; though Lansbury, the genuine, if muddle-headed revolutionary, who had tried to work with them and knew them better than Bevin did, dismissed their pretensions with contempt. 'That lot run a revolution?' he said. 'They couldn't run a whelk stall.'[3]

There was little, in fact, for Britain to be complacent about. It had

---

[1] See Hugh Dalton, *Call Back Yesterday*, pp. 202–3, for an unusually convincing picture of conditions at this time.

[2] Pelling, *op. cit.*   [3] Raymond Postgate, *Life of George Lansbury*, p. 238.

been proved at least that, as Jack Jones remarked, 'a general strike is a general nonsense'; or, in wider terms, that the people of Britain had no taste for revolutionary methods of achieving political change. It checked the epidemic of constant strikes which had so interrupted and hampered industry since the war: the number of those involved in stoppages dropped from an average of 500,000 a year to below 100,000. But this was little enough to balance against the permanent embitterment of large and important sections of the community. For not much more was to be heard of the 'square deal for all parties' and 'even justice between man and man'. Baldwin, nervous and highly strung, and a far more delicate mechanism than was suggested by the imperturbable, pipe-smoking front he presented to the public, had exhausted himself in the fortnight of the crisis itself. Even his enemies have had to admit that his handling of Cabinet and Parliament, both frequently over-excited and recalcitrant, and his conduct of public relations generally were throughout the strike masterly. Its peaceful conduct and early end were universally admitted to have been largely his personal triumph. But with his last big speech against victimisation his fit of energy was past and he relapsed into lethargy. To a plea from Steel-Maitland that something constructive should be done to create better conciliation machinery in industry and a new spirit of co-operation and mutual trust he responded not at all. Instead he allowed the extremists of his Party to do just what Steel-Maitland had pleaded against: 'We cannot wield a sword in one hand,' he had written, 'even if it be in reality but the phantom of a sword—and at all convincingly proffer an olive branch in the other.'[1] The sword which the Conservatives proceeded to brandish—and it was indeed a phantom sword—was the Trades Disputes Act of 1927.

This measure declared all sympathetic strikes illegal and made the funds of any Union engaging in such a strike liable for civil damages, while the Union rights of blackleg workers were legally protected. It sought to limit the right of strikers to form peaceful pickets. It forbade Civil Service Unions to become affiliated to any other Union or any political movement; and it embodied Macquisten's projected Act of 1925 by insisting that Union members should contract 'in' and not 'out' for the political levy. It thus combined almost every disadvantage an Act of Parliament could have. Vicious and vindictive in tone and inten-

[1] G. M. Young, *Stanley Baldwin*, p. 121.

tion, it created the maximum grievance possible among Trade Unionists
—a grievance which was to simmer on for twenty years and play a large
part in the vote which so disconcerted Conservative expectations in 1946.
On the other hand its language and threats were, in the opinion of many
eminent lawyers, so vague as to defy legal analysis and definition.
Literally applied, it would have tended to turn every small industrial
dispute into a minor revolution. Yet in a major crisis, such as the nation
had just weathered, it would do little to strengthen the powers the
government already had and much to drive men to the extremes of
violence which it must always be the object of governments to avoid.
And in any case a repetition of the disastrous experiment of the General
Strike was the one thing no British government had to fear for a
generation to come.

Baldwin not only allowed this Bill to go through without recorded
protest; he actively intervened in its support and in the end forced it
through by the sledge-hammer method of applying the closure to the
debate in June of 1927. By so doing he forfeited almost all the goodwill
he had gained by his brave stand against Macquisten's Bill in 1925 and
by his patient tolerance during the course of the strike. He allowed
what he had himself proclaimed as a victory for common sense, and
especially a victory for the nation as a whole, to be exploited as a Party
triumph, identified the government in the minds of all good Trade
Unionists with the coal owners, and by that one ill-judged, practically
valueless Act lost more votes than the good work of Chamberlain and
Churchill on pensions and housing would be able to win back for him.
Moreover his collapse, which was physical as well as moral, left both his
Party and the nation without leadership for two critical years.

For 1927 was one of the few moments of hopefulness in the dreary
inter-war period, when it seemed that both in Great Britain and in the
world at large the drift back to chaos might be arrested. In spite of unemployment and the strike, trade was reviving and was better than it
had been for years. Sir Alfred Mond, who had now forsaken the Liberals
for the Tories, and the new Chairman of the T.U.C., Ben Turner, were
able to bring together a committee of employers and Trade Unionists
to discuss practical methods of co-operation in industry, and to produce
the National Industrial Council on which both sides were represented,
in an attempt to remove grievances before they became disputes.

Abroad, the signature of the Treaty of Locarno had seemed to open up some real possibility of easing the tension imposed on Europe by Versailles, of getting Germany into the League of Nations, and of making a real start with disarmament. Unfortunately nowhere among the statesmen was there the vigour and clarity of mind needed to take advantage of the situation.

The evacuation of the Rhineland and the entry of Germany into the League were indeed achieved, but only at a very dangerous price. It had been well known to the Allied governments, though not on the whole to their peoples, that the Germans had from the first resisted and evaded their promise to disarm. The governing caste of the old German army remained unbroken and implacably determined on revenge. Using every device—hectoring rudeness, deliberate lying and concealment and self-piteous appeals for the poor workmen who would starve if the lathes of the armament factories were dismantled, the old Army Command managed to keep intact a great portion of its pre-war organisation, all its artillery, supply, munition, and remount depots, a great part of the industrial plant which could be turned back to the manufacture of armaments at a moment's notice, and a cadre of trained officers and N.C.O.s which would serve for an army ten times the size of the 100,000-strong Reichsheer which was all that the Treaty of Versailles allowed. Every company in this small, professional, treaty force bore the number and badge of one of the regiments of the old army; every officer drew the pay of at least one rank higher than that of his official employment; and behind them there was an equal number of men trained, armed, and organised on exactly the same lines, but disguised under the name and uniforms of the Security Police.

The Reichsheer's commander, General Hans von Seeckt, was the organising genius behind all this. Behind him again there was a network of concealed, unofficial organisations: volunteer bodies of senior officers and likely recruits, unnecessary departments of the civil service which housed and concealed the administration of the army of the future, and committees which co-ordinated the plans of the senior soldiers with those of the big industrialists. The coalition governments of the Weimar Republic were composed of ordinary, middle-class folk who had been accustomed all their lives to spring to attention at a rasped military command and to clear the pavement in front of any officer in uniform.

They were aware that they themselves existed as politicians largely on sufferance until the old governing class found it expedient to move into the open again. They still took their orders in a crisis from the generals; and any workman of socialist or communist leanings who denounced concealed dumps of arms to the Allied Control Commission was given a savage sentence of imprisonment for treason, while those who had concealed the arms were never even prosecuted.[1]

Not even German historians now dispute the truth of all this, and it was all perfectly well known to the ex-Allied governments in 1926. But the British government had preferred to suppress the facts rather than rouse the hostility of the great and growing body of pro-German opinion in the country, while the French merely used them as a convenient justification for prolonging the occupation of the Rhineland beyond the dates laid down in the Treaty. It was even known quite definitely that Germany, passing beyond the mere non-fulfilment of her disarmament promises, had begun actively to rearm. Stresemann, the new German Foreign Minister who had signed the Locarno Treaties, passed with the Western powers as an honest, peace-loving statesman whose greatest ambition was to bring Germany back as an equal into the comity of nations. He was in fact a sincere, nationalist-minded patriot whose policy was not so much 'fulfilment' of the Treaty of Versailles, as an acceptance of 'The Treaty as signed' so as to give himself a bargaining position for revising it. He undoubtedly knew of the rearmament and on the whole approved of it, since it further strengthened his hand in playing for his two major objectives: the entry of Germany into the League on her own terms, and a revision of her eastern frontier before that, too, became fixed and frozen by guarantee treaties on the lines of Locarno.

In the first of his two objectives Stresemann was wholly successful. Whereas, in 1925, German evasion of the disarmament clauses had been made the excuse for prolonging the occupation of the Rhineland, in 1926 that evacuation was begun in the full knowledge that Germany had already begun to rearm, and in the hope of inducing a German change of heart by reasonable treatment. The arrogant German claim to be admitted to the League without undergoing the prescribed examination

[1] All this is set forth and documented in J. H. Morgan, *Assize of Arms,* esp. App. V to Vol. I. See also J. W. Wheeler-Bennett, *The Nemesis of Power.*

by the Admissions Committee which must have disclosed the truth about disarmament, was conceded as a further sop to German susceptibilities. The French acquiesced in the British policy of concession and appeasement. Germany became a permanent member of the League Council, though she did not abandon her ceaseless complaint—hypocritical in the circumstances—against her compulsory disarmament while the Allies ignored the implied promise of Article VIII of the Treaty that they, too, would disarm. Stresemann also used Germany's theoretically disarmed condition as an excuse for reservations on participation in sanctions, so as to preserve the special relationship she had built up with Russia.[1]

Meanwhile, in order to meet the recurrent German complaints, there had been some preparatory discussions at Geneva to pave the way for a full-scale Conference on Disarmament, though little progress was made. No single touchstone could be found by which to measure, either quantitatively or qualitatively, the differing military strengths of the powers. Neither expenditure, nor numbers of effectives, nor quantities of war material found any general acceptance as a measuring standard, and an attempt to combine all three proved impossible. Furthermore it was impossible to assess the value of armies, navies, and air forces in relation to each other. The only sensible and practical suggestion was made by M. Litvinov, when Russia was invited to participate in the fourth meeting of the so-called Preparatory Commission. He proposed that the nations should stop arguing about formulas and actually start to disarm. But this seemed to all grotesque—a joke in not very good taste; and the suggestion was rejected by the only unanimous vote the Commission ever achieved. A conference in 1925 between the naval representatives of Great Britain, the U.S.A., and Japan, on what ought to have been the much simpler problem of limiting warships other than battleships, also broke down in disorder, largely because of Britain's claim for a relatively greater cruiser fleet to guard her long, vulnerable trade routes. Thus by 1929 no progress at all had been made in the direction of general disarmament, and only Great Britain had made any practical contribution, stripping down her Air Force in particular far beyond the margin of safety. The 187 Squadrons of 1919

[1] For the facts set out in this and the preceding paragraph, see the agreed conclusions of the 4th Anglo-German Historical Conference, *Internationales Jahrbuch für Geschichts Unterricht*, Band V, p. 281.

had been so reduced in the post-war years that by 1923 only 18 Squadrons remained for home defence. Hoare had then started an expansion aimed to produce the 52 Squadrons estimated as essential by the Air Ministry, but progress was very slow, and by 1929 there were still only 31. The Navy had only 50 obsolescent cruisers, though the Admiralty put its minimum needs at 70; and the Army was back to its peace-time normal, barely sufficient for its police duties throughout the Empire and on the Rhine. But the Germans were for the moment much more preoccupied with the strength of the French army and of those of her allies in the Little Entente, and so were left with their grievance, which many Englishmen thought to be justified, intact.

The only apparent step forward towards ensuring permanent peace was in fact a very dangerous one. The Kellogg Pact, worked out in Paris by the American Secretary of State and M. Briand, the French Premier, sought in two short and simple clauses to outlaw war for ever. All signatories solemnly renounced the use of war 'as an instrument of national policy', and agreed to seek only pacific means of settling disputes among themselves. There was no attempt to define such pacific means or the methods to be adopted to force any recalcitrant power to keep its promises. This in reality left everything a little worse than before. No statesman who had made up his mind to the gamble of war would be deterred in the slightest degree by a mere paper promise, however solemn; whereas thousands of unthinking people were persuaded that something effective had been done to 'outlaw war' and began to oppose all expenditure on armaments thenceforward as unnecessary. Until the Conservative Party in Great Britain and the government and people of the U.S.A. could accept the necessity of general commitments and the use of their armed forces by some international authority not under their control, no real advance could be made on 1914. The Covenant of the League provided machinery perfectly adequate for the prevention of war; but so long as the member states retained the right to withhold support where their own interests seemed to demand it, statesmen would guide national policies by the old, XIX-century criteria. Sixty-three nations joyfully subscribed to the Kellogg Pact—six more than had accepted the League Covenant—for the very reason that it committed them to precisely nothing.

It was during this period that both the main Parties in Britain helped to create the conditions which were to reduce British policy to impotence in the critical years after 1935. The Labour clamour for total disarmament would not have been wholly logical even if they had managed to carry Parliament with them in ratifying the Geneva Protocol, for they would have rendered British support of the Covenant valueless. George Lansbury once went the length of proposing the abolition of the Navy and Air Force altogether. True, on this sort of occasion, responsible Socialists would agree with Chamberlain's judgement of Lansbury that 'where reason reigns he has no place'. But he reflected that temperamental and irrational mood of hatred for anything admitting the possibility of war which permeated the Labour Party and gained an increasing hold on the younger generations which were coming to maturity and the vote. It can be argued that the Labour leaders would have been more prepared to entrust the disposal of armed forces to the Assembly of the League than to a Conservative British government. But there can be no doubt that until something resembling the Protocol provided reliable machinery for preserving international security, clamour for total and unilateral disarmament was irresponsible and dangerous. It was of course an added complication of their views that they believed that a capitalist government could only pursue imperialist foreign policies, and therefore could not be trusted with armaments. Their tone remained that of the Peace Letter of 1927: 'Convinced that all disputes between nations are capable of settlement by diplomatic negotiations, or by some form of international arbitration, we solemnly declare that we shall refuse to support, or render war service to, any Government which resorts to arms.' They thus totally ignored the fact that, if they themselves got into power, their policies would need the backing of armed strength perhaps even more than those of the Conservatives; and navies and air forces cannot be created and abolished in conformity with the results of general elections.

The Conservative Party and their leaders forfeited any right to protest at the Socialist attitude by their own equally irresponsible contribution to a situation of which they were to complain so bitterly ten years later. By rejecting the Protocol and insisting that the British government must retain its freedom of action in a crisis, they accepted responsibility for ensuring that when the crisis came the government had the means of effective action. Thanks to what Neville Chamberlain testily called 'the activities of that preposterous League of Nations Union', they dared not admit that they had rejected the methods and ideals of the League and that they preferred to pursue an old-fashioned balance of power, which would necessitate the maintenance of reasonable armed forces, at least on the seas and in the air. They joined instead in the prevailing lip-service to Geneva. With the industrialist and taxpaying elements of their own Party clamouring for economy, they were unwilling to face the public with the logical but unpopular consequences of their own policy. With the majority and the time and the means to have maintained the fleet and Air Force at strengths which gave some security, they funked the issue; and by signing and extolling the Kellogg Pact, and by going through the motions of participating in disarmament conferences, they helped to foster the illusion that paper instruments would halt armed forces which lay at the root of the pacificism of the thirties.

Thus, in spite of appearances, the long-term outlook for Europe was not reassuring. Germany was in the League and since 1926 had been making regular payments of Reparations. The French and Italian debts to Britain had been reduced to feasible figures and funded. The beneficent effects of American capital advances were making themselves felt and it seemed that, however belatedly, the economic blunders of Versailles which had so exasperated Mr. Keynes were being put right. The French appeared to have committed themselves to more conciliatory policies, and the Kellogg Pact at least marked the end of America's complete isolation from European politics. But there remained all the time the two factors which were the real source of all danger in the future. No practical steps had been taken to remedy Germany's main political grievances arising out of Versailles; and at the same time the attempt to keep her disarmed had been tacitly abandoned. In the long run French and British policies cancelled each other out. French intransigence was strong enough to prevent concessions—the Anschluss with Austria, for example—which British opinion increasingly felt to be justified. But the British government, driven on by this rising opinion, was able to frustrate the French desire for a tough line on disarmament. Thus we got the worst of both worlds. It is customary still, as Mr. Churchill does, to treat what he calls 'the Economic Blizzard' of 1931 as the main cause for Hitler's easy and hysterical triumph. But there was no reason why any German statesman, Stresemann or anyone else, should be able to control the powerful forces working for Treaty revision in Germany unless he could win from the late Allies the concessions which would take the sting out of it. The economic crisis only accelerated and precipitated what was inherent in the logic of the situation once the opportunity offered by the favourable diplomatic climate of 1927 for a genuine policy of appeasement had been lost. It is conceivable that generous concessions then, made from strength and not weakness, might have averted calamity. The height of folly was to refuse them, and yet let Germany regain the strength which would be able to exact them by force.

At home in Britain there reigned in these years an equally hopeful and deceptive calm. Chamberlain in administrative obscurity and Churchill in a series of spectacular budgets worked away at their huge programme of pensions and local government reform which were a masterpiece of 'disinterested statesmanship', but from the vote-catching point of view almost valueless. Indeed, Attlee recalls that in committee on the Rating and Valuation Bill it was often he and his Labour colleagues who saw Chamberlain through in the teeth of Conservative opposition.[1] The electoral reforms of the past century were brought to their logical conclusion in the grant of what Lord Rothermere's newspapers indignantly denounced as 'The Flapper Vote', giving women an equal right with men to vote at the age of 21. Lord Balfour rounded off a long career of distinction in a suitably philosophic way by finding an acceptable definition of the Dominions—'equal in status, in no way subordinate one to another in any respect of their domestic or external affairs, though united by a common allegiance to the Crown, and freely associated as members of the British Commonwealth of Nations'. Rather surprisingly this proved for many years perfectly satisfactory to all except the Irish; and indeed throughout this period the British Commonwealth of Nations grew in effectiveness far more satisfactorily and harmoniously than the League of Nations, partly, perhaps, because it did not rouse the same widespread missionary zeal, but applied itself with practical common sense to problems as they arose. And in 1927 the first big step was taken towards implementing the Montagu-Chelmsford promises of 1919 and bringing India one step nearer to Dominion status.

The first stage was purely preparatory: two visits to India by an all-

---

[1] *As It Happened*, p. 63.

party Commission under the chairmanship of Sir John Simon on a purely fact-finding mission, on the basis of which they were to prepare recommendations. But even that was enough to rouse the suspicious hostility of both extremist wings. The Congress Party in India boycotted the whole proceeding because there were no Indians on the Commission; and the die-hard Tories began a warning grumble which unfortunately aroused the sympathy of that distinguished ex-Liberal, Mr. Churchill. But Baldwin, here as always conciliatory and reasonable and middle-of-the-road, was determined to go forward towards some sort of federation which would enable British India and the Indian States to work together, and to ignore the communal differences which perpetually threatened to plunge India into civil war between Hindus and Moslems. He was determined, too, to ignore the Churchillian, Kiplingesque clamour for a 'robust assertion of British Imperial greatness'.[1] Here again there was the note of sound, but quite unspectacular progress which was rapidly shaking the faith of Conservatives in their own leadership. They wanted something more exciting and dynamic to appeal to an electorate increasingly post-war in generation and outlook, whereas, as Colonel Moore-Brabazon put it, 'the snores of the Treasury Bench resound through the country'.

For the two years which followed the General Strike the government in fact drifted gently, but always further out of touch with public opinion. To the vociferous, self-confident, inexperienced younger generations, whether they emerged from the Union Societies of Oxford and Cambridge or the London School of Economics, the prevailing tone of the Cabinet appeared stuffily Victorian and its policies a feeble rehash of ideas which had already led the world to disaster in 1914. Austen Chamberlain's notorious pro-French tendencies, and indeed the whole trend of his foreign policy, which was away from the alarming general commitments of Geneva and towards an old-fashioned balance of power, outraged the most cherished beliefs of the growing number who saw in the League the only hope for the world's salvation. His failure to make progress with disarmament, understandable enough in view of the unreasonableness of all the powers concerned, was attributed to lack of enthusiasm, and was to cost the Tories many votes at the coming election.

[1] *The Second World War*, Vol. I, p. 26.

The Home Secretary, Sir William Joynson-Hicks, a rugged, die-hard individualist who rejoiced in the nickname of Jix and was always treated by the newspapers as a rather better comic turn than he deserved to be, made things no better by a dramatic raid on Arcos, the head-quarters of the Russian Trade Agency in London. An army of police officials, ransacking its archives and bursting open its safes, found plenty of evidence that Arcos was used as a centre for the dissemination of Russian Communist propaganda, which everyone knew anyway, but failed to discover the incriminating secret document relating to defence which the Russians were alleged to have stolen. The episode created a tremendous stir, but it excited little sympathy except among elderly Conservatives who had all along detested MacDonald's Russian Trade Agreements, and, oddly enough, the T.U.C., which broke off fraternal relations with the Russian trade unions as a reprisal for Communist infiltration into Union management. The public as a whole had no taste for fresh quarrels, would rather have seen Russian trade expanded, and was increasingly impatient with a view of Russia which could see no further than the murder of the Tsar.

This was the period when the loss of the 'missing generation' began to make itself really felt. To the more intelligent young it seemed that, as in Kipling's time, they were being 'sugared about by the old men ('Eavy-sterned, amateur old men)', who were not even of their fathers', but of their grandfathers' generation. They wrapped in a comprehensive condemnation all that smacked of the pre-1914 world—its clothes, its conventions, its manners, its armies and navies, its politics and its morals. Too young and inexperienced themselves as yet to force an entry into the management of affairs, they were intelligent enough and well enough informed to perceive in every department of the national life the same out-of-date, backward-looking leadership: admirals cling-ing pathetically to obsolescent battleships, and generals with their minds still rooted in Passchendaele mud; industry a hundred years behind the times in equipment and production methods, complacently contemp-tuous of the stream-lined techniques and organisation of American big business and of the rebuilt, rationalised foundries and factories of Ger-many and France, run by men who had inherited family firms in the days when cut-throat competition from abroad had seemed a remote and inconsiderable contingency. These were the men who had to be reminded by the Prince of Wales at the British Industries Fair that their salesmanship and their marketing methods were out of date, and that the happy, Victorian days, when the world had had to take British goods even if they were not exactly what was wanted and were delivered at a time convenient only to the manufacturer, were gone for ever. Naturally enough, the rebelliousness of youth took forms so outrageous and extravagant that it had only the effect of making the older generation hang grimly on to all the power it could keep. It is likely that the young preached far more free love than they practised. They wore their Oxford trousers and their skimpy evening frocks and smoked and swore more to shock their elders than to express any coherent rebellion; and many of the young men who proclaimed pacificism so loudly in 1929 were to die gallantly enough in defence of one freedom or another between 1935 and 1945. There was none the less substance in their grievance. But the old took the antics at their face value and only strengthened the impression that they were as stupid and stuffy as they sounded; and there was no effective middle generation, reared in the tradition of Liberalism, yet disillusioned by the experience of war, to give the young a lead or to tread hungrily on the heels of the old and force a compromise between the extremes. The outcome in political terms—that is in the terms decisive for the fate of the country, and in part for the world as a whole —was a widening gulf between the politicians and the voter. The full effect was not to be felt until the mid-1930s, when sane policy came to mean electoral suicide. But it was opening already in 1928 widely enough to lead Baldwin and his Party to a quite unexpected débâcle.

In these circumstances it is perhaps not surprising that the two measures which aroused the hottest controversy during these years were not really contemporary or Party matters at all, and that they revealed a traditionalism wholly unexpected and quite irrelevant to the complacently materialistic and rationalist Britain of the twenties. The first and less important was an attempt to reform the House of Lords so as to make it both more democratic in structure and more powerful in action. It was a measure foreshadowed in the Parliament Act of 1911 and then described by Mr. Asquith as one which 'brooked no long delay', and which was to go on being overdue for many years after 1927. The Tories had long cherished a desire to restore to the second chamber the power of acting as an effective brake on too rapid and ill-considered legislative changes, but had had to recognise that the domination of a hereditary peerage must first be at least modified. This scheme, which was sponsored by Lord Chancellor Cave and Lord Birkenhead, sought to meet inevitable opposition from Liberals and Socialists by providing for a mixed House, partly elected by the existing peerage, partly nominated for 10 years by the Crown on the advice of the government of the day. In return the House was to have its absolute veto restored on any measure affecting the constitution or limiting its own powers. All the passions of 1910 were reanimated by what seemed a shameless Conservative attempt to reverse the Parliament Act. Even the younger Conservatives were shocked, and Mr. Garvin in the *Observer* likened the Party to Gadarene swine rushing upon their doom. So Baldwin, who had all along remained curiously detached from the project, pronounced an elegant funeral oration upon it and it was dropped.

The other great controversial measure of 1927 roused passions which stretched far back beyond 1910. Ever since the beginning of the Oxford Movement there had been disquiet in Church of England circles at the discrepancies which existed between the services conducted by the clergy of what had come to be known as the Anglo-Catholic persuasion and what had been sanctioned by Parliament and embodied in the Prayer Book of 1662. Disraeli's Public Worship Act of 1874 had in practice failed to suppress what he called the 'mass in masquerade', and a Royal Commission of 1906 had admitted the need for a more effective discipline over the clergy, but had postulated the necessity of first bringing the Prayer Book, as the 'disciplinary norm', more into conformity with 'the religious life of the present generation'.

Prayer Book revision had been a matter of intermittent debate ever since in Church Assemblies and committees of various kinds, the main controversy being centred throughout on the vestments and ritual to be permitted in the Holy Communion service, and more particularly on the practice of reservation of the sacrament. Randall Davidson, Archbishop of Canterbury since 1903, would have preferred himself to 'let it alone', and 'adhere to what has satisfied English people for more than three centuries'. He also believed, probably quite rightly, that this was 'the view of the overwhelming majority of English Churchmen through-

out the country'.[1] But he was scrupulously anxious to give full weight to
the strongly held convictions of many of his fellow ecclesiastics: men
who, as he said, had 'studied the subject and cared about it most'. Under
his non-committal chairmanship an alternative canon for the Prayer
Book had finally been produced, sanctioning reservation of the sacrament for sick persons only, and making other, less important changes;
and this received final sanction from the Church Assembly by large
majorities in all three Houses, the only considerable opposition being
in the House of Laity.

By the time that the Prayer Book measure had been piloted through
the House of Lords by the Archbishop all Protestant Britain had been
roused to an unexpected frenzy of opposition. All the irrational, deep-
seated prejudice against Popery, which had survived in the most remarkable way from the XVI and XVII centuries, came suddenly again to
the surface. The still powerful Evangelical party within the Church
found solid support from the non-Anglican Protestantism of Scotland,
Wales and Ulster, unrepresented in the Church, but powerful in the
House of Commons. Thanks to this support, Joynson-Hicks and Sir
Thomas Inskip were able to rally a majority in the Commons against the
measure: 238 votes to 205 in December, 1927, and 266 to 220 when it
came up again, slightly revised, in June, 1928. The passionate feeling
provoked by this measure was all the more extraordinary since nobody
really believed that the Bishops would be able to enforce strict conformity with the new book any more than they had with the old. The
House of Commons vote had in practice no effect at all. Those who
wished to use the New Prayer Book have done so ever since with impunity; and most Anglo-Catholics for whom it did not go nearly far
enough, have also continued the liturgical practices, illegal even by the
New Book, which they prefer, with an almost equal impunity. 'Reservation of the sacrament', it has been truly said, 'remained in the same
category as driving a motor-car at more than twenty miles an hour. It
continued to be illegal and it continued to be allowed.'[2]

Amidst these excitements, which tended to underline Conservative
disagreements and did nothing to enhance the government's prestige,
the solid, practical achievement of Chamberlain and Churchill passed

[1] Bell, *op. cit.*, p. 1332.
[2] Somervell, *op. cit.*, p. 408.

almost unnoticed. The crowning piece of their work, the Local Government Act, only became law a few weeks before the dissolution of Parliament, and far too late for any beneficial effects of the policy as a whole to make themselves felt in the country. Much more important from the electioneering point of view was the suspicion that Churchill was actively opposed to disarmament and the knowledge that he deplored any rapid move towards Indian autonomy. Boredom, and a sense that the Conservatives were old, tired, spent men, swung opinion strongly away from the government; and Baldwin's unimaginative slogan of 'Safety First', his reliance on his own personal reputation, his honesty, and his pipe, proved a grave miscalculation.

Yet the result of the curious election of 1929 was safety first carried to an illogical extreme. The electorate, larger than ever before, responded apathetically to the most dynamic of the Party appeals, that of the precariously reunited Liberals, embodied in Lloyd George's pamphlet, *We Can Conquer Unemployment*. A bold programme of large-scale, deficit-financed public works proved to have even less appeal than unadventurous conservatism or watered-down socialism. Slightly over $8\frac{1}{2}$ million votes went to the Conservatives, rather fewer to the Socialists, and only $5\frac{1}{4}$ to the Liberals. Thanks, however, to the vagaries of the British electoral system, the numbers in Parliament in no way reflected these figures. Each party had put over 500 candidates into the field, and the result of this genuinely three-cornered fight was to make the Socialists the largest group in the Commons with 287 members, the Conservatives second with 260, and to give the Liberals a mere 50. The Communists lost even their one member, Mr. Saklatvala. The Liberals were thus forced back into the trap from which they had tried to escape in 1923. Once again they found themselves almost inevitably maintaining a Labour government in office and had to console themselves with the barren illusion that they held the balance of political power. The Tories were left to wrangle among themselves over the failures of their uninspired leadership; and the electorate got what, presumably, it wanted: a government condemned to no decisive action of any kind. It had, as a contemporary put it, 'rejected the slogan of Safety First, but achieved the result';[1] and all parties could console themselves with the thought that government activity would be restricted to the sphere

[1] *Round Table*, quoted Somervell, *op. cit.*, p. 412.

of foreign affairs, where Mr. MacDonald could be counted on to support the League and the cause of disarmament with distinction, but without any undesirable commitments, or any positive contributions to the maintenance of world peace.

CHAPTER 8

The Second Labour Government and the Crisis of 1931

Since Labour was now the largest Party in the House, Baldwin did not this time wait to be defeated, but resigned forthwith; and on June 5th MacDonald set about his very difficult task of forming a government. The inner circle of the Labour Movement was always a hotbed of jealousy and intrigue, much of which in recent years had been concentrated against MacDonald. The Trade Union wing of the Party sympathised not at all with his dream of establishing Labour as the second great Party working within the existing Parliamentary machine and of inducing his wilder followers to join him in convincing the electorate that they were perfectly capable of responsible and statesmanlike government. The extremists would have preferred to refuse office altogether until they had a working majority. They mistrusted the compromises and manœuvres to which a minority government was inevitably condemned, and this hostility was to play a decisive part in the crisis two years later. Then there were the personal difficulties. Henderson, though he had loyally co-operated with MacDonald in building up the Parliamentary Party, and never relinquished its chairmanship, remained to the end a Trade Unionist rather than a politician. The Webbs and the young men like Dalton who sat at their feet maintained a constant sniping campaign at their leader, whose adaptability and tactical skill they dismissed as snobbery and an absence of principle. Jimmy Thomas's boisterous, easy familiarity with men of all kinds and classes brought him under the same intellectual lash; and Snowden had a talent for bitter invective which, under the growing strain of illness, he was apt to unleash on left-wing colleagues who would not see that the time had come to substitute the responsible attitudes of mature states-men for what he called 'propaganda patter'.

For three days MacDonald battled with these intransigencies, 'courteous and dignified' and 'surrounded by that wall of reserve, accompanied by a sort of injured innocence'[1] which so irritated his critics, but which was only probably the inevitable consequence of the isolation of leadership. He was uncertain, he told the King, if he would be able to form a government at all. At one point he even offered to surrender the premiership to Henderson in exchange for the Foreign Office. But in the end it sorted itself out. Henderson got the Foreign Office and Thomas was consoled with the Privy Seal and an overall responsibility for dealing with unemployment. Philip Snowden, inevit-ably, was Chancellor of the Exchequer and Deputy Leader. Clynes, honest, charming, hard-working and ineffectual, went to the Home Office, and Lansbury got his one great political opportunity, of which he was to make unexpected and spectacular good use, at the Office of Works. Sidney Webb, reluctant and embarrassed, went to the Upper House as Lord Passfield, and the remaining quota of peers and law officers was found, partly by recruitment of opportunist Liberals. On June 8th they all went down to Windsor Castle, where the King was still convalescing after a long and dangerous illness, and the second Socialist government in English history was inaugurated under what then seemed far better auspices than the first.

It was obvious that, if government was to be carried on at all, there would have to be a large measure of co-operation between all three Parties; and for this MacDonald made a statesmanlike plea at the out-set, inviting the new Parliament to decide how far it was possible 'to consider ourselves more as a Council of State and less as arrayed regi-ments facing each other in battle'. To this plea the leaders of the other two Parties would have been largely ready to respond. The difficulty was that none of the three leaders was at that moment in effective con-trol of his own back benchers and extremists. The very idea of co-operation was anathema to the I.L.P. which was now, under Jimmy Maxton's leadership, trying to build up an *imperium in imperio* within the Labour Party, which had denounced the Mond-Turner Industrial Council as 'class collaboration', and had vowed itself to 'unceasing war

[1] Boothby, *op. cit.*

against capitalism'. Throughout the next year the Government was constantly in danger from the indiscipline of its own left-wing supporters and was frequently saved from defeat only by Tory abstentions. The Liberals, nominally reunited, were torn not only by personal feuds dating back to 1916, but by deep cleavages of principle. For Keynes outside Parliament and Simon within it had become convinced of the temporary need for a 10% revenue tariff as the only way of averting an industrial crisis and stemming the rise of unemployment, while the purists stood doggedly for Free Trade. Thus Lloyd George and Samuel also had the greatest difficulty in leading a united body into the lobbies. Baldwin meanwhile was under heavy attack from the Press Lords, Beaverbrook and Rothermere, largely on this same issue of a tariff, and at the same time quite unable to get the support of his right wingers for what would nowadays be called a bi-partisan policy on India and on disarmament.

It was nevertheless on these two issues of India and disarmament that the greatest measure of Party collaboration could be secured; and on these, not unnaturally, MacDonald concentrated at once, leaving Thomas, assisted by Lansbury, Sir Oswald Mosley, and Tom Johnston, the Secretary for Scotland, to work in private on the intractable figures of unemployment. As far as Indian affairs were concerned, the government had merely to pick up the threads of all-Party investigations and negotiations which had been going on for three years. The responsible leaders of all three Parties were agreed that it was desirable to begin the move towards Indian self-government implicitly promised in the Montagu declaration of 1917; and a Commission under Sir John Simon had been investigating the possibilities since 1927. It was thus easy for MacDonald, soon after he took office, to agree enthusiastically with Simon that the terms of reference of his Commission be extended to include relations between British India and the Indian native states, and so allow them to produce, in effect, a sketch-plan for a future all-Indian constitution. The opposition leaders, when duly consulted, wholeheartedly agreed; and the Viceroy, Lord Irwin, made the momentous announcement that the 'natural issue' of the Montagu declaration was 'the attainment of Dominion Status' by India.

From then on, considering the complexities of the Indian situation, the religious and communal difficulties, the suspicions of the Indian

Princes, and the intransigence of Mr. Gandhi's Congress Party, matters as far as India was concerned went forward with surprising smoothness. The first Round Table Conference sat in London from November, 1930, until January, 1931, and, under the very able chairmanship of the Prime Minister, produced agreed proposals which went far beyond the Simon Commission's and which opened up such possibilities for the future that the whole Indian atmosphere was momentarily transformed. But the progress of India towards self-government is a subject in itself. The important impact of these events on the immediate course of British history was twofold. In the first place they resulted in a decision to resume the Round Table Conference in the autumn of 1931; and the absolute necessity that there should be a responsible and representative government to conduct it was to be an important—in Ramsay MacDonald's mind perhaps even a decisive—factor affecting every phase of the great political crisis of that summer. Secondly it intensified the leadership crisis within the Tory Party by provoking a die-hard revolt which did more than all the intrigues of the Press Lords to bring Baldwin to the verge of resignation. Above all Churchill, in one of his several less responsible speeches of this period, made himself spokesman for the malcontents in the House of Commons, in the certainty 'that we should lose India in the final result and that measureless disasters would come upon the Indian peoples'.[1] In consequence he felt obliged to resign from Baldwin's Shadow Cabinet and thereby condemned himself to a fateful isolation throughout the decisive years when the second world war was being prepared.

In the sphere of spectacular foreign policy, which was once again to be Labour's strongest card, it was, oddly enough, Snowden who first captured the limelight. The 1925 Dawes plan for Reparations had so far worked well, in that it did at least produce regular payments of instalments from Germany. But it only thinly veiled the fact that these payments were in reality financed by American loans, much of which found its way back to the United States as 'inter-Allied Debts'. Moreover the cumulative effect of these large payments on both payers and payees were much what Keynes had predicted; and they threw a disproportionate burden on Britain, still struggling to discharge her American debt in full. The Allied experts had therefore prepared an-

[1] *Second World War*, Vol. I, p. 27.

other plan, the Young Plan, which would reduce the charges on Germany, but so spread them that the last instalment from Germany would only become due in 1988. Because the new plan might lead to an early evacuation of the Rhineland, it had the enthusiastic support of Henderson and his Under Secretary, Dalton, who had pledged themselves that 'our British Tommies shall eat their Christmas dinners at home'.[1] But because it also redistributed reparation payments in favour of France and Italy and to Britain's disadvantage it was uncompromisingly opposed by Snowden; and it was Snowden who got first innings when the Finance Ministers met in international conference at the Hague in August of 1929.

Snowden had become with the years more and more the orthodox Liberal financier, and he was intent on balancing his budget by, as Dalton contemptuously put it, clawing back some millions a year from the French and Italians. He also brought to international negotiation the cantankerous asperity to which colleagues and opponents had become accustomed at home, but which struck a new note in European diplomacy. His description of the French proposals as 'grotesque and ridiculous' created a first-class international row. It also made him, rather unexpectedly and for the first time, a popular national figure in Britain. His stand for 'England's rightful place in international affairs' in the best Palmerstonian manner delighted the newspaper-reading public; and by sitting alone in his hotel glumly refusing to negotiate he rather surprisingly won his point. 'You are asking me to condone a felony,' he said to the German delegation when they begged him to yield for the sake of the Rhineland evacuation; 'I cannot do it.' On August 27th he got the agreement he wanted and on the 28th, as Dalton gleefully noted in his diary, his 'face was hissed at a Paris cinema. The Prefect of Police has forbidden its further exhibition.' On the other hand, he was given the Freedom of the City of London. And in spite of all Dalton's moanings of the disastrous effects of this 'swollen-headed and fanatical policy', Henderson, too, had his way over the Rhineland, when it was duly evacuated some five years earlier than had been laid down in the Treaty of Versailles. This, however, proved merely to be the first step in what was to become the policy of appeasement. Whether a generous peace with Germany in the first place would have evoked a

[1] See Dalton, *op. cit.*, p. 235.

generous response can now never be decided. Certainly in 1929 merely generous gestures came too late and did not even evoke the pretence of gratitude. The Allied withdrawal from German territory was greeted by outbursts of self-assertive nationalism which showed clearly enough to all but the wilfully blind that the dream of restoring German power was not confined to a military and Junker class, but permeated all classes and shades of German opinion.

Meanwhile, in comparative obscurity, Arthur Henderson, the official Foreign Secretary, toiled away with varying success at the objects dearest to his heart, most of which centred on disarmament and the League of Nations. From 1929 to 1931 the pace and tone of proceedings at Geneva were largely set by Great Britain, and during those years Henderson acquired a prestige abroad which he was never able to command in his own country But at the end of two years of speeches and resolutions, there was alarmingly little to show in the way of practical advance towards collective security. Parliament had been induced to ratify the signature by Great Britain of the so-called Optional Clause, which bound its signatories to resort in all cases to international arbitration before using force, and was a step back along the road towards the Geneva Protocol. But no real progress could be made without general disarmament. The Preparatory Commission for this did not meet until November, 1930, and it was only in the summer of 1931 that the framework of a Disarmament Treaty was sufficiently worked out for a full conference to be called, to meet in February, 1932. Meanwhile Henderson had successfully implemented one Labour election pledge by reopening diplomatic relations with Russia, only to find himself involved in endless unfriendly incidents and complaints. He succeeded in launching Irak on the precarious path of independence without any immediate difficulty. But he failed altogether to get satisfactory terms for the full evacuation of Egypt, in spite of the dismissal of Lord Lloyd, the British Agent in Cairo, whose imperialistic and pro-consular independence had long been a thorn in Labour flesh. For even the most democratically elected Egyptian government would not abandon the claim to sovereignty over the Sudan, and on this point all the prolonged negotiations ultimately broke down.

It was a competent, but not an overwhelmingly impressive record; and once again, as in 1923, it was MacDonald himself who did most to establish Labour's claim of success in foreign affairs. When he reluctantly surrendered the Foreign Office to Henderson he had specifically reserved Anglo-American relations as his own especial province;[1] and his decision was triumphantly justified when he visited President Hoover in October, 1929. Since the squabble over cruiser strengths in 1927, Anglo-American relations had seriously deteriorated, and there was even wild talk of naval armaments leading to war. In a series of very able speeches in Washington and elsewhere MacDonald swept away all this rubbish and really did restore an atmosphere of mutual trust and co-operation in which it might be possible to go forward to another round of talks on general naval disarmament. It was, it is true, all very cloudy and rhetorical, based dangerously on the illusory promises of the Kellogg Pact—'a great event', he told the Senate, 'which I believe will stand up like a monument in history'. The very humbleness of his origins was endearing to the self-conscious democracy of his American audiences; and the vagueness of his thought and phrasing was reassuring to Americans and Canadians who had no wish to face the harsh facts of a looming economic crisis. American naval touchiness was soothed by the promise of a parity of fleets 'category by category', though this was precisely what the Admiralty had been anxious to avoid, American and British needs being radically different in almost every category. But since no British government of this period had any intention of building the number of cruisers the admirals demanded, American goodwill was cheap at the price. For once MacDonald's personal success silenced even the waspish critics in his own Party. 'He has made for himself an eternal niche in the temple of history,' Dalton wrote in his diary after welcoming him home at Euston on November 6th.

But, successful though some of this activity abroad really was, it was no substitute for a social and economic policy, and actually it helped to blind both ministers and public to the imminence and seriousness of the approaching crisis. The relative inexperience and instability of the American banking system, combined with the illusion of perpetual prosperity fostered by an unprecedentedly rapid industrial expansion, produced during 1928 and 1929 an outburst of speculation on Wall Street which quickly became uncontrollable. The huge fortunes made in the twenties in genuine industrial and commercial speculation had in

[1] Nicolson, *op. cit.*, p. 435.

any case created a situation of great potential danger, since the production of consumer goods was already growing far beyond what the existing distribution systems would permit the world to buy. Everything indicated that a slump of the normal trade-cycle pattern was impending anyway; and in that American world where share values and the movements of stock exchanges were in many circles the only topic of interest and conversation, the pressure of further speculative investment was working already to magnify and precipitate the crash. The rapid growth of hire-purchase had mortgaged the future buying power of the American consumer almost to capacity; and the hysterical, purely stock exchange boom of 1928, when men gambled wildly on the inflated market values of shares which bore no relation to the facts of industrial production or commercial possibilities completed the disaster.

The American boom was already having dangerous repercussions in Europe long before the crash came. Events since 1918 had made European, and especially German, industry perforce largely dependent on American capital for its reorganisation and expansion; and this had eventually been made available on a scale even more generous than Keynes had hoped for. Still more dangerously, the German government had formed the habit of paying reparation instalments and the interest on earlier loans by further borrowing from the United States; and, since the industrial reconstruction of Germany's creditors was in turn based on reparation payments, the whole of European industry had come to depend very largely on substantial annual subsidies from across the Atlantic. A separate, inevitable, and interrelated crisis thus loomed also in Europe when the Wall Street hysteria suddenly diverted every available penny of American capital into speculation in largely worthless scrip. Not only was the flow of American capital into Europe suddenly stopped. American gamblers who had formed the habit of financing their speculations on borrowed money began to raise loans in Europe, too, so that there was a twofold shrinkage in European capital investment. This had been one cause of the breakdown of the Dawes plan, which had brought the Finance Ministers together at the Hague; and at the beginning of November, just as MacDonald landed for his triumphal tour of America, the bubble burst.

The magnitude of the inevitable repercussions does not seem to have dawned on Ramsay MacDonald when they broke it to him that he would not be given the traditional ticker-tape welcome in Wall Street, since no office had time to spare from the ruin which had just overtaken them all. The same lack of apprehension seems to have affected most of his senior colleagues, in spite of warning grumbles from Snowden, the senior Treasury officials, and the bankers. Obsessed, perhaps, with the conviction that the Party stalemate in the Commons made any effective action on the Home front impossible for them, they let Thomas and his committee dally with the problem of unemployment, which for Great Britain was the crux of the matter, without formulating any constructive or comprehensive policy. Lacking the courage to apply the Lloyd George remedy, which had Keynes's blessing, of deficit-financed public works and large government spending, which would have to be forced through in the teeth of the Treasury and the Bank of England and the orthodoxy of Mr. Snowden, they were equally too fearful of their own Trade Unionist wing to apply the traditional remedy of ruthless economy. Immediately on taking office they had thrown a sop to the Trade Unions by raising the dole, abolishing the tests designed to prove that a man was 'genuinely seeking work', and transferring the burden of the old 'uncovenanted benefit'—now called transitional benefit—from the Insurance Fund to the Exchequer. This merely palliative measure served only to get them into trouble with extremists on both wings. Trade Unionists grumbled that they had still done far too little for the unemployed; and Mr. Churchill rallied the Tory opposition in another of his wilder speeches of this period, the phraseology of which he was one day to adapt to a greater crisis and a worthier purpose. 'By every device', he said, 'and by every dodge, by every shift and, almost, by every turpitude, they have managed to keep on paying for the longest time in the loosest fashion the largest doles to the largest number.' But that was all that was done.

So the Labour government proceeded on its modest but creditable way. Snowden postured in Palmerstonian attitudes abroad and in the Cabinet preached a financial doctrine which was almost Gladstonian. MacDonald used his American goodwill to get a real Naval Disarmament Treaty out of the United States and Japan, based on a 5:5:3 ratio for all categories of warship; and Henderson cautiously nursed the growing confidence of the League and cultivated trade relations with Russia. Lansbury made himself quite unexpectedly the government's star turn by taking down park railings, opening the Serpentine for mixed bathing, and providing public refreshments in Hyde Park. Dr. Addison, who took over from Noel-Buxton in 1930, laid the foundations for the whole future recovery of British agriculture with his Land Utilisation and Agricultural Marketing Bills. But Mr. Thomas's committee spent its time in acrimonious discussion and the unemployment figures rose remorselessly: from 1,122,700 in June, 1929, to 2 million in July of the following year, and a year again after that to over 3 million. Both Mosley, who very soon resigned and set off to found a new Party of his own, and Lansbury subsequently claimed that they had produced for Thomas any number of schemes which would have abolished unemployment: retirement pensions for all workers, the raising of the school leaving age by one year, emigration to Western Australia, and government-financed public works were between them to absorb the whole number of the unemployed. But all these schemes and many others took no account of the falling balance of trade which was at the root of all the trouble, and which was not within the government's control, unless possibly by tariffs, to which Socialists were traditionally as deeply opposed as were the Liberals. Something was done in the way of public works, but any ground gained was instantly lost again as the volume of exports and revenue alike declined.

In spite of the increasing burden thrown on to the Exchequer by the rising cost of transitional benefit, and of the fact that the Unemployment Insurance Fund was itself running into debt at the rate of £40 million a year, the government, thanks perhaps mainly to its own internal dissensions, reacted only sluggishly to the situation. Snowden's Budget of April, 1930, showed no sense of impending crisis. He found the extra £30 million he needed by putting 6d. on the income-tax and raising the rates of surtax and death duties, and he expressed the belief that he would not the following year find it necessary to impose any further burdens. The government did, indeed, appoint a three-Party committee, subsequently turned into a Royal Commission, to investigate unemployment; and in May MacDonald again appealed for collaboration and suggested a three-Party Conference. This the Tories refused. The Liberals, however, agreed, though nothing much came of their closer collaboration with the Socialists which prevailed throughout 1930. Lloyd George refused to consider a Coalition government, which would anyway have been very unwelcome to the Labour rank and file, and he courteously rejected a plea from Lansbury to join the Labour Party with such Liberals as would follow him. He also denied to the government the only help which would have enabled them to push through their more controversial measures with any speed—the voting of the closure.

In consequence Commons debates were endlessly acrimonious, and by 1931 there was what Postgate described as 'an almost Canadian log-jam of held-up bills in Parliament':[1] the Repeal of the Trade Union Act, the Coal Mines Bill, the Education Bill, and many others were being slowly picked to pieces in either the Commons or the Lords, and the mounting exasperation and sense of frustration among government supporters were to have their effect on tempers and reactions when the crisis came in the summer. They felt already that they were the victims of capitalist intrigues in which their leaders incomprehensibly acquiesced; and this was to make it easy for them to seize on the theory of the 'Bankers' Ramp' when the financial break came and to believe that MacDonald and Snowden had all along been betraying them. It is certainly true that Lloyd George hoped to exploit the dissensions within the other two Parties so as to retain a balance of power for himself. He had already exacted a bill for electoral reform as the price of his continued support, giving the Liberals, not the proportional representation which they wanted, but at least the alternative vote which would alone enable them to survive as a great Party. In view of the attitude of the House of Lords the passage of this bill was likely to take two years; and the knowledge that Lloyd George would have to keep them in office for that period may have contributed to the complacency and patience with which the leading members of the Government pursued their various objectives. It was probably as well for Britain that both they and Lloyd George had miscalculated. For the legislative deadlock which prevailed for the two years of this government's life was an admirable demonstration of the disadvantages of a three-party system such as the alternative vote would have tended to perpetuate; and this, not capitalist intrigue, was the real cause of Socialist discontent and frustration.

At the beginning of 1931 it really seemed that Lloyd George's gamble might come off. The financial situation was worsening so slowly and

[1] *Op. cit.*, p. 265.

imperceptibly that it had as yet produced no general sense of panic. When the withdrawal of American credits threatened the Germans with ruin the London banks had stepped in with a short-term loan to save one of Britain's best customers. Britain's own financial position, and indeed the whole of her economy, both seemed and were sounder than those of any other nation in the world. It thus appeared possible that this slump might be left, like others before it, to get better of itself by the immutable operation of the trade cycle which XIX century thought had got into the habit of treating as a fact of life. Only a few experts with inside knowledge were seriously perturbed. Tory dissensions were at their height on both India and tariffs and reached their climax in an attempt to displace Baldwin from the leadership at the end of February. In spite of the conversion of Simon and one or two others to the idea of a 10% revenue tariff, the Liberals and the government had a common rallying principle in the Free Trade to which Socialists of all shades were fanatically attached—Snowden and his school by passionate conviction, and the Trade Unionists by long-standing tradition. It seemed, therefore, that the government might after all coast along, accepting defeats on the details of legislation, in the hope of emerging as the men who had weathered the storm.

It was largely the evidence of Sir George Hopkins, the Treasury representative, before the Royal Commission on Unemployment which falsified all such hopes and expectations, and started the train of events which superimposed on the existing economic crisis a financial, and then a major political, crisis. Hopkins, whose views Snowden shared, tersely described the vast loans to maintain the Unemployment Insurance Fund as 'State borrowing to relieve current State obligations', which were 'the ordinary and well-recognised signs of an unbalanced budget'. This confirmed all the worst suspicions of both Conservative and Liberal oppositions and led directly to a Conservative motion of censure on government spending on February 11th. It strengthened the growing mistrust abroad of British financial stability, already shown by large withdrawals of foreign deposits from London; and it laid the foundations for the belief among the rank-and-file Socialists that they were being made the victims of an intrigue by Treasury officials and the bankers, who were manufacturing a crisis as a handle for reducing unemployment benefit. In the debate of February 11th it became clear that the leaders of all Parties agreed that some joint action should be taken to deal with a problem too big for any one of them to solve alone; and also that the core of the problem—what Snowden called 'the vulnerable spot in our position'—was the danger of a wholesale loss of confidence abroad, leading to a run on the £. Both Snowden and Worthington-Evans took up MacDonald's earlier plea that the House might act in this as a Council of State rather than as a partisan assembly, thereby provoking vigorous protests from back benchers on both sides. The government, W. J. Brown said—and he spoke for the mass of Labour members—had become 'the humble custodian of the capitalist interest which we were sent here to destroy'. Here were laid the foundations of the obstinate Socialist delusion, which was to persist throughout the thirties and to some extent persists to this day, that the crisis could be handled as a purely internal affair, without reference to foreign confidence and the financial and commercial necessities of a nation which lived by exporting. For the moment, the government survived by accepting a Liberal amendment to the vote of censure that a 'small, independent committee' should investigate the situation and draw up a programme of all possible economies. Sir George May, of the Prudential Assurance Company, was appointed to preside over this, and two members were appointed by each of the three Parties.

There, somewhat uneasily, matters rested for the next few months. The unemployment figures continued their remorseless climb towards the three million mark. Few men realised how potentially dangerous the international financial position was; and it did not perceptibly worsen during the spring. In one of his cleverest and most statesmanlike speeches, on India, Baldwin recaptured control of his Party and ensured that the Round Table Conference in London, called for the following autumn, should not become a subject of inter-Party battle. Snowden produced a budget which in no way reflected the gravity of the crisis in the certainty, as he afterwards explained, that the May Committee's report would necessitate a supplementary budget in the autumn. He therefore balanced his accounts for the moment by increasing the petrol tax and some rather shady juggling with his book-keeping. For Snowden knew perfectly well that falling revenue and rising expenditure on unemployment were creating a situation much graver than it seemed. He had said during the debate in February that he could write the May

Committee's report himself in advance. He believed that the delicacy of our foreign exchange position made unorthodox experiments in deficit-financed public enterprise impossible, and that only a budget balanced by ruthless economies and equally ruthless increases in taxation could restore foreign confidence in the £. But until the grim realities of the situation were brought home by some drastic shock, there would be no chance of reconciling the country at large and his own Party in particular, to the necessity for such draconian remedies. He also knew, as did the responsible leaders of all three Parties, that no one Party could be expected to incur the odium of demanding such large sacrifices. His next budget must be a non-partisan affair, however much irresponsible back benchers might long to leave their opponents holding the baby.

Unfortunately for Snowden's gamble, the May Committee took over five months to draw up its conclusions; and during that time events abroad had made the gamble very much riskier. On May 11th the Austrian State Bank, the Credit Anstalt, broke under the strain, so starting a run on the German banks by hysterical people who had not yet forgotten the era of inflation. The London finance houses gained a little time by lending to the Germans what they could borrow on short term from the French, while old President Hindenburg appealed to Hoover for a moratorium on reparation and war debt payments which in the end, after much French haggling, was agreed. But it came too late to prevent financial panic and chaos in Germany, whose citizens converted over 100 million Marks into foreign exchange in two days; and its effect was to make the London banks appallingly vulnerable. Thanks to two successive bursts of lending, a large part of their assets were frozen in Germany under the Hoover moratorium, while their own liabilities, in France and elsewhere, were unprotected. It was a crisis of confidence. A real loss of faith in British solvency among the governments and finance houses which habitually kept a portion of their reserves in sterling for safety could produce a run on the £ and bring Great Britain virtually to insolvency, with incalculably damaging effects on her trading position.

Almost everywhere abroad belief in the fundamental soundness of Britain, financially, had long been wavering. The rigid and indeed complacent conservatism of both employers and workers and the consequent inflexibility of the wage structure, the widespread reluctance to modify or modernise commercial and industrial practice, or even to replace obsolete machinery, had been noted by foreigners with misgiving; and the industrial disputes of the twenties had further fostered the belief that the British people no longer had the energy and the capacity for self-sacrifice to weather a major crisis. In these circumstances any attempt to bring home to the nation the real gravity of the situation was bound to bring it home also to foreigners. It might have been possible to do so in February without upsetting the delicate balances of foreign confidence. In the prevailing hysteria of July it could hardly be done. Already, on June 4th, an interim report from the almost forgotten Royal Commission on Unemployment Insurance had revealed enough of the dangerous facts to start a mild run on the London banks. The breakdown of the German banking system and the complete failure of a conference of Finance Ministers in London during the following week started the deluge. By July 22nd the Bank of England had lost £22 million of gold. The Bank Rate was raised progressively from 2½% to 4½%, and £50 million was borrowed from France and the U.S.A.

The situation was thus almost irretrievable when, on July 31st, the May Committee at last published its report. Its estimate of a deficit on the current budget of £120 million by the following April shocked even those who were best informed on the position. Its proposals were, to the Socialist ministers, even more alarming. £24 million was to be found by increased taxation; the remaining £96 million by economies in expenditure. All official salaries and those of civil servants and teachers were to be cut, along with servicemen's and policemen's pay; but the largest sum—£66 million—was to be found by reducing expenditure on unemployment. Ministers had already received their copies before the last Parliamentary debate of the session, and both Snowden and Neville Chamberlain had delivered carefully prepared speeches on lines agreed between them beforehand and calculated if possible to emphasise the gravity of the situation without provoking a panic.[1] Snowden was already particularly insistent that this was an all-Party matter. No government, and least of all a minority government, could be expected to incur the odium of inflicting hard sacrifices on the

---

[1] Snowden, *Autobiography*, Vol. II, p. 929, and Feiling, *op. cit.*, p. 190.

nation if the other Parties were to be free to make political capital out of them. In fact, throughout the ensuing crisis the Socialists leaders were at all times assured of whole-hearted support from Conservatives and Liberals, always provided that their economy proposals were drastic enough to give a reasonable certainty of balancing the budget. But there was still no great sense of urgency among the politicians. The Cabinet appointed an Economy Committee, which was not to meet until August 25th, when the various government departments would have prepared their comments and suggestions; and it was not proposed to introduce detailed economy plans until Parliament reassembled in October. Mr. Baldwin went off, as usual, to Aix-les-Bains, MacDonald and Chamberlain to Scotland, and only Snowden held the fort in London.

Events moved much too fast for this somewhat leisurely programme. Heavy withdrawals of foreign balances used up the latest loan with alarming speed, thanks largely to the impact of the May Committee's report, which had confirmed the already widespread impression abroad that the British budgetary position was fundamentally unsound and that the insolvency of the Unemployment Insurance Fund was the root of the trouble. There was an obvious and imminent danger of Britain being forced off the Gold Standard. This, in spite of all the panic which centred round it, would not in itself have mattered very much. The best opinion, both at home and abroad, had long held that the £ was over-valued. This was probably what Montagu Norman had in mind when he remarked privately that 'if I thought the dole had really got out of control, I would let the pound go'.[1] The loss of the Gold Standard was the bogey to frighten government and nation into saving the situation. But the danger lurking behind the bogey was real enough: that, with an unbalanced budget and no agreed policy for stabilisation, there would be no means of stopping the panic if once the Gold Standard went, and that uncontrollable inflation would lead rapidly to such a rise in prices that British industry would be brought to a standstill. What threatened was not a mere financial crisis engineered by a sinister com-bine of international bankers, but a complete commercial collapse which would engulf employed and unemployed in a common ruin. The Bank warned the government in the middle of August that its own

[1] To Mrs. Grigg. See Thomas Jones, *A Diary with Letters*, 1931–1950, p. 11.

borrowing power was exhausted and that, if immediate disaster was to be avoided, the government itself must borrow £80 million or make up its mind to declare a moratorium—in other words, to admit bankruptcy. The cause of the crisis, the bankers insisted, was political, not financial; and it would continue until the government managed to restore confidence abroad in its own honest intentions.[1] By August 13th the Cabinet Economy Committee had been hastily recalled, and Chamberlain, Hoare, and Samuel[2] were all in London, in close touch with the Bank and the Prime Minister.

From then on, for the next fortnight, the crisis, financial and political, increased in intensity not merely daily, but hourly. No other episode in British history has given rise to more embittered controversy or to more partisan and misleading statements than this one; and the actual facts have been so obscured by the passion and prejudice of the participants, some of whose misrepresentations, deliberate or otherwise, persist thirty years after the event, that the thread of events can only now with difficulty be disentangled. Whole volumes could be, and indeed have been devoted to this subject alone, and it is difficult for the most impartial historian to recount the salient facts without distortion.[3] Broadly speaking, the crisis passed through three distinct phases: for the first week it remained concentrated within the Cabinet Economy Committee; it then became successively a Cabinet crisis and finally a national crisis, involving the Crown and the leaders of all the political Parties in very difficult decisions.

The Economy Committee, consisting of MacDonald, Snowden, Henderson, Thomas and Graham, met for the first time in the afternoon of August 12th and presented its conclusion to the Cabinet on August 19th. It had had to face a probable deficit not of £120 million, as the May Committee had calculated, but, on Snowden's revised figures from the Treasury, of £170 million. Its members seem to have reached agreement almost at once that about half this sum should be raised by additional taxation and the remainder be found by cuts in expenditure;

---

[1] See Chamberlain's letter to Cunliffe-Lister of August 15th. Feiling, *op. cit.*, pp. 190–1.

[2] Acting Leader of the Liberal Party during Lloyd George's illness.

[3] It would be quite impossible, but for the work of J. R. Bassett, *The Nineteen Thirty-one Political Crisis*, which effectively disposes of all the chief misrepresentations and legends, including the Morrison assertion that King George V acted unconstitutionally.

and further, though here Henderson dissented, that they would concentrate on the detailed economics to be laid before the Cabinet, leaving it to Snowden to indicate the general lines on which he would frame his budget for increased taxation. In any event, it was over the economies that all the difficulties were to arise; and the Committee's discussions of these had to take into account certain background factors which considerably reduced their freedom of manœuvre. The report of the May Committee had already incurred the bitter and implacable hostility of certain sections of the Labour Movement, particularly in the Trade Unions; and though the Treasury recommendations had reduced the May Committee's proposed 20% cut in unemployment benefit to 10%, it was clear that even the reduced figure would be opposed, whatever happened, by a large number of the Labour Members in Parliament. On the other hand, whatever they proposed had to command the support of one and preferably, in view of the probable mutiny in the Labour Party, both the opposition Parties. The Conservatives, after some preliminary uncertainties, had closed their ranks on the issue of Protection, and held the view that a tariff was in the long run indispensable to any national recovery. But they were prepared not to make this a condition of support for the government's proposals, provided that these proposals were drastic enough to balance the budget and restore immediate confidence abroad; whereas the Liberals would go into uncompromising opposition if there were any tampering with the sacred principle of Free Trade. On this last issue Snowden stood firmly with the Liberals. The rest of the Committee, if faced with the alternative, would have preferred a 10% revenue tariff to any cut in the rate of unemployment benefit.

The Economy Committee thus produced no agreed recommendations when the Cabinet met on August 19th, but only a number of possible economies which it submitted for debate. Broadly these fell into two parts. There was an overall cut which would take from 10% to 15% from ministers, civil servants, teachers, servicemen and police. This, with levies from the road and other funds, was estimated after modification in the Cabinet, to save some £34½ million. Along with this went a £22 million contribution from the Unemployment Insurance Fund, to be made up by limiting insurance benefit to 26 weeks and thereafter imposing a means' test; by increased contributions from all insured workers; and by removing various 'anomalies'. On all of this by the evening of August 19th, after nine hours' debate, the Cabinet was broadly agreed and remained so to the end. But this only amounted to £56½ million, and another £22 million had to be found to bring the total up to the £78½ million which the Economy Committee and the opposition leaders alike believed to be the essential minimum. For this the only two possible sources seemed to be a 10% cut in the standard rate of unemployment benefit or a 10% revenue tariff; and on neither of these could the Cabinet reach any agreement. Faced with an absolute choice between these two, 15 out of 20 members of the Cabinet would have voted for the tariff, at any rate on manufactured goods. But the five 'unalterable Free Traders'[1] included Snowden, and their resignation would have brought the government down. Furthermore—and this in MacDonald's mind was decisive—it would have thrown the Liberals into uncompromising opposition. It was therefore abandoned; and for the next four days discussion, both in the Cabinet and outside it, turned almost exclusively on the 10% unemployment benefit cut.

Inside the Cabinet the deadlock which had been revealed by the first day's discussion remained throughout substantially unchanged. There was a small majority in favour of carrying through the Economy Committee's suggestions and imposing the 10% cut in the standard rate of unemployment benefit. There was a powerful minority against. MacDonald himself was passionately anxious to hold his government together and to weather the crisis without having recourse to any form of coalition. He had devoted his life to building up the Labour Party to take its place as the mature and responsible rival to Conservatism, and this, for him, was the supreme test. He wanted for his government the credit and prestige of dealing single-handed with a great crisis and rising above partisan and tactical issues to do so. As the nation's government they must accept responsibility not only to their own Party and voters, but to the nation as a whole. Snowden, his staunchest supporter, saw the issue in more strictly financial terms, with a balanced budget as the paramount objective. Henderson and those who joined him in opposing MacDonald could not see beyond their duty to the working class; and, rather than court unpopularity, they would have preferred to resign and 'leave the Conservatives to hold the baby'. Moreover, the

[1] *Daily Express*, August 22nd.

pressures working outside the Cabinet served only to intensify the deadlock.

On the one hand there were the three representative organs of the Labour Movement, the Consultative Committee of the Parliamentary Party, the National Executive of the Party, and the General Council of the Trades Union Congress. On the other were the opposition leaders, Neville Chamberlain and Sir Samuel Hoare for the Conservatives,[1] Samuel and Sir Donald MacLean for the Liberals. These were informed of the Economy Committee's proposals for saving £78½ million on the morning of August 20th and committed themselves to the extent of finding them 'a bold and courageous scheme', though they asked for time to consider and consult, and Chamberlain said that the total figure was not high enough. In the course of their discussion Snowden agreed with him that falling prices had raised the value of benefit by over 30%, and that the cuts would still leave the unemployed better off than in 1924. That same morning the Parliamentary Labour Party's Consultative Committee, having been informed of the facts, decided unofficially, but unanimously, that if the opposition conditions were met it was 'very doubtful' if the government would get any but the lawyers among the Labour Members to vote for them. In the afternoon a joint meeting of the National Executive and the General Council of the T.U.C. was similarly informed, though there was ambiguity in some of Snowden's phrasing, and some of those present believed that he had assured them that the Cabinet had decided against unemployment cuts. Subsequently the National Executive decided to leave the issues entirely to the Cabinet; but a deputation from the General Council informed the Economy Committee that evening that they must 'oppose the whole thing'. They produced an alternative, four-point plan which, Mac-Donald said in a letter to Citrine the next morning, 'instead of reducing expenduture, would substantially increase it'.

Thus by the time the Cabinet met again on August 21st the terms of its dilemma were hard and clear. The scheme on which they were working would be opposed by both the left wing of their own Party and by all the industrial elements within it. This knowledge hardened Henderson and his supporters against any unemployment cuts. On the other hand, it was extremely unlikely that, without the cuts, the govern-

---

[1] Baldwin did not get back from Aix until August 23rd.

ment would get the support of the other two Parties essential for the implementation of any economy scheme whatever. After five hours of discussion, the Cabinet did reach provisional agreement. In the teeth of the General Council's root-and-branch condemnation of the whole Economy Committee scheme, a decision was reached to go forward with all of it, save for the direct cut in unemployment benefit; that is to say, the whole Cabinet agreed on £56½ million of economies substantially as recommended. On the question of the remaining balance of £22 million they discussed possibilities of extra direct taxation, of raids on the Sinking Fund or on Chamberlain's Derating scheme, and they unanimously rejected a revenue tariff. Somewhat illogically, they then reiterated their view that the deficit should be met half by savings and half by taxes, as against Chamberlain's view that three-quarters should come from economies; and they conveniently ignored the fact that the £56½ million, which was their last word on economies, was only about a third of what was needed. Webb and Henderson and a good many others were to say later that when they dispersed in the afternoon they thought that they had finished with the matter: that they would announce this plan as their last word in the hope of halting the foreign panic, and that they would face Parliament with the plan when it met on September 14th. If defeated on the issue, they would then resign. But if this is so it is hard to see why they authorised MacDonald and Snowden to lay their proposal immediately before the other Party leaders. It is equally odd that MacDonald seems to have thought that these modified proposals would be accepted by Chamberlain and Samuel. Yet he allowed the Cabinet to disperse for the week-end; and only when the Conservative and Liberal leaders expressed misgivings and asked for time to consult their friends were the emergency calls sent out to summon ministers back to Downing Street.

When the Party leaders met at 5 p.m. that evening Samuel's reaction was one of 'surprise and deeper regret'. Chamberlain asked what would happen if this announcement of the government's modified scheme as the last word failed to restore foreign confidence. Snowden answered, 'the deluge'.[1] The Conservatives and Liberals withdrew to consult their friends, agreeing to meet again at 9.30. The Cabinet was hastily recalled, but since some of the members could not be reached, an

[1] Feiling, *op. cit.*, p. 192.

emergency meeting was fixed for 9.30 the next morning, August 22nd. And at 9.30 that evening Samuel and Chamberlain made their position absolutely clear. 'I opened first', Chamberlain recorded in his diary, 'and intimated, (1) that if these were the final proposals . . . we should turn them out immediately the House met: (2) that before then we anticipated that the financial crash must come: (3) that we considered that it was the P.M.'s bounden duty to avoid that crash: and (4) that we were ready to give him any support in our power for that purpose, either with his present, or in a reconstructed government. Samuel followed on exactly the same lines'.[1] Lloyd George had also been consulted in the interval and from his sick-bed had pronounced the government's proposals to be 'derisory'.

The news which MacDonald gave the Cabinet on the Saturday morning of the reaction of the opposition Parties provoked an outburst of resentment, which has echoed down to the present day, at what they chose to interpret as an attempt to dictate their policy. In reality, of course, Chamberlain and Samuel had presented no ultimatum or demand, but had merely stated the facts as they saw them, and as they undoubtedly were. But a reluctance to face facts had all along characterised the approach of the Trade Unionist wing of the Party to unemployment problems. It was that which had largely stultified the activities of Thomas's committee; and resentment at the discovery that national policy could not be framed exclusively in the interests of one section of the population produced a hunt for scapegoats and ultimately the legend of the 'Bankers' Ramp' which, surprisingly, still persists.[2] For at the long and exhausting Cabinet on Saturday, August 22nd, MacDonald had another piece of information for his colleagues. The Bank's credits were expected to run out on the following Wednesday; and unless Messrs. J. P. Morgan, the government's agents in New York, could by then negotiate a loan of £80 million a moratorium would be inevitable and the crash would have come. There could, therefore, be no question of waiting three weeks for the reassembly of Parliament. The government could either, as Henderson wished, resign immediately, admitting that it was 'being asked to handle a situation that it will be quite impossible for us to carry through', and, as Webb put it, 'let the Tories come in and stand the racket', or it must make con-

---

[1] Feiling, *op. cit.*, p. 192. [2] See, e.g., Attlee, *As It Happened*, published in 1954.

cessions to meet the wishes of the opposition and of the New York investors who were, after all, being asked to put up the money. It was common knowledge that they would only do so if satisfied that adequate steps, commanding the support of a majority in Parliament, were being taken to balance the budget.

So the old, dreary battle on the unemployment cuts was resumed; and in the end, unwilling either to resign immediately or to open negotiations for some form of coalition, the Cabinet authorised MacDonald and Snowden to make a last approach to the other Parties. A modified scheme, put forward by Snowden, which would find £12½ million by cutting the standard rate of unemployment benefit and a further £7½ million from other sources, was to be offered them while the Cabinet adjourned for lunch. But it was clearly understood that nobody was committed to this proposal, which was purely tentative. The reply from the other Party leaders during the lunch break was equally tentative. They thought such a scheme 'might' command Parliamentary approval, satisfy the bankers, and stop the run on the £. This was at any rate sufficiently encouraging for the resumed Cabinet to authorise enquiries of the Bank. Here again the answer was encouraging enough to justify further enquiry in New York; and the Cabinet adjourned until the following day to await the result of transatlantic telephone calls and cables on which a final decision might be made.

It is unnecessary to follow out in detail the negotiations which then took place between the various bankers concerned, though it should be emphasised that George L. Harrison of the Federal Reserve Bank was only an intermediary, and that there was no question of his bank lending the money. It was the investing public of America which, ultimately, had to be satisfied with the soundness of the British government's intentions. When the Cabinet met at 7 p.m. on Sunday, August 23rd, the final answer from J. P. Morgan was still awaited. It was an oppressively hot night, and ministers strolled in the garden of No. 10 Downing Street until 8.45, when news came that the telegram was on its way from the Bank of England. It provoked, when it was read aloud, so vociferous an outburst of anger that Sir Edward Harvey, of the Bank, waiting in an ante-room behind double doors, thought that 'pandemonium had broken loose'. Yet it was, on the whole, a favourable response. Morgans' clearly thought that, on the basis of the economy scheme put up to them, they would be able to raise both the short-term credits immediately needed and, later, a publicly floated, long-term loan. But—and this was what roused the resentment—they insisted that the programme proposed must not only command Parliamentary support, but also 'the sincere approval and support of the Bank of England and the City generally'. Thus the opponents of the economies were brought once again face to face with the unpalatable facts; and this, really, was what they resented.

MacDonald seems to have put the final issue to his colleagues perfectly fairly. He believed that the government could, if it stood together, command the support of the bulk of the Party, provided they clearly understood the alternative available. They were assured in advance of support from outside the Party; and they would gain immensely in moral prestige if the unemployed, too, had to accept the principle of equality of sacrifice. Failure to accept the terms proposed must entail immediate resignation; and the resignation of any one of the senior ministers would produce the same result by splitting the Cabinet. He carried a majority with him, but only a bare majority. Nine members out of a Cabinet of twenty were unalterably opposed to the 10% cut in unemployment benefit. This left no possibility of carrying on with a reconstructed Labour government, and inevitably MacDonald asked his colleagues to place their resignations in his hands. He did not, it seems clear, announce his immediate intention of resigning, but only of informing His Majesty of the situation and of advising him to confer the following morning with himself, Baldwin, and Samuel; and to this, whatever impression some members may have had later, they also agreed. He left Downing Street soon after 10 in a state of high nervous tension —'distraught', as Sir Edward Harvey described him in a telephone message to the Palace—and at 10.40 he was back again. He told them then that the King had agreed to hold a conference of the three Party leaders the next morning, and summoned them to meet again at noon. So, though the Labour government had clearly thrown in its hand, it remained in existence in fact until the following day.

CHAPTER 9

The National Government and Recovery

Out of the events which followed Mr. MacDonald's first visit to Buckingham Palace on the night of Sunday, August 23rd, there has been manufactured the second of the great Socialist legends of this period: that, on top of the Bankers' Ramp, there came the Great Betrayal. Almost all the leading Socialists of that time have given some currency to the story that Ramsay MacDonald had always hankered after social distinction and personal advancement, for which the Labour Party had been a convenient ladder; that he would always rather have led a Tory government than a Socialist; and that his colleagues had always been in his mind poor dupes, to be thrown over when the great opportunity came. Beatrice Webb, who had always considered him 'rotten stuff',[1] even professed to see the first leanings towards coalition in the years before 1914. Jealousy of his Parliamentary skill, which put them all in the shade, of his charm, and of the ease with which he could adjust himself to any social background, undoubtedly inspired much of the hostility. The very fact that he had set himself to make Labour respectable—to build it up into a Party which would command votes in a society which was largely non-socialist —made him suspect. As the leader of two minority governments he had inevitably been forced to consider working arrangements with other Parties and to discuss the ways and means of inter-Party co-operation. Every move he made in that direction, and everything he had ever said on the subject, were to be brought up as evidence of a long-matured plot to ditch colleagues whom he had long despised and to emerge, in Disraelian phrase, as the 'leader of the gentlemen of England'.

---

[1] *Beatrice Webb's Diaries*, ed. Margaret Cole, p. 283.

The lies and the insinuations would not be worth repeating if, twenty years after the event, they did not still appear in the memoirs and so find their way into the textbooks, where words like 'insincerity' and 'betrayal', 'snobbery', and 'desertion' constantly and quite unjustifiably echo the political passions of 1931. Even the phrase in which he begged, at the outset of his 1929 ministry, for some abandonment of partisan politics and for a Parliament which would behave as 'a Council of State', was brought in as evidence of a premeditated betrayal; and Snowden, who repeated the phrase himself in the House of Commons two years later, ultimately joined the ranks of the accusers. The enemies and the critics have survived to perpetuate the sneers and innuendoes into the 1950s: Dalton tracing the first warning back to some ambiguous words of MacDonald's in 1923, when he first had to consider the problems of minority government and the possibility of a 'national government', 'nearly a Coalition, but not quite';[1] and Attlee, dismissing the whole complex, agonising situation in a paragraph as 'the greatest betrayal in the political history of this country'.[2] The damning sentences in which Snowden, during the next election, castigated the men who had preferred Party to the national interest and their own popularity to what they had explicitly accepted as their painful duty have got forgotten. But it seems probable that the considered judgement of posterity will be more nearly Snowden's than Attlee's, when he characterized the 'brazen way' in which ex-Labour ministers were repudiating their own actions in the Labour Government as 'an instance of political depravity without parallel in Party warfare'.

To anyone who, in 1931, thought about politics at all, speculation on possible coalitions must have been familiar ever since the result of the 1929 election had been known. A measure of co-operation and restraint had been inherent in the situation itself, since clearly no one Party held any sort of mandate from the voters; and whoever governed could do so only with the goodwill of one, at least, of the other Parties. The possibility of a Liberal-Labour government must have been from time to time in the minds of the leaders of both. When the crisis came, and it seemed probable that the Labour government would be unable to produce a solution of its own, it is equally obvious that both the possibility of a Conservative-Liberal coalition, or, better still, of a three Party

[1] Dalton, *op. cit.*, p. 148.   [2] Attlee, *op. cit.*, p. 74.

agreement, to include the Labour moderates, was in the forefront of the minds of every leading politician. On certain fundamentals all were clearly agreed. All of them thought that the best solution would be for the existing Labour government to put through the necessary programme of economy and taxation with the declared goodwill and support of the other two parties. Failing that, it was desirable that whatever government took its place should have the widest possible basis of support, and that no one party should be in a position to make political capital out of sacrifices and hardships which all in their hearts knew to be in the national interest. Nor was it surprising or improper that King George V, who could draw by now on a very long-accumulated fund of political experience, should have reached the same conclusion.

The King had gone from Sandringham for his usual holiday at Balmoral on the previous Friday, largely on MacDonald's advice that, if he cancelled his arrangements, he would merely increase the sense of panic which it was important to allay. Almost immediately on his arrival, however, a telephone call from Downing Street made it clear to him that a Cabinet crisis impended, and he came south again on the Saturday night, remarking characteristically that 'there was no use shilly-shallying on an occasion like this'.[1] He had seen MacDonald early on the Sunday morning and had been put in possession of the relevant facts, including the probability that, even if the American bankers' answer was favourable, Henderson and Graham and some others were likely to resign and so bring the government down. With his Prime Minister's consent and approval, and therefore with perfect constitutional propriety, the King then saw first, because he was the first to be located, Samuel,[2] and then Baldwin; and both gave the same advice. Both wanted the Labour government to remain, and both guaranteed the support of their parties for any policy sufficiently drastic to command the confidence of the banking world. Both thought that, even if the government fell and a coalition became necessary, Mac-Donald should lead it and bring to its support such Labour votes as he

---

[1] Nicolson, *op. cit.*, p. 460.
[2] Fortunately as it happened. The King, quite rightly, found Samuel 'the clearest-minded' of the three leaders. The best summary of his very able appreciation of the situation is to be found not in his own *Memoirs*, but in his biography, *Viscount Samuel*, by John Bowle.

could command. Only if this proved impossible was Baldwin prepared to head a more narrowly based coalition to do what was necessary. But both emphasised that what was wanted was not really a coalition of parties, but a National government, composed of members of all three parties, pledged to the sole duty of 'overcoming the financial crisis' and to the avoidance of all controversial legislation. It was expected that such a government would last only for a month or two, when it would be safe and reasonable to hold a general election, and the parties would be free to resume their own policies.

This, broadly speaking, was what the King proceeded to implement when he saw the three leaders at 10 o'clock on the Monday morning. By noon they had worked out the framework of a government and a policy; and a communiqué to the press from Buckingham Palace told the world that the formation of a National government was 'under consideration'. Much ink has been spilt in recording the 'stupefaction', the 'stunned resentment', the 'astonishment' and the 'shock' experienced by various of his colleagues—in spite of their subsequently declared belief that the move had been long premeditated—when, five minutes after leaving the Palace, the Prime Minister informed them of the situation. All of them, of course, had been under very great strain, and perhaps none of them was thinking very clearly. But even Snowden, who afterwards professed to have been as surprised as anybody, records that the last act of the Cabinet had been to authorise the conference with the King and the other party leaders; and it is difficult to see what they thought such a conference would do except discuss arrangements for the continuance of the King's government and the surmounting of the crisis. At the time they seem to have behaved with admirable decorum. They received MacDonald's announcement, with its frank admission that he was committing political suicide and going into the wilderness, where he would be 'doubtless denounced and ostracised',[1] in silence, the only recorded comment being a shrewd one by Morrison: 'You will find it easier to get into this combination than to get out of it.'[2] Formal business was wound up and Sankey, the Lord Chancellor, carried a vote of thanks to the Prime Minister. The stunned resentment was all to come later, and particularly when the electorate had passed

[1] Sidney Webb to his wife immediately after the meeting, quoted, Bassett, p. 160.
[2] Morrison, *Autobiography*, p. 127.

decisive judgement both on MacDonald and on his opponents, in the following autumn.

For what MacDonald had done was to see the national crisis and the national interest as his one, overriding responsibility. In the last few weeks he had worked harder and more patiently than any of his detractors to preserve his party's unity and prestige. In the end, whatever he did, he could not prevent a Labour split in the coming months. He and his Cabinet supporters were bound in honour to stand by the measures of economy to which they were already pledged, whoever introduced them; and it was clear that Henderson and his friends would go into opposition, though it was not then anticipated that they would also bitterly denounce what they had previously agreed to in Cabinet. In any case, the interest of Trade Unionists as much as that of everybody else demanded that the national economy should not be engulfed in a financial panic; and an uncontrolled devaluation of the £ would have ruined many others outside Britain whose economies had been geared to sterling. Baldwin, who also had to contend with some uneasiness in his own party, put the real issue fairly enough: 'Here am I, the leader of the Conservative Party, who took my political life in my hands nine years ago to escape from a Coalition, asking you to support a government led by a Socialist Prime Minister, and to enter myself under him in another Coalition. I think, if any proof that there is a crisis is necessary, that is sufficient answer. There are greater things than consistency with one's past. There are greater things than loyalty to one's party. I am an Englishman first.'[1] It is impossible not to sympathise with MacDonald's rueful remark, years later: 'Any man in my position at the time, knowing all that I did, would have acted as I acted. However, I wish sometimes that someone else had been in my position at the time.' When the dust of controversy at last settles it seems probable that historians will agree with the judgement of a dispassionate American observer that MacDonald's was 'one of the best performances in the history of democratic politics and one of the best examples of action responsibility decided on from a correct appreciation of an economic and social situation'.[2]

Three ministers were asked to stay behind after the last meeting of

[1] Quoted in Arthur Bryant, *Stanley Baldwin*, p. 173.
[2] J. A. Schumpeter, *Capitalism, Socialism, and Democracy*.

the Labour Cabinet and invited to take office in the new government's small Cabinet of twelve: Snowden, Thomas, and Sankey, all of whom had faithfully supported the Prime Minister in his battle for economies. Snowden was particularly important as the architect of the fiscal policy which was to balance the Budget and save the nation; and it was his financial convictions rather than loyalty or friendship to the Prime Minister which induced him to remain at the Exchequer. Sankey was perhaps equally important as an expert pilot for the resumption of the India Round Table Conference in the autumn—another factor which made it highly desirable to avoid acute party controversy in the next few months. All three agreed to serve. Of the Junior Ministers, whom MacDonald saw that afternoon, very few pledged their support for a National government. But this may have been partly because Mac-Donald himself advised them not to follow him into 'the wilderness', but for the sake of their own careers to stand by the party he had risked so much to hold together and whose future was still for him of paramount importance, whatever his enemies might say.

Assured of this vital minimum of Labour support, MacDonald was able, when he tendered the resignation of his government to the King at 4 o'clock that afternoon, to accept office again immediately as the new Prime Minister; and by the following evening the government was more or less complete. In a Cabinet of ten the four Socialists all kept their previous offices. Baldwin became Lord President—a position which exactly suited his increasing lazy disposition, since he had the reality of power as the leader of the largest block of government supporters and could dictate policy, but avoided much of the tedious business of co-ordination and day-to-day tactics which fell to the Prime Minister. Sir Samuel Hoare was very properly given the important responsibility of the India Office, Neville Chamberlain went back to the Ministry of Health, and Cunliffe-Lister got the Board of Trade. The Liberals contributed two members, Samuel as Home Secretary, and Lord Reading at the Foreign Office, and received rather more than a fair share of minor offices on account of the large number of votes which their small numbers in the House of Commons so inadequately reflected. Parliament was summoned for September 8th; and on August 25th MacDonald broadcast to the nation an exposition of the dangers which they were hoping to avoid. The kernel of his argument was that 'if the pound were to fall suddenly and catastrophically, not by plan, as some people suggest, but by the force of economic circumstances and without control—should that happen, prices would rise much faster than wages and incomes could be adjusted', and conditions similar to those of the German inflation 'would arise by the widening of a vicious circle'. His case has never seriously been challenged. As he said then, the time to argue about new and better theories of banking was when the crisis was past. The immediate necessity, with world conditions what they were, was a solvent British government.

As soon as Parliament met the government moved briskly to the first essential measures. On September 8th it secured the necessary vote of confidence from the House by 309 votes to 249, though already there were signs of opposition belligerence; and even the *Manchester Guardian* expressed regret that the back benchers had 'got the bank complex very badly', and that every time MacDonald used the word 'Bank', 'the Opposition benches boiled over with wrath'. On the 10th Snowden presented his Budget. It was an austere, straightforward measure calculated to provide £100 million in a full year. The standard rate of income-tax was raised from 4/6 to 5/- and personal allowances were severely slashed, while higher duties were imposed on beer, tobacco, petrol, and entertainments. This left £20 million to be raised by a raid on the Sinking Fund and £70 million to be found by economies, which were separately dealt with in a National Economy Bill. This last was the seriously contested part of the government's plan. Bitter opposition was to be expected to the raising of £14 million by cutting unemployment benefit from 17/- a week to 15/3 for men, from 15/- to 13/6 for women, and from 9/- to 8/- for adult dependants; for this was the specific issue on which the Labour government had split. What was not expected, and what in the long run proved extremely damaging to the national credit, was the venomous attack, led even by ex-ministers, on the remaining £56 million of economy cuts which were essentially what the Labour Cabinet had already accepted in principle, and some of which the departmental ministers had already begun to implement before they resigned. This led to endless, undignified, and improper wrangles over what had in fact taken place in the Labour Cabinet. The government's Bill of course went through. But by the end of the debate the Opposition, leaders as well as rank and file, had repudiated all responsibility for it and declared their undying hostility to all the cuts.

The formation of a National government, however, only slowed down the run on the £. It did not stop it; and as soon as Parliament met certain factors combined to start it again at an alarming rate. The first, and probably the most important, was the attitude of the Labour Opposition. During the fortnight before Parliament met the official organs of the Party had declared their absolute hostility to the whole range of economy cuts. The expulsion from their various organisations of the Labour members of the government and the dozen ordinary M.P.s who supported them was clearly on the way; and even those members of the late Cabinet who had refused to accept the unemployment cuts were severely criticised by the T.U.C. General Council for having accepted so much else. In consequence even the ex-ministers were carried away with the tide and, regardless of what they knew to be the facts, were gradually led to an embittered, root-and-branch attack which denied the reality of the crisis altogether, plugged the line of the Bankers' Ramp, and in general set themselves to do just what all the responsible leaders had originally been seeking to avoid: to make party capital out of the unpopularity of inevitable sacrifices.

Foreign doubts of the genuineness of the British change of heart were thus revived before the crisis had been weathered. Conservative clamour for a quick election intensified the fear abroad that Labour might after all win by offering voters an apparently painless avoidance of hardship; and the loss of confidence was completed by what the press injudiciously handled as a 'mutiny' in the fleet at Invergordon. The Admiralty, always the most inept of government departments in its handling of public relations, had allowed the news of certain impending cuts in naval pay to reach the crews of the battleships at Invergordon by the wireless and the newspapers without any preliminary explanation or discussion of possible cases of hardship. A sort of passive resistance declared itself throughout the fleet. The crews of the battleships still in port refused to sail on the summer exercises, though they scrupulously avoided violence and remained entirely respectful to their officers. As far as the Navy was concerned the matter was from then on handled with the greatest skill and tact. The ships already at sea were ordered home; a thorough investigation was held; and an equitable settlement was reached. Even the questions and answers in the Commons showed a commendable restraint. But the damage abroad had been done. The Navy symbolised all that was the most solid and most reliable in Britain; and if that were disaffected, what faith could be put in paper plans for retrenchment and national sacrifices? The result was a renewed run on the £ which speedily exhausted the extra credits from New York and Paris. Since the basic economy of the country was still sound, and arrangements for balancing the budget were in hand, there was no longer any danger of a major crash. But the abandonment of the Gold Standard and the stabilisation of the £ at about two-thirds of its previous gold parity were obviously desirable from all points of view. On September 20th the necessary steps were taken; within a month the situation was settling down, and those countries which had pegged their currencies to sterling were making the necessary adjustments.

None the less there remained an uncertainty as to the real will of the British people, and it became more than ever desirable to test the matter by a general election. Already, on September 15th, Dalton had formally challenged the government to put its popularity to the proof, and there were many among his friends who thought that Labour would more than hold its own in an immediate election. Aneurin Bevan voiced the bitter, aggressive mood prevailing on the Opposition benches and at the same time struck the note which was to lead his party to almost total disaster. Rejoicing that events had at last 'clearly exposed the class issue', he proclaimed their intention to 'carry it through to a final conclusion, be the circumstances what they may'. The difficulties which beset the government during the following fortnight strengthened this defiant optimism. The suspension of the Gold Standard, Bevan said in an even more irresponsible speech on the 21st, had finally proved that the government was 'not a National Government at all'. 'The world does not believe in it,' he said; 'it does not take it on trust; it thinks it is unrepresentative of the British electorate. It is considered that at all costs an election must be postponed, because the government would be kicked out.' Such a challenge had to be met. Though MacDonald had promised that there should be no 'coupon election' and that the parties supporting the National government should be set free to pursue their own aims and policies as soon as the crisis was past, it had already become clear that the mere balancing of the budget was not enough to restore confidence. Moreover the National government would not have done its job until it had corrected the adverse trade balance; and for that it needed a mandate.

The final decision was long delayed by the difficulty of uniting the government on the long-term measures needed to restore the economy. Conservatives had all along clamoured for tariffs as the only safeguard. The Liberals, and with them Snowden, were still convinced free-traders. They would, indeed, have liked to postpone the election altogether. Several times MacDonald was tempted to throw in his hand, but the King exercised a bracing influence, and in the end a formula was found. The National government was to seek from the electors a 'doctor's mandate' to do whatever seemed necessary to relieve Britain's trading position. Under this umbrella each of the three parties was free to make its own statement of policy. This would avoid a renewal of the age-old battle between Free Trade and Protection as the main issue of the election, and would place the main problem fairly to the electors: were they prepared to back the men who had little to propose but sacrifices and higher taxes as the road back to prosperity, or did they prefer to risk disaster, as the Labour Party proposed, by defying the 'conspiracy of the international bankers' and refusing to shoulder the burdens which were being offered to them. On October 7th Parliament was dissolved, and polling day was fixed for the 27th.

There resulted, inevitably, a very confused general election and an extremely abusive one. The official machines of the Labour Party had reacted vigorously and efficiently to the crisis presented by the split in their Parliamentary membership in September. The National Executive rapidly induced the constituency executives to conform to the Party line, as laid down by the General Council of the T.U.C.: that the crisis was an artificially manufactured one, based on a bankers' ramp, and designed deliberately as an assault on the standard of living of the industrial workers. The fifteen Labour M.P.s who had either joined or supported the National government were formally condemned by their constituency organisations and called on to resign; and many members of the party who could see two sides to the question and in their hearts sympathised with and admired the disinterested courage of MacDonald and his friends felt bound, either by the need for Party unity, or through fear of abuse and unpopularity among their old associates, to toe the line. Sir Norman Angell was afterwards to admit that he had only re-fused MacDonald's requests for support because he 'shrank from facing the censure of old friends in the Labour ranks—censure for "ratting", for betrayal of "the cause", for failing to stand by old comrades'. 'I have felt since', he wrote, 'that it was no credit to me that I did refuse.' There must have been many others with similar misgivings. But the front of party unity was maintained on a basis of bitter hostility to every detail of the new government's programme. Ex-members of the government repudiated responsibility even for policies they had been prepared to sponsor in Cabinet, and in seeking to justify themselves started a deplorable series of revelations and wrangles on Cabinet discussions which should have been inviolably confidential; and their campaign of personal abuse of their former colleagues reached a shrill climax during the election.

On the face of it the government had a much less straightforward and more difficult case to put. It had been formed to save the £ and it had let the Gold Standard go. Its leaders had said over and over again that they intended only to balance the budget and stave off the crisis before resigning and letting the parties resume the old battle. Yet here they were, seeking a mandate for prolonging their own power indefinitely. The overwhelming mass of their candidates were Conservatives, pledged to tariffs, and it could plausibly be said that this was a bare-faced attempt to foist a Tory government on to the nation under a National label; and this view was given added strength by the open propaganda for tariffs carried on by Mr. Amery and his friends, who would outspokenly have preferred to fight the election on old-fashioned, party lines. Then Liberal dissensions further confused the issues pre-sented to the electorate. Simon led a group which had already forfeited the party whip and was rapidly being absorbed by the Conservatives. Samuel and the majority of the Party's M.P.s remained loyal to the government, though still insisting on the principle of Free Trade, whatever temporary protective measures might be necessary. Lloyd George, 'beside himself with fury' at the decision to hold an election at all, controlled all the Liberal funds and advised his own slender follow-ing to vote at all costs for Free Trade, if necessary supporting Labour candidates against Tory protectionists.

In the upshot the electorate showed how remarkably it can be independent of the party machines and impervious to misleading propaganda. It refused quite clearly to treat the issue as one of Free Trade versus Protection. It rejected the appeals to class interest and self-interest, and for a 'solid, working-class vote'; and all the Labour propaganda recoiled upon itself. What should have been the 'popular' line failed, perhaps for the very reason that the appeal seemed so deliberate. Voters, impelled, as Mrs. Pethick Lawrence had remarked in 1918, by 'a passion for abstract justice', preferred men who risked unpopularity by offering hardships and sacrifice: what one defeated Labour candidate, more honest than most, called 'an essentially non-materialist appeal'. Snowden, in a broadcast appeal on October 17th which was both one of his most venomous and most effective interventions in the campaign, narrowed the issue for electors to one simple question: 'whether we should have a strong and stable government in this time of national crisis, or whether we shall hand over the destinies of the nation to men whose conduct in a grave emergency had shown them to be unfitted to be trusted with responsibility'. On this the nation gave a uniquely decisive verdict. The government returned with 556 supporters, 471 of them Conservatives, 68 Liberals, and 13 National Labour followers of MacDonald. The Opposition was reduced to 56, of whom 6 belonged to the I.L.P. group and 4 were independent Liberals, which really meant Lloyd George and his family. In terms of votes the Conservatives were the biggest gainers, the Liberals the biggest losers.

It looked on the surface as if the gibe that a National government was merely a Conservative one under another name had been proved true. But the truth was that the whole election was a personal triumph for Ramsay MacDonald, and for that very reason produced a government which really was 'national', whatever label was tied to its individual supporters. The majorities by which the 13 National Labour candidates had won their seats in the teeth of the official party machine gave them an importance in Parliament out of all proportion to their numbers. Almost all of them represented 'safe' Labour seats where the voters were most vulnerable to the materialist and sectional appeal of the accredited party candidates. The miners of Seaham Harbour gave MacDonald a majority of 5,951, and Thomas headed the poll at Derby with a majority over his nearest opponent of 27,416. The mere fact that these 13 embodied the government's main claim to call itself 'national' enabled them to put a permanent brake on any Conservative tendency to exploit the situation for party purposes. Moreover large numbers of the Conservatives and many Liberals clearly owed their seats to the votes of the very unemployed whose hardships were the main theme of Labour propaganda. In 'depressed' County Durham, as Dalton wrote, 'the contagion of Seaham spread like a plague',[1] and Labour held only 2 out of 19 seats. At Gateshead, where Labour had a majority of over 16,000 in 1929, Bevin was defeated by nearly 13,000 votes. Hayday, President of the T.U.C., who had a majority of 10,000, lost Nottingham West by 5,000. Lansbury was the only ex-Cabinet Minister elected, and so became the Leader of the Opposition; and only two of the junior ministers were there to support him—Attlee and Cripps. Only in Wales, South Yorkshire, and East London did Labour hold its own.

Amery and his rabidly Protectionist friends were almost certainly right when they claimed that the Conservatives could have won the election by a narrow margin fighting by themselves on a policy of tariffs. They were quite certainly right in feeling that they were far more trammelled and enjoyed far less freedom of action as supporters of a National Government than they would have under a purely Conservative administration. The knowledge that they would never have won their seats fighting merely as Conservatives or Liberals had a vastly sobering effect on many of the government's supporters. All the victorious leaders, in their messages after the election, emphasised that this was not a triumph of party, but of national common sense. It imposed, particularly on the Conservatives, a new sense of responsibility and did much to modernise the Party and enlarge its understanding of the need for flexibility and compromise in modern politics. Labour, too, was given an admirable lesson to learn—the lesson MacDonald had striven to teach for a lifetime: that a British electorate cannot be stampeded in terms of class warfare; and that a government, whatever its label, is responsible for and to the nation as a whole and not only to its own supporters. Subsequent history has shown that this lesson, too, was faithfully learnt, in spite of the soothing phrases with which the leaders salved and still salve the wounds of 1931: assuring each other that the voters had merely been bewildered by the Labour split and had failed to understand the issues involved.

[1] *Op. cit.*, p. 296.

The National Government and Recovery

In the re-formed government MacDonald and Baldwin resumed their partnership as Prime Minister and Lord President. Snowden, whose health was failing, had not sought re-election and went to the Lords as Lord Privy Seal; and Neville Chamberlain took over the Exchequer. Hoare kept the India Office, but Reading gave up the Foreign Office to Sir John Simon, and Austen Chamberlain and Lords Crewe and Amulree all stood down voluntarily to make room for younger men. Sir Herbert Samuel, rather against the King's will, stayed at the Home Office, somewhat precariously, since it seemed obvious that he and his 32 followers would desert the government the moment they were brought seriously to face the tariff issue. As MacDonald told the King, he preferred to let sleeping dogs lie and preserve for the time being the character of the National government. On the immediately necessary legislation—the Abnormal Importations Bill to stop the massive foreign dumping of manufactured goods which threatened to ruin British industry—the Samuelites waived their objections on the understanding that it was a strictly temporary measure. At the same time Sir John Gilmour was able to begin a tentative rescue operation for British agriculture, which was facing the completion of the ruin begun in the 1860s, with a Horticultural Imports Act, which the Liberals again reluctantly accepted, on the grounds that the fruit and vegetables concerned were luxuries and not necessities; and they even allowed him to promise a wheat quota before the next harvest, though this was much trickier, since it threatened to compromise in advance the Dominions' Economic Conference due to meet at Ottawa in the summer of 1932.

The sleeping dogs lay for long enough to enable the government to get the second phase of the Round Table Conference on India completed. This did not, unfortunately, achieve what had been hoped. The first session had in effect committed the British to create in due course an all-Indian, self-governing federation; and on the strength of this the Mahatma Gandhi, then at the peak of his unique prestige, had been released from gaol and had had a series of profitable talks with the Viceroy, Lord Irwin. In the autumn of 1931 Gandhi arrived in London as the sole representative of the Congress Party—in effect of Hindu India. But he had come determined to resist the idea of federation, to reject the government's plan for proportional representation for the Hindu and Moslem communities, and to insist on an all-India government directly elected by universal suffrage. Clearly neither the Princes nor the Moslems could accept this; and in the course of acrimonious debates the hope of an agreed solution receded altogether. The Moslems put forward impossible claims for self-government which would have created a sort of Indian Ulster, called Pakistan. At the same time Congress shied away decisively from any federal solution, fearing that they would find themselves outweighted at the centre by a combination of Princes and Moslems. So MacDonald's high hopes came for the moment to nothing. He could only announce at the end that the government would proceed along the lines laid down a year earlier regardless of Indian differences. Civil disobedience broke out afresh, and before long most of the Congress leaders were back in gaol.

In the light of subsequent history it is a matter for profound thankfulness that both MacDonald and Baldwin refused to give way, either to the clamour of the right-wing Conservatives or to the touchy intransigence of all sections of Indian opinion. Probably the larger share of the credit belongs to Baldwin. It was he who launched the Simon Commission on its venture in 1927; and it was he who had to deal with the suddenly aroused romanticism of Mr. Churchill who denounced with scorn the Viceroy's conferences with that 'naked fakir', Mr. Gandhi, and passionately believed that 'we should lose India in the final result and that measureless disasters would come upon the Indian peoples'.[1] Baldwin's was the voice of sanity when he retorted that the generations of devoted Englishmen whose work, Churchill said, was being wrecked, had been 'at the greatest pains to educate Indians in our political theories and in the study of democratic institutions'; and this alone made it impossible to say to them in 1931: 'Democracy is for us and not for you.'

So, while a new Viceroy, Lord Willingdon, with long pro-consular experience behind him, blunted the effects of the civil disobedience campaign by a policy of judicious firmness, the government plugged away at implementing the main conclusions of the Simon Commission, proving at least its own impartiality by provoking at every stage vociferous protests from every section of Indian opinion and from extremists on both sides in the House of Commons. A White Paper in 1933, carefully examined and re-edited by a Select Committee of both Houses on which there sat three ex-Viceroys, laid the foundations for

[1] *World Crisis*, Vol. I, p. 27.

the Government of India Bill, which went through at last in 1935 in the teeth of Churchillian clamour that it went much too far and Socialist protests that it did not go nearly far enough. The first part of the Bill gave India a federal government with an Assembly elected indirectly by the separate religious communities, separate representation for the Princes, and all but two of the All-Indian ministers directly responsible to the Assembly. The second part provided the provinces of British India with similar Assemblies, to which, however, all the Provincial ministers were responsible.

In spite of the reiterated promise that this was a step towards 'full Dominion status', which remained the ultimate objective, the first part of this plan fared badly. The more powerful Princes could not bring themselves, when it came to the point, to surrender sovereign rights to an Assembly and government which Congress would probably dominate. Congress resented the introduction of the Princes as a possible bar to their exclusive exercise of power and also objected to the communal representation as a deliberate attempt by the British to retain power on the 'divide et impera' principle. The Moslems, also mistrusting Hindu domination more than British, continued to clamour for Pakistan. In the provinces things went much better. After an initial boycott, Congress bowed to Gandhi's decision that there was an opportunity to acquire experience and to make progress with some useful, particularly educational, programmes. It is, indeed, conceivable that the whole experiment might have worked itself out successfully, had India been given the needed years of peace and progress, in spite of the intolerant handling of minority problems by Congress governments which fully justified British caution. But the ifs of history are imponderable, and all that can be said is that its Indian policy and achievement were one of the strongest justifications for the National government.

It was not, of course, an achievement which contributed anything to the main problem of 1931: the adverse trading position which was the main issue. Three million unemployed, an excess of £409 million of imports over exports and a net adverse balance of trade of £113 million, thanks to the fall in the value of the invisible exports represented by shipping and foreign investment, made up a situation which, unremedied, would lead to ruin. A committee, presided over by Chamberlain, met in December and presented its conclusions to the Cabinet on

January 21st. They proposed a flat duty of 10% on all goods not on a special free list, which would include wheat, meat, cotton, and wool. On top of this the Treasury were to have powers to impose extra duties on luxuries and on goods which could be produced cheaply and in sufficient quantity at home—what were called 'non-essential goods'. There would thus be a flexible weapon always available against foreign discrimination or to induce foreigners to open their markets by a reciprocal lowering of tariffs.

As was inevitable, such a scheme came up against the dour opposition of all the Samuelite Liberals and, of course, Snowden; and the tension in the Cabinet was acute. MacDonald, feeling that the whole National character of the government would be lost if four non-Conservative ministers[1] resigned at that stage, actually warned the King to stand by for his resignation. But on the 22nd Lord Hailsham saved the situation, to the King's great relief, by suggesting that in the very exceptional circumstances the doctrine of joint Cabinet responsibility might go by the board: that the Bill might go forward as a government measure, but that individual ministers should be at liberty to speak and vote against it. It was a solution which theoretically cut at the roots of English constitutional doctrine and offered an easy target for opposition gibes at a disunited National government, but, as King George remarked, the ordinary Parliamentary system was in suspense, and in fact in the 'abnormal circumstances' it worked very well. The free-traders had their say and the Import Duties Act went through, to the great glory of Neville Chamberlain, who had the satisfaction of implementing at long last policies for the sake of which his father had ruined his political career.

What is more important, on the whole the new Act achieved its purpose very well. The cost of living did not go up, as the embittered free-traders had prophesied. There was even a slight, though temporary drop in unemployment. The financial situation improved so fast that by the spring half of the £80 million loan of the previous summer had been repaid and the bank rate had been brought down from 6% to 2%. One valuable result of this was that Chamberlain was able in June, 1932, to put through a huge conversion operation which had already been devised in detail by Snowden, bringing down the interest on £2,000

[1] Snowden, Samuel, Maclean and Sinclair.

million of 5% War Loan to 3½%, thereby saving the nation £40 million a year. His Budget had been a sober, undramatic, realist affair, calling for 'hard work, strict economy, firm courage, unfailing purpose' as the qualifications for national salvation. But all this left agriculture on the verge, still, of ruin, with an annual average of 20,000 farm workers leaving the countryside to swell the numbers of urban unemployed. Liberal feeling and the government's election pledges prevented any direct taxation of foodstuffs, so Walter Elliott, the Minister of Agriculture, had to achieve the same effect by the devious method of quotas and controls. The guaranteed price for wheat had already done something to salvage arable farming. Now the Agricultural Marketing Act set up marketing boards for each of the other agricultural products—milk, bacon, potatoes, stock-breeding, and sugar-beet. Production was curtailed to meet demand, foreign imports being limited by fixed quotas; and prices were guaranteed by various expedients: sometimes by subsidy, as with sugar-beet; sometimes, as with milk, by compulsory purchase of the entire output by the appropriate government board. Oddly enough, the fact that the controls established by these marketing boards, along with others which took over the direction of public utilities, such as the Electricity Board and the London Passenger Transport Board, and planning legislation such as the Ribbon Development Act of 1935 and the Public Health Act of 1936, represented a tremendous advance along the road towards a modified socialism seems to have passed almost unnoticed. They were accepted as common-sense solutions of practical problems, and the only doctrinaire clamour came from the dwindling band of Samuelite Liberals.

Actually, by the time Walter Elliott put through his great measure, in the summer of 1933, the Samuelites had already left the government. The earlier Protectionist measures had strained their consciences to the limit. The agreements reached with the Dominions at Ottawa in August, 1932, though they only represented a very small instalment of the Imperial Preference for which Beaverbrook was campaigning so vigorously, were too much for them. The threatened resignation of Snowden and Samuel, together with ten less important Liberals in the government, threw MacDonald into a panic. 'What will the new government be?' he wrote despairingly to Baldwin, holidaying as usual at Aix. 'How can it be National? How can I remain?' And to the King, 'I cannot

hide from your Majesty my apprehensions of the result of resignations
at this time. . . . The country will have a shock; the Opposition Parties
a score; and the outside world will see cracks in the national unity.'[1] But
Baldwin, urbane and not seriously disturbed, declined to come home
until he had had a proper holiday. 'I see *all* the difficulties,' he wrote,
'but though the boat may rock when our allies jump off, it may well sail
henceforth on a more even keel.'[2]

Both MacDonald's apprehensions and Baldwin's unruffled calm were
justified by the event. Manned almost exclusively by Conservatives, the
boat did indeed rock less, and the real power in the government passed
to Baldwin. MacDonald's prophecy to the King that his position would
become 'more and more degrading' was fulfilled. He had one moving
ovation from his supporters in the House of Commons when Parliament
reassembled in October, 1932, after the Liberal resignations. Thereafter
he became steadily more lonely and ineffectual. Headaches and trouble
with his eyes sapped his power of concentration; and he became more
and more vulnerable to the vicious attacks of his former friends and
colleagues, more and more of a liability to his Conservative allies, until
in the summer of 1935 he at last resigned, leaving Thomas and Simon
as the last non-Conservatives in the Cabinet.

He had not deserved that his career and life should end on such a
note of anticlimax. The debt owed to him by the Socialist Party was
greater than most of its younger leading members have ever been prepared to admit. It was in the minority administrations which he nursed
so carefully that men like Morrison and Attlee and Dalton learned the
technique of government and the art of compromise which enabled
them to take over full responsibility so successfully in the years following
the Second World War. The nation as a whole owed him, perhaps, an
even greater debt, both for leading Labour into constitutional paths and
away from violence and revolution, and above all for the disinterested
sacrifice of his political future and personal happiness in 1931, when
nobody but he could have achieved what was necessary without arousing
far greater bitterness and dissension. For then on he was shunned by his
friends and treated at best with a distant courtesy by his new allies,
though he gained and kept the affection and esteem of the King, who

[1] Nicolson, *op. cit.*, p. 498.
[2] Both letters are printed in full in G. M. Young, *Stanley Baldwin*, pp. 170–2.

visited him in hospital towards the end, and always strongly resented what he felt to be unfair attacks on a great public servant.

Nor is it fair to dismiss his performance during his last period of office at the head of a National government as that of a mere figurehead, throwing the cloak of his name and reputation over the activities of a Tory government. He shares with Baldwin and Hoare the credit for making what progress was possible in the intractable circumstances then obtaining in India, and so enabling the peaceful concession of independence much sooner than could have been anticipated in 1931. And by the time that his health broke down the fruits of his action in 1931 had been safely harvested. Britain's economy had by then been restored far more rapidly and completely than that of any other nation in the world. The budget of the previous year had shown a surplus of £31 million, which Chamberlain used to knock off income-tax the extra 6d. imposed at the crisis, to restore the unemployment rates of benefit to their old figure, and half of the service pay cuts. A year later all the cuts were restored. By then the volume of industrial production was higher than it had been before the crisis; and the number of employed workers was higher than it had been since 1921.

But Keynes had not yet formulated *The General Theory of Employment, Interest, and Money*,[1] which was to be the textbook from which the world might eventually learn the technique of maintaining full employment, and complete national recovery was singularly difficult to achieve in a world which still wrestled with the breakdown of its distribution system: in which tons of unsaleable wheat were tipped into Canada's great lakes, and the Brazilian government found it more economic to run its railway engines on coffee. Thus in Britain there remained 1½ million unemployed, largely concentrated in the black areas of South Wales, Tyneside and South Lancashire; and this figure seemed irreducible. Moreover, in a well-meaning attempt to rationalise the whole system of Unemployment Benefit in 1934, Chamberlain had created a Family Means Test for those who had exhausted or had never qualified for Insurance payments, and had thereby started a deep, bitter, long-lasting grievance among the poorer classes such as had not manifested itself since the Poor Law Reform of 1834. It meant that the whole income of a family had to be declared before the father of the family

---

[1] Published in 1936.

could draw the dole; and that a rise in pay for any member of the family would automatically be deducted from the householder's benefit. To the heavily burdened tax-paying classes it seemed reasonable enough that there should be no 'profiteering on the dole'. In families struggling on the verge of starvation the Means Test was bitterly resented and was remembered long after its repeal in 1937.

Furthermore, some of the steps taken to restore British prosperity during these years made the general situation outside Britain worse, particularly in their political consequences. The attempt at Ottawa to lay the foundations of Imperial Preference closed the British market to many European nations, which were thus thrust at a critical moment into an undesirable economic dependence on Germany; and it was not possible simultaneously to develop trade with Canada and trade with Russia. While British thought and effort had been concentrated on industrial and commercial recovery and on Imperial affairs, the international situation had been worsening with unbelievable rapidity; and by the time that MacDonald retired there already threatened a crisis abroad far more dangerous than the one which seemed to have been safely weathered.

CHAPTER 10

The Breakdown of the Post-War International System

WHILE Britain struggled back to something approaching prosperity much of the world was still going downhill, in many cases with political consequences which were to prove disastrous. Perhaps the worst result of this general breakdown of the world's distribution system, which left producers without markets for their accumulated stocks and consumers without the means to buy, was the intense national self-interest which it engendered. Keynesian dreams of internationally managed currencies evaporated in the rat-race, in which each nation turned in upon its own problems and let the rest go hang. In this sense the cry of the free-traders, which made no sense at all in a world of economic nationalism run mad, was in the long run the voice of sanity and reason. In the commercial complexity of the modern world only a temporary and precarious prosperity can be bought by one nation at the expense of its neighbours, and economic nationalism is ultimately self-destructive. So, though the protectionists who successfully shepherded Britain out of the worst of the slump had little choice of means or ends in the world conditions then obtaining, their very success helped to create an international situation which by 1935, when the country had weathered its own particular storm, was very alarming indeed.

The world's crisis had begun with the collapse of the American stock market in 1929, and it was worsened and prolonged by the subsequent collapse of the whole American economy. Animated by a sort of old-fashioned mercantilism, the rulers of the United States had not only accumulated within the vaults of the Federal Reserve Bank more than half the world's stock of gold, which ought to have been available to oil the machinery of the international exchanges, but had built up behind tariff walls a system of production almost as artificially inflated as the stock market. In due course this bubble, too, burst, and the glut and slump brought half the highly protected American industry to a standstill. With some 12 million unemployed workers, for whom there was no system of state relief, but only haphazard local arrangements and private charity, the United States were in no position to give decisive help to a European economy already debauched by vast American loans. It was only from the beginning of 1933, when Franklin Roosevelt took over from President Hoover and launched the National Recovery Act, that the American economy began its slow and painful restoration. In Britain, wholly dependent as she was on international trade, huge, deficit-financed schemes of public works could not, in the critical situation of 1931, be safely or effectively applied, as even Keynes himself admitted, though they might have done something to mitigate the catastrophe if boldly and swiftly applied in 1929. In the much more self-contained U.S.A. such a remedy, almost accidentally applied by a President without financial experience, did in fact do what Keynesian economists had always predicted. The huge New Deal programmes of public works could not in practice be financed entirely from taxation; and the large loans which thus became necessary gradually created the purchasing power needed to get the factories back into production. 'You have made yourself the trustee', Keynes wrote to the President, 'for those in every country who seek to end the evils of our condition by reasoned experiment within the framework of the existing social system. . . . If you succeed, we may date the first chapter of a new economic era from your accession to office.'[1]

The experiment did succeed, and by 1935 the United States, too, were struggling out of the morass. But by then the cessation of the flow of American capital had ruined a Europe debauched by five years of easy credit. As in America, so in Austria and Germany, the financial breakdown was followed by a general economic collapse. A large part of German industry ground to a standstill. The Republican government produced no New Deal, but by applying the classic remedy of economy and retrenchment and cutting down the civil services threw a fresh body of unemployed on to the labour market. In a desperate effort to

[1] *New York Times*, December 31st, 1933, quoted Harrod, p. 447.

find the money for Reparations payments under the Young plan government credit was drastically restricted, so further discouraging trade and throwing more millions out of work. By 1932 a third of Germany's labour force was altogether unemployed and another third was working on short time only. Wages were down and prices were up, and conditions began to resemble all too closely those of the frustrating years immediately after the war, though the psychological effects were perhaps worse, thanks to the sudden disillusionment after the artificial boom of the middle twenties.

Inevitably, moreover, the collapse of the great industrial countries produced a similar crisis for the world's primary producers. Canadian farmers could not sell their wheat nor Australians and New Zealanders their mutton, and there was no market for Brazilian coffee and Argentinian beef. Moratoria and debt repudiations in one South American country after another did yet further damage to the British economy by cutting off a large part of the income from foreign investments. Inevitably the German collapse produced similar effects throughout central Europe; and in Hungary, while the masses in Buda-Pest starved, the corn stood uncut in the fields, since it was not worth transporting it even to the capital. Economic wretchedness, in the still unstable post-war Europe, was translated into political discontent. It was out of this situation that the Nazi triumph in Germany was manufactured. Revolutionary rumblings threatened the aristocratic régime in Hungary; and in Spain widespread discontent overthrew the military dictatorship of General Primo de Rivera in 1931, that popular sportsman, King Alphonso XIII, was forced to abdicate, and a Liberal Republic was launched on its precarious career.

It was in the years of the great depression that the international system on which the post-war world had built such hopes really foundered. Up till then it had still been possible to believe that problems and disputes were all capable of settlement round what Castlereagh had called 'the green cloth' of the council table, either at Geneva, or at one of the great conferences which took place, as it were, under the wing of the League: that the nations would hold themselves bound by their 'free commitments, openly arrived at', and that they had learnt once and for all the folly of war. Frenchmen might protest that the phrase 'sécurité collective', first coined by the Czech Prime Minister,

Benes, was not French, but it was eagerly seized on by all those who talked scornfully of 'power politics' and hoped to save themselves from ever having to face the brutal logic of force. In 1929 it was permissible to hope that American and Russian isolationism would gradually be broken down and that the League, strengthened by the accession of Germany, would prove itself capable of dealing with issues graver than mere boundary disputes between Poland and Lithuania. In the *sauve-qui-peut* atmosphere of the economic blizzard, in which every nation strove ruthlessly to save itself at whatever cost to the rest of the world, it could clearly be seen how illusory these hopes and beliefs were; and the failure of three great international conferences in the space of a single year underlined the lesson.

The meeting at Lausanne at the beginning of June, 1932, was really called to end the whole business of Reparations and war debts which had so bedevilled international relations for more than ten years and contributed so largely to precipitate and intensify the world's economic catastrophe. Ramsay MacDonald was in the chair, but he was already largely incapacitated by headaches and was hampered by knowing no French, so that the main burden fell on Neville Chamberlain and Herriot, the French Prime Minister. Even the French knew in their hearts by now that complete cancellation of all the debts arising out of the war was the only feasible solution, and it should have been easily reached. But the Germans, while willing to make one final payment of £150 million in the form of government-guaranteed 5% bonds, made such a payment conditional on the recognition by the other powers of their right to 'equality' of treatment in the matter of armaments; and the United States, in spite of the hope held out by the Hoover Moratorium of the year before, now resolutely refused the cancellation of the debts still owed to her by Germany's creditors, without which they neither could nor would remit Germany's obligations.

The German line aroused the worst of French suspicions, and that of the other powers the latent truculence of America, always touchy at any suggestion of a 'line-up' of European powers which seemed to make the United States the villains of the piece. In the end a settlement was cobbled together, Chamberlain sitting up until three in the morning in Herriot's bedroom to achieve it. The German final payment was accepted in return for a dangerous phrase promising 'justice' in the matter of armaments; but the four creditor nations agreed not to ratify this agreement until they had reached a satisfactory settlement with America. In the upshot this did produce the required result, but with the maximum ill-will and grievance all round. Reparations and war debts ceased to be paid for the simple and brutal reason that, as long as America refused payment in goods or services, they just could not be paid. Since Hoover, on his way out of office, could not renew the moratorium and Congress would not, Britain sent one heroic final payment of £33 million in gold in January, 1933, and a small token payment of £3½ million in silver later in the year in return for a statement from Roosevelt that he did not consider we were defaulting. But the American public, apart from a few bankers and economists, still in the hysteria of a bank panic and crashing prices, firmly regarded it as a default; and at this most dangerous moment American isolationism and suspicion of foreign entanglements were fatally strengthened, while European grievances and mistrust of American intentions were strongly confirmed.

In the end the Lausanne failure had been engulfed in a still larger failure: that of the World Economic Conference. The representatives of 66 nations assembled in the Geological Museum at South Kensington, with MacDonald once again in the chair, on June 12th, 1933, and dispersed on July 27th having achieved nothing. Everyone agreed on the symptoms of the world's illness: high tariffs, quotas, subsidised industries, low wholesale prices and exchange restrictions, all resulting from the frantic efforts of each nation to escape from ruin at whatever expense to others. There was even a broad agreement that the foreign exchange arrangements were at the root of the trouble. But there was no agreement on the appropriate remedy. What was needed was something in the nature of a world bank which would be in a position largely to manage the world's currencies—the sort of solution towards which the non-Communist world has been groping its way since the Second World War. For that, in 1933, no nation was prepared to risk abandoning its own particular safeguards. France would not sacrifice tariffs unless the foreign exchanges were first established in a fixed relation to gold; and she carried with her all the countries of the so-called 'gold bloc'. Roosevelt came suddenly to the opposite conclusion—that to peg the dollar to a fixed relation with gold would endanger his gigantic experiment in public works, only just launched in the U.S.A. Britain, more intent on expanding Imperial trade and doubtful of the efficacy of public works, moved cautiously among half measures: reciprocal tariff treaties between individual nations and regional agreements. So the conference adjourned in what Maisky, the Soviet Ambassador, described as 'disorderly rout', lacking even the courage to record its own failure, while M. Bonnet, so Chamberlain recorded in his diary, swore at 'American perfidy', and Keynes published a provocative article in the *Daily Mail* under the headline: 'President Roosevelt is Magnificently Right'.

But the most important failure of that year, at any rate in its immediate moral repercussions, was that of the Disarmament Conference at Geneva. It is, in fact, very doubtful if any degree of disarmament by the former allied powers would have satisfied German pride. The German desire to rearm was not rational, but temperamental. It sprang fundamentally from a determination to reassert German power and to wipe out from the national memory the defeat of 1918 and the degrading humiliations to which it had led. The failure of the former enemy to disarm only gave a plausible excuse for what would have taken place anyway. But it must, equally, be agreed that the diplomacy of the peace-loving powers would have been vastly strengthened had this plausible excuse been removed. Particularly in Britain, where the sense of guilt about Versailles did not subside, but gained in force over the years, the continuing armaments of the world powers seemed to justify every excess of German bombast; and this attitude of mind dominated the vast majority of those who thought about such things at all, irrespective of class or party. Equally widely spread was the belief that disarmament must necessarily lead to peace: that armaments were invariably the cause and not the consequence of international mistrust.

It had been hoped that by the time the Disarmament Conference met, on February 2nd, 1932, the vexed question of naval parities would have been got out of the way. The three great naval powers had already settled for a 5:5:3 ratio in all classes of warship. Any extension of this agreement depended on France and Italy consenting to be treated as equals. To this the French would not agree, arguing that they must be able to match the Italians in the Mediterranean and still retain a margin of strength for possible commitments on their Atlantic seaboard. The

Italians, on the other hand, would accept nothing short of parity, lest the French should be able to concentrate a greater strength than theirs in the Mediterranean, which they had already begun to regard as 'their' sea. Thus the whole question of naval parities was left over to provide one of the most complicating factors in an already complex problem. After seven years of discussion, the Preparatory Commission had succeeded in preparing a Draft Convention, and to this every one of the powers had made some objection. It was easy for everybody to agree that purely offensive weapons should be abolished. The trouble was that there was no weapon of any kind which one power or another did not regard as essential to its defence. France sought to justify the retention of a large submarine fleet for the protection of a long, vulnerable coast line. Britain even insisted that the bomber aircraft had become vital for policing the Empire, raids on villages on the Indian frontier being much more salutary and economical than the old punitive column. Meanwhile the Japanese delegation enthusiastically supported the prohibition of naval aircraft-carriers, which could alone bring bombing aircraft within reach of their homeland, and the Germans protested vigorously against the clause maintaining in force 'all earlier treaties by which certain of the High Contracting Parties had agreed to limit their armaments', which would have perpetuated for ever one of what it was now fashionable to call 'the injustices of Versailles'.

It was more than two years before the Disarmament Conference formally admitted failure. But the fact of failure was apparent long before the end of 1932, and it was only the heroic patience and dogged persistence of its President, Arthur Henderson—out of Parliament now and soon to give up the leadership of the Labour Party, but still the possessor of a unique European prestige—that kept it going at all. It is difficult not to conclude from a study of the detailed proceedings of the Conference, that a large part of its failure was due to the chilly, negative approach of Sir John Simon and the British delegation. But the fundamental cause of the failure was simple and unchanging: it was not possible to reconcile the German demand for equality with the French insistence on security. The withdrawal of Japan at an early stage both from the Conference and the League did not help matters. The fall of the German Chancellor, Brüning, and the rapid transference of power via von Papen to Hitler had the effect of stiffening both the German demands and the French resistance. Thus, when Simon finally produced a plan, French in origin and carrying the blessing of the United States and Italy, for a two-phase disarmament which would delay for a four-year probationary period any German possession of the heavy weapons prohibited at Versailles, the other great powers remaining fully armed, German patience was exhausted. In October the German delegation withdrew and the German government gave formal notice that it was withdrawing from the League.

Obviously this breakdown at Geneva and the more or less simultaneous breakdowns at Lausanne and London were closely interrelated. Taken as a whole they strongly suggested, to those who were prepared to face international facts at all, the breakdown, temporarily at least, of any system there had ever been of collective security. However uninspiring and unimaginative the British initiatives at Geneva, the nation had at least set the world a practical example of disarmament. The Air Force was still ten squadrons short of the modest programme laid down ten years before. The fleet was short of cruisers and mostly obsolete. The army barely sufficed to police the Empire and the mandated territories and was without modern equipment. As Neville Chamberlain wrote at the time, 'Mussolini is playing the usual double game, the Americans are chiefly anxious to convince their people that they are not going to be drawn into doing anything helpful to the rest of the world, the Germans are propaganding with a view to dividing France and England. . . . I think we must be very cautious, for it would be very easy to make a mistake. But common prudence would seem to indicate some strengthening of our defences.' Opinion in Britain was far from accepting even this modest estimate of the situation. Sir Herbert Samuel led his band of 33 into formal opposition on the grounds of the government's failure in the matter of disarmament. And not even the Japanese attack on Manchuria and the rise to power of Hitler in Germany seriously modified the view so strongly held in Britain that there was still safety in the League and in its sanctions.

A great many eminent men have since said or written that 1931 was a turning-point in the post-war world's affairs: that up to that point, in spite of many set-backs and disappointments, the general outlook both for Britain and the world had steadily improved, and that thereafter it steadily worsened. It is certainly true that the consequences, both international and in the internal affairs of every important nation in the world, of an economic crisis of unprecedented gravity were disastrous. They introduced a new tone into international politics, and they altogether sapped the faith of those who had hitherto been able to believe that they were building a new and better world. The failure of the three great conferences of 1932, and most especially that of the Disarmament Conference, derived largely from the same causes and enormously increased the sense of disillusionment and frustration which characterised the thirties everywhere. In that general breakdown the Japanese intervention in Chinese affairs, the establishment of a new puppet kingdom in Manchuria, and the failure of the League of Nations to enforce an acceptable solution played a considerable part. It has, indeed, come to be regarded by many as the turning-point—the moment at which it ceased to be possible by pacific means to prevent the outbreak of a second world war; and it may well have been so. But the actual events have been so overlaid with a mountain of later propaganda that even now it is difficult to formulate an accurate narrative.

It is incontestable that Japan, in the summer of 1931, was ripe for mischief. The alliance with Britain in 1902, the success of the Russo-Japanese war, and the events of 1914–18 had all encouraged in Japan a militant, aggressive, modernistic imperialism, largely represented and controlled by the army and navy chiefs, and very difficult for the more liberal parliamentary leaders to hold in check. The insult of the sudden repudiation of the alliance by Britain in 1921 for the sake of a naval understanding with the United States had stimulated this latent nationalism; and the world depression, which almost wiped out the foreign trade on which the teeming millions of Japan depended, gave the army leaders an unexpected measure of popular support. Inevitably it was towards China that both imperialists and industrialists looked as a field for expansion and economic exploitation. For twenty years there had been no effective Chinese government and the Empire had become little more than a geographical entity within whose frontiers rival war lords fought their endless and meaningless battles. The Communist forces which were ultimately to overrun the country were still at a very rudimentary stage of development; and the only effect of the emergence of a rather stronger national government under General Chiang Kai-shek was to intensify the anti-foreign propaganda and agitation and to make the maintenance of peaceful trading relations infinitely difficult for foreign powers.

On top of this general situation there were for the Japanese particularly provocative conditions in the great province of Manchuria, which they themselves had saved for China at the time of the Russian war, and where they enjoyed, in consequence, special trading rights and had developed large commercial interests. It was never disputed by any impartial observer in 1931 that the Japanese had real and justified grievances. The Chinese government was incapable of controlling the periodical outbreaks of xenophobia, and seemed indeed to encourage them by a deliberately sponsored boycott of Japanese goods. When the Japanese army, on September 18th, 1931, set about establishing throughout Manchuria the order which the central government neither could nor would maintain, they undoubtedly felt that they were doing little more than the British and Americans had done when they found it necessary to safeguard the international settlement at Shanghai. It was also incontestable that in doing so they committed an openly warlike act against a fellow-member of the League of Nations and that they flagrantly violated the Covenant, the Kellogg Peace Pact, and the Washington Nine-Power Treaty of 1921.[1]

Here, then, was what seemed the first big test of collective security; and it could not have come at a more inconvenient moment, or in a more inconvenient part of the world. The only two great powers which were really effectively placed for direct military or naval intervention in Manchuria were Russia and the U.S.A., neither of them members of the League. Moreover, Russia had her own designs in that part of the world, and any intervention on her part was far from likely to restore or strengthen the existing Chinese government. The wave of isolationist feeling in the United States was to be steadily strengthened in the next two years, partly by the default of her European creditors, partly by her own imminent economic collapse. They were also approaching one of their periodical intervals of political paralysis consequent upon a Presidential election. The only League member who could conceivably apply military sanctions was Great Britain, and for her, too, the moment was ill-chosen. The so-called Invergordon mutiny took place two days before the Japanese coup; the abandonment of the Gold Standard three

[1] See above, pp. 75–6.

days after it; and for the next month the country was plunged into the excitements of a general election. The whole Manchurian Incident, as the Japanese preferred to call it, was played out against a background of continuous world crisis with its accompaniment of world conferences; and before it was over the triumph of National Socialism in Germany had given the statesmen graver preoccupations nearer home. In the circumstances no power, great or small, was at all inclined to embark on adventurous policies in the Far East.

Throughout the eighteen months of the Manchurian episode the British government pursued two objects with considerable skill and on the whole with success. The first was to act only within the framework of the League; the second to co-ordinate such action, if possible, with that of Mr. Stimson, the United States Secretary of State, who was not concerned with infringements of the Covenant, but only with violations of the Kellogg Pact and the Nine-Power Treaty which threatened the principle of the 'open door' in China. Even on these issues the state of American opinion compelled Stimson to move with the greatest caution, and effectively his intervention never went beyond the terms of the Note he addressed to the Chinese and Japanese governments on January 7th, 1932, warning them that the United States would not recognise any treaty or settlement which would impair the treaty rights of American citizens, which infringed Chinese sovereignty, or which deprived the Chinese of territory by means outlawed under the Kellogg Pact.

The League also moved with extreme caution. From the very first it was recognised that, however improperly Japan had behaved juridically in ignoring the League rules and procedures to which she had subscribed, this was not a straightforward case of the invasion of a neighbour's territory by armed force; and it was never in fact treated as such by the League. Japan had a clearly defined status and rights in Manchuria which the Chinese had equally clearly and persistently infringed. Though the phrase on the lips of Sir John Simon and others roused the fury of the Left and of the apostles of the League of Nations' Union, all she had done was, quite literally, to take the law into her own hands; and Article XVI, which listed the penalties for a 'resort to war in disregard of the Covenant', was never at any stage invoked against her. Action was taken by the League Council on October under Article

X, which required members to 'respect and preserve' each other's territorial integrity, and Article XV which provided for compulsory arbitration by the Council—a slow and unmilitary procedure remote from sanctions. In spite of the rising clamour for 'active intervention', 'firm handling', and 'bringing Japan to heel', the Council merely ordered her to withdraw all her troops to the railway zone in Manchuria; and since the Japanese seat on the Council enabled them to block the necessary unanimous vote, the matter automatically went forward to the Assembly at Geneva in the following March.

By the time the Assembly met Stimson had issued his famous 'Non-recognition Note', which infuriated the Chinese by its moderation. It had, one of them said, 'the head of a dragon and the tail of a rat'. Stimson had invited the British government to send a note in similar terms, but Simon very correctly pointed out that the matter was now in the hands of the League and that Britain could not properly anticipate its decisions by independent action. Japan had clearly declared her intention of maintaining the 'open door', and the question of whether there had been an infringement of Chinese sovereignty was now a matter for the League. Simon did not, however—though he has often been accused of it—leave the American initiative unsupported. It was he who persuaded the twelve neutral members of the Council on February 16th to endorse the American stand on non-recognition and who carried a unanimous resolution through the Assembly on March 11th. Then, still uncommitted on the rights and wrongs of the case, the Assembly appointed an international Commission of five members under the chairmanship of Lord Lytton, an enthusiastic supporter of the League, to investigate the facts on the spot and report back to a nineteen-member committee appointed to supervise the matter until the next Assembly meeting.

It was not until October of 1932 that the Lytton Commission published its long, scholarly, and scrupulously impartial report. All that summer the governments and press of the world were preoccupied with the effects of the American banking collapse, with war debts, and with the World Economic Conference, and finally, to the exclusion of almost everything else, the Disarmament Conference. For more than a year Japan was thus left with virtually a free hand in China. She overran the Province of Manchuria with little difficulty, and on March 9th set up a provisional Government for the new state of Manchukuo, with the dim figure of Mr. H. P'u, who had once been briefly titular Emperor of China, as 'Regent'. The Japanese thesis that this was no war, but merely an 'incident' in the vindication of her just, extra-territorial rights was, however, seriously weakened when, under pretext of breaking up a threatened Chinese counter-offensive, they broke south of the Great Wall and seized the Province of Jehol, which was certainly an integral part of China, whatever might be said of Manchuria. There was an ugly interlude, too, in March, when the Japanese commander at Shanghai seems to have lost his head and used the Japanese sector of the International Settlement as a base for an assault on the Chinese city. The attack was launched with quite inadequate forces and was strongly resisted; and there was an immediate danger of the whole Settlement being overrun by a horde of maddened Chinese. Here the British and Americans had no difficulty in co-ordinating effective action. Their own garrisons and fleets in Shanghai were promptly reinforced, but, beyond protesting at the dangerous misuse of the International Settlement, they remained scrupulously neutral; and it was on the British flagship at the end of March that the truce was signed under which the Japanese withdrew into their own zone.

The Lytton Report, which came up for discussion at the League Assembly in December, 1932, did full justice to Japan's grievances and recognised that there had not been in China for some years, and there was not at that time, a government capable of controlling the situation and securing the special interests which Japan justly claimed for herself: 'allowance is made', it said, 'for the provocation she had to endure when engaged in activities warranted by treaty; and it is explicitly stated that a mere restoration of the *status quo ante* would be no solution.' On the other hand, the Japanese method of redressing these grievances was categorically condemned. It was emphasised that the local population was anti-Japanese, and that Manchukuo was in no way the product, as the Japanese claimed, of a spontaneous popular move towards independence: 'the sovereignty and administrative integrity of China are (according to this report) to be maintained; all armed forces other than gendarmerie are to be withdrawn; and temporary international co-operation is recommended in the internal reconstruction of China.'

The Breakdown of the Post-War International System

The Lytton Report had an almost universally good press in Britain, even from the wildly pro-League *Manchester Guardian*. Sir John Simon recommended the Report as it stood to the Assembly on December 7th in a statesmanlike, scrupulously passionless, and balanced speech, which Lord Cecil later denounced, very unfairly, as 'a forensic defence of Japan', and which Mr. Stimson found wholly praiseworthy as an attempt to 'offer conciliation in a genuinely conciliatory manner'.[1] Unfortunately the Japanese were not prepared to accept either the Lytton Report or any interference from the League. Under the Minseito government, with the comparatively liberal Baron Shidehara as Foreign Minister, a compromise might perhaps have been found. But that government was engulfed in the rising tide of Japanese nationalism in December, 1932. In January, 1933, the Japanese delegates were ordered to withdraw if the League accepted the report of its Committee of Nineteen, which, having exhausted all conciliation procedures, had drafted a resolution condemnatory of Japan; and in February the Japanese army moved into Jehol. Rightly determined to uphold the Covenant at all costs as what Simon had called the 'fundamental law' of their existence, the members of the Assembly accepted their committee's report unanimously on February 24th, and the Japanese delegation duly withdrew. It should be emphasised that all the Assembly had done was to record its strong moral disapproval of Japan's action and to indicate the lines along which it believed the situation might be remedied. Japan was not 'branded as an aggressor' within the meaning of the Covenant, and Article XVI, which alone made provision for sanctions, economic or military, was never invoked against her. In a spirit of strict realism the statesmen at Geneva avoided any action which might involve them in a war which they could not possibly fight.

Reluctant though the Labour Opposition in the Commons and the growing number of League of Nations' Union enthusiasts in the country were to accept the fact, there was nothing that anybody could do to interfere effectively in the Japanese proceedings. The Washington Treaties had endowed Japan with an absolute strategic supremacy in the western Pacific. The Americans were allowed no base west of Honolulu, the British none east of Singapore. Even supposing there had been the slightest chance of American opinion allowing the State

[1] Printed in full in Bassett, *Democracy and Foreign Policy*.

Department to declare war on Japan, naval experts were all agreed that the American fleet by itself could not defeat the Japanese in their own waters. This was even truer of the British, even had they moved the entire battle fleet into the Pacific to operate 11,000 miles from home and thousands of miles from its nearest base. The Japanese were perfectly aware of their immunity, and there is not the slightest reason to suppose that they would have allowed themselves to be strangled by economic sanctions rather than declare a war in which they were in a position to inflict far more damage than they suffered. In any case President Hoover, in a memorandum written in the autumn, had ruled out sanctions 'either economic or military, for these are roads to war'.

In the event the only concession the British government made to opposition clamour for further effective action was the announcement on February 27th of an embargo on the export of all arms and munitions, either to China or Japan, which they were asking all armament-manufacturing nations to support. The difficulty about this was that, though it delighted out-and-out pacifists like Lansbury, it discriminated heavily against China, which manufactured no armaments, and did not affect the Japanese who could make all they wanted themselves. A discriminatory embargo against Japan only, such as the Opposition wanted and a Geneva committee was trying to work out, was difficult in view of Japan's absolute control of the seas, and impossible for a single nation acting alone. In fact no agreement was reached, and the embargo was lifted on March 3rd. The U.S. Senate's Foreign Relations' Committee approved a similar embargo on May 28th, but it came too late to have any effect. For, three days later, on May 31st, the Japanese achieved that direct settlement with China which had been their declared object all along, and signed the Truce of Tangku which brought the Manchurian phase of their great East-Asia venture to an end.

It is important to understand the actions of the League, and particularly the part played by the British government, in the Manchurian question, because it was to become one more of the many legend-encrusted episodes of inter-war British history. Sir Geoffrey Mander, in a book published in 1941 and specially reprinted for the 1945 election, entitled *We Were Not All Wrong*, wrote that 'the pathway to the beaches of Dunkirk lay through the wastes of Manchuria'. In a sense he was right, for there were vital lessons to be learnt from Manchuria. They were: that the League still had clearly definable limitations and that there were cases of international lawlessness and aggression with which it was powerless to deal; that only if it included in its membership all the great powers, and if the majority of these powers were prepared in the last resort to go to war to enforce its decisions, could such a body hope to check a determined aggressor; that there were nations which would not be deterred by the moral disapprobation of the world; and that the risk of major war was implicit in the use of sanctions, however economic. It was, of course, a corollary of these that, until general disarmament became a reality, the peace-loving members of the League must arm themselves at least heavily enough to give it effective support when necessary.

But the lessons which Mander and many like him drew were very different. They rested throughout on three great delusions, all of which were so sedulously and skilfully propagated that by 1935 they had been accepted as articles of faith by the overwhelming majority in Britain who thought about politics at all. The first was that the League could have acted more effectively: could have forced Japan to disgorge her ill-gotten gains and reach an equitable settlement with China. The effective actions recommended—though only, be it noted, well after the event—ranged from the withdrawal of all ambassadors from Tokio, as a gesture of moral disapproval, to discriminatory embargoes amounting to full economic sanctions, and even in the last resort military sanctions. The feasibility of all this rested, of course, on the second delusion: that the United States were ready, and even eager, to support the League in all or any of these courses, and even at one stage offered to take a lead which the nations failed to follow. Finally a heavy share of blame for all these failures was laid upon the National government on two counts: first, for failing to take the initiative at Geneva and to 'give an effective lead'—Sir Stafford Cripps was even to go so far as to accuse them of 'sabotaging or undermining the League of Nations'; and second, for not backing up 'Mr. Stimson's courageous lead'.

None of these propositions stands up for a moment to a close analysis of the actual events and circumstances of 1931.[1] It is just conceivable that an immediate condemnation of Japan's action and a firm statement

---

[1] This has been done, with almost unnecessarily thorough scholarship, in R. Bassett, *Democracy and Foreign Policy*. His conclusions, which are the basis of the judgements in this chapter, are incontestable.

on non-recognition right at the outset might have strengthened the hands of Japanese Liberal statesmen and enabled them to get the militarists under control. Mr. Wickham Steed at any rate claimed at the time to have found strong support among Japanese politicians for this view. But it is not conceivable, Japanese pride and intolerance being what they were, that any gesture of moral indignation, such as the withdrawal of ambassadors, would have had any effect but to strengthen their determination. A discriminatory arms embargo sounded splendid in theory, but nobody was ever able to explain how it was to be effective except against China, in the teeth of a Japanese naval blockade of the whole Chinese coast. As for sanctions—the Socialists and the leaders of League of Nations' Union thought rejected the idea of military sanctions at the time as whole-heartedly as did the government's supporters. Only a very few voices were raised in tentative suggestions of economic sanctions, and then only on the strict understanding that there should be no risk of war.[1] It was only after the Tangku Truce, when there was no longer any fear of the matter being put to the test, that the clamour arose that economic sanctions ought to have been applied, and that they would not have led to war. By then, of course, such suggestions could be made to appear far more plausible by the invariable addition of the phrase 'provided that the co-operation of the United States were assured'. At the time of the crisis nothing was clearer than the determination of the American government to avoid any such action, and it was not even possible to argue seriously that economic sanctions would be effective.

For of course at no point in the history of the Manchurian episode was the State Department in a position either to give a lead to world opinion or strongly to support any lead given by the League. American opinion was more intensely suspicious of any suggestion that the United States' fleet might be put at the disposal of the Council of the League than at any time since 1919. Manchuria was at that time still remote and almost uncomprehended, and in any event unimportant when American banks were closing their doors and half American industry faced total ruin. Though Stimson personally, and many of his

[1] Bassett's final conclusion, after an exhaustive analysis of all that was said and written at the time, is worth quoting: 'During the period of the Manchurian dispute advocacy of economic sanctions had been tardy, hesitant, spasmodic, limited and safeguarded by unrealisable conditions.'

high officials, followed the League action with close attention and some-times with openly expressed approval, their public statements had to be guarded; and there was never any suggestion of American participation in League action or that America was concerned with breaches of the Covenant. The only important American initiative was the proclamation of the doctrine of non-recognition. There was never the slightest question of participation in sanctions, economic or military.

The whole thesis that Simon failed to support the American lead has grown out of the one incident of this very proper refusal to send an identical note to Stimson's on non-recognition; and even this accusation is without substance, since he went one better and engineered the much more impressive endorsement of the American principle by both the Council and Assembly of the League. Moreover there was no funda-mental difference between Simon's proposals at Geneva and those of other leading statesmen, and there was no serious proposal of further action by the League which was hindered or sabotaged by the British government. The conclusive paragraph of Simon's speech at the Assembly in December, 1932, laid the whole emphasis on the need to vindicate League principles, whatever the mitigating circumstances put forward to justify Japanese action; and the course of events at Geneva fully justified his claim, constantly reiterated in the House of Com-mons, that the government's main objective was the vindication of those principles. When Mr. John Strachey wrote in 1938 that Simon, 'using to the full his great forensic powers, and, more important, of course, by using the whole influence of Britain, stopped the League from taking action', and that 'the U.S. government, as Mr. Stimson, then Secretary of State, has since revealed, was actually pressing the British for sanc-tions against Japan',[1] he said what was demonstrably untrue, and was flatly contradicted by the facts.

The magnitude of the self-deception achieved by Labour members and ardent League supporters in the following years, and the ease with which they forgot what they had said, written, and recommended when the crisis was actually on, is scarcely believable. Even Lord Lytton, whose record of balanced, statesmanlike impartiality throughout the crisis was impeccable, later denounced the line taken by the British government as 'absolutely destructive of the whole basis of collective

[1] *Left News*, April, 1938. Quoted Bassett, *op. cit.*, p. 625.

security'. Yet at the time, in a series of speeches and under cross-examination at League of Nations' Union meetings, he had no further steps to recommend beyond what the Assembly, largely under the leadership of the British government, had already carried out. Economic sanctions he repeatedly rejected as 'a peculiarly cruel form of war' waged in the main against women and children. He also said that an economic blockade 'would almost certainly precipitate an actual state of war'. An arms and financial embargo was the most extreme step he was prepared to contemplate. 'The bellicose pacifist system' and the use of 'the big stick' he utterly deplored. 'The League', he declared, 'must say what the obligations of the Covenant are and what action is consistent with them.' It could then only say to China and Japan: 'We offer the chance with both hands of using the machinery of the League to settle the dispute. If you don't take advantage of that, we can only wait until the day comes when you will take advantage of it.' And this was precisely what Simon had throughout advocated and what the League had actually done.

Lansbury, who throughout the Manchurian episode eclipsed even his colleagues in muddled, self-contradictory, often quite incomprehensible utterances, unlike them reached the right conclusion in the end with astonishing clarity. 'If Japan is allowed', he said in July, 1933, 'to remain in possession of that territory after the protest of the whole world, it seems to me to prove that the League as a means of preserving justice and fair play is really impotent.' It was a conclusion which the mass of the British people was passionately anxious to avoid. It was Mr. Mander and the National Peace Council, the more extremist League enthusiasts, and the leaders of the Opposition in Parliament who first signposted the road from the wastes of Manchuria to the beaches of Dunkirk by encouraging them to reject the lesson and to cling to the belief that the League Covenant, properly handled, could by itself and without the use or risk of force prevent armed aggression; and that it had failed in Manchuria only because it had not been properly supported. By persuading the electorate that all demands for navies and air forces were the propaganda of war-mongers and armament manufacturers and that the League could function effectively without armed support, they delayed the rearmament of Britain by three, almost fatal years.

The impact of this propaganda was instantaneous and devastating. In the October following the Tangku Truce the Labour Party Conference had pledged itself to take no part in any war and to foment a general strike to prevent Britain engaging in one; and three weeks later the National government candidate in the East Fulham by-election was defeated, with a turnover of 19,000 votes, by a pacifist, and solely on the issue of disarmament. The Oxford Union carried its famous motion refusing to 'fight for King and Country', causing, perhaps, a disproportionate commotion outside the university. But the situation was urgent, and there was no time for hysterical outbursts of this kind. On the 30th of the previous January Hitler had become Chancellor of the German Reich; and February 27th—the day of the great Commons debate on Manchuria—was also the date of the Reichstag fire.

It will probably always be a matter of dispute among historians as to how far Hitler and his Nazi movement were a logical sequel to the bombastic nationalism of XIX-century Germany and how far the product of a particular set of circumstances in 1931. Certainly among Bismarck's legacies, whether he himself would have approved of it or not, there was a national aggressiveness, a worship of power, embodied in military terms, for its own sake, and a belief that political success was its own justification; and of all these convictions Hitler was the heir. His plans, at the outset as much Socialist as Nationalist, could be adapted very well to the ideals of the old military caste which had refused to accept the fact of defeat in 1918. They also seemed, with their promise of unconditional and unrestricted rearmament, to offer golden opportunities to the industrialists of the Ruhr.

But it was popular support which swept him into power, largely drawn from the petty bourgeoisie, the small shopkeepers and the black-coated unemployed, who made up the mass of Brownshirts, officered by disillusioned men who had never settled down after the war. Germany has always tended to over-fill her universities and to produce a larger crop of graduates than she can usefully employ. There was thus a powerful educated element among the millions of German unemployed whose numbers were further swelled by the government's desperate economies of 1931, when the last Dawes Plan payments were due, which threw large numbers of second-grade civil servants on to the labour market. In the desperate atmosphere of panic and disillusion-ment engendered by the nation's second economic collapse within ten years, these were the men who felt most bitterly frustrated. They could not dig, to beg they were ashamed. It seemed to them all too clear that they had been deprived of their birthright of an orderly, peaceable existence in a pensionable job by the injustices of Versailles and the exactions of the victorious powers. With such material to work on it was easy for Hitler to turn the disillusionment with war prevailing in 1919 into a mere resentment of defeat. Their minds and outlook had been formed against the background of the continuing blockade and starvation of 1919 and the wholesale ruin by inflation of the solid, dependable German middle class. For them democracy meant only the feebleness of the Weimar governments which had failed to stand up to the Allied powers; and the tentative internationalism embodied in the League they saw all too easily as a hypocritical device to enable the French to perpetuate their domination of Europe. Finally, given the German historical and social background, any suffering not laid at the door of the late Allies was easily attributable to the Jews.

The process by which the Party infiltrated itself into power and stampeded the German electorate into giving them and their Nationalist allies the bare 51% majority in the Reichstag which sufficed for the destruction of democratic government is all too familiar history. But for diverse reasons British public opinion was very slow to draw the appropriate conclusions. The nagging sense of guilt about the Versailles Treaty, which had grown steadily stronger as the memory of 1918 receded, combined with a growing exasperation with a French outlook and policy apparently rooted in a dead past, blinded Englishmen to the fact that the European balance of power was destroyed and that all the safeguards which had seemed to justify stripping British armaments to the bone were gone. Hitler's withdrawal killed the Disarmament Conference stone dead, and in due course he also withdrew from the League. It was too easily assumed that the rearmament of Germany would be a token affair only, designed to establish her right to equality in the eyes of the world, and that in time, as the hysteria died down and the injustices of Versailles were clearly rectified, it would be possible to bring her back into the international system and resume the interrupted negotiations. Even Hitler's first great diplomatic coup, the ten-year non-aggression pact with Poland in 1934, destroying at a blow the last of France's devices for national security, her system of East European alliances, made little impression on people who had never seriously understood the passionate French desire for some form of international guarantee.

Another factor was, of course, the intense self-preoccupation induced in all nations by the magnitude of the economic collapse. Absorbed in their own comparatively successful struggle back to prosperity, Englishmen tended to look with a sympathetic eye on the rigid state control of every branch of the national activity which was Hitler's method of achieving the same thing in much more difficult circumstances. By forbidding the employment of women in industry, by compulsory labour service on public works, and by directing all German production towards the purpose of a self-sufficient Germany, Hitler did gradually master the unemployment problem. State control of currency and investment, the compulsory reduction of dividends, the direction of capital into fresh industrial production, and the limitation of all foreign trade to large-scale barter agreements which secured the necessary imports of raw materials, miraculously set the national economy working again; and in due course the fighting services and the armament factories absorbed the remaining margin of unemployment. It was too easily assumed in Britain that all this represented merely a single-hearted effort to restore prosperity, without ulterior motive.

Even the beginning of Jewish persecution and the 'night of the long knives' of June 30th, 1934, when Hitler, Goebbels, and Goering reasserted their control of the Party by the massacre of some 700 potential rivals and dissidents, did not for a time seriously disturb British complacency. As he came to write the closing chapters of his admirable chronicle of the reign of King George V, which he published in 1935, even so distinguished a historian as Mr. D. C. Somervell was more preoccupied with the monstrous behaviour of Mr. de Valera in breaking away from the British Crown than with any potential threat from Germany. He probably spoke for the mass of the voters who supported the National Government when he dismissed the threat of the Nazi movement as being as unreal as had been the French clamour for *revanche* after 1871: something that appealed to the German 'love of uniforms and quasi-military pageantry', but was 'mistakenly interpreted by those who read into Hitler's speeches an intention of ultimately refighting the Great War. Hitler talked in military metaphors because they are the favourite metaphors in Germany, but his actions were much more pacific and conciliatory, at any rate in the sphere of foreign policy. It may even be maintained that his movement has served the cause of international peace by sublimating the militaristic complexes of his people. He supplied brown shirts instead of battles and diverted the violent impulses of his fellow countrymen from the Polish frontier on to the Jews and Marxians in their midst.'[1]

Against such complacency the warnings of Churchill and Boothby and a few others, that the strength of the *Luftwaffe* was already such as to cause alarm, broke in vain. 'We deny the need for increased armaments,' Mr. Attlee said in the House of Commons on July 30th, 1934. 'We deny the proposition that an increased British Air Force will make for the peace of the world, and we reject altogether the claim for parity.' Sir Herbert Samuel was even more complacent: 'Nothing we have so far seen or heard would suggest that our present Air Force is not adequate to meet any peril at the present time.' The Prime Minister was able to report with self-satisfaction to the King that support for Mr. Churchill's warnings 'came from only a very small group of members'. Not for the first time the King was wiser than any of his ministers. 'His Majesty feels', ran a message to the Ambassador in Berlin in the following January, 'that we must not be blinded by the apparent sweet reasonableness of the Germans, but be wary and not be taken unawares.' Sir John Simon, for one, was not in any way impressed with Churchill's sense of urgency. Time, he wrote to the King in October, 1933, might well bring Germany back into the Disarmament Conference, and: 'Fortunately time is available, for Germany is at present quite incapable of undertaking aggression. Europe forewarned is, in a sense, Europe forearmed.'[2] The breakdown of any organised system of international security had passed as unnoticed in government circles as it had among the Opposition.

[1] *Op. cit.*, p. 475.   [2] Nicolson, pp. 521–2.

CHAPTER 11

The End of the Baldwin–MacDonald Régime

L ooking back over the inter-war years with easy, after-the-event
wisdom, almost everybody who has thought about them agrees
that the turning-point in the world's affairs was in 1931. It was
then that the hopes of 1919 for better standards of living, for democratic
progress, and for a saner international order finally foundered. In most
parts of the globe it was clear enough at the time. The effort of the 1920s
had been in practice largely an effort in reconstruction: an attempt to
recover a stability and a sense of security which men felt had been lost
in 1914. The world of the 1930s looked, either with apprehension or
excitement, forwards. In crude, historical terms, the first period was one
of restoration and recovery from the effects of the First World War; the
second one of regrouping and preparation for the next. Germany and
Italy were the extreme cases, where the problems and strivings of the
past were clearly and abruptly written off and the nations plunged into
new and, as it proved, lunatic adventures. But almost everywhere the
impact of the change was vivid and immediate. The economic crash had
broken the old world beyond repair; and France, the traditional weapons
with which she had sought to protect her Rhine frontier broken in her
hands, groped with diminishing hope for some new method of achieving
the security which eluded her. Even Russia, in her suspicious isolation,
had to think in terms of new and urgent dangers on her western
frontiers; and the United States, almost equally isolated, had launched
into the gigantic adventure of the New Deal which, in that old-
fashioned world of *laissez faire* and free enterprise, represented a revolution.

Only Britain remained, for five almost fatal years, immune. No revolutionary methods were evolved to deal with her crisis. Her recovery was achieved with the classical, well-tried remedies and without political upheaval: a process of dogged rebuilding which still looked backwards, expressing even its success in terms of the past, as the volume of trade crept back to the 1919 level and the number of employed rose towards the record figure of 1921. Absorbed in this task, which was indeed in itself a notable achievement, lulled into a false sense of security by a century of immunity from danger behind the shield of the Channel and an unbeatable fleet, the British woke very slowly and reluctantly to the fact that they were living in a new world. Indeed, the national thanksgiving to mark the Jubilee of King George V and Queen Mary in May, 1935, was an almost defiant assertion of their determination to live for as long as possible in a past which everywhere else was being repudiated with loathing by statesmen and people alike. It was a last assertion of the British belief in venerable, well-tried institutions, under which near-revolutionary changes in social relations and standards of living could be carried through without political upheaval, almost unnoticed, before the storm outside reached a pitch which even they could no longer ignore.

Few people in 1910 would have expected George V to make a very distinguished mark in the national history or to capture more than a dutiful affection in the hearts of his people. He and Queen Mary were then known to be a shy, retiring, domesticated couple, a little aloof from the Edwardian world, and with none of the apparent glamour needed to captivate the masses. It was even doubted if the inexperienced King would weather the early storms of his reign at all, succeeding as he did in the midst of a constitutional crisis and to an Irish situation which trembled on the verge of civil war. In practice he had not only a remarkable understanding of the constitutional duties and limitations of his position, but a very valuable capacity for giving decisive leadership at critical moments. What was even more unexpected, he showed a remarkable adaptability in a world of growing publicity and social adjustments which were producing a society very different from the Victorianism in which he had grown up. Though irascibly conservative in small things, such as the niceties of dress and etiquette, he had a large tolerance for the major changes which were gradually eliminating the worst of the XIX-century social injustices. Labour ministers, who had expected to be received with hostility and suspicion, found themselves instead charmed and then impressed; and this quality had enabled him to do for the monarchy in the XX century what his grandmother had done for the Hanoverian monarchy a hundred years before.

It was all done so quietly and unobtrusively that it was almost with a shock of surprise that the nation discovered, after twenty-five years, the depth of its affection and esteem for the Royal Family. The British Monarchy had become one of the most remarkable institutions in the modern world, not only as a useful ceremonial symbol of all that great framework of constitutional and political agreement within which party rivalries and party government can alone function effectively, but as a sort of national possession, intimately linked with almost every aspect of the nation's life. However valid the sneers of the intellectuals and the psychological analyses of the need for a 'father figure', it remained a simple fact that the mass of the people had come not only to value, but to love their King and Queen. The intense public anxiety and the pre-occupation with the medical bulletins during the period of the King's long and serious illness had given an inkling of the strength of these feelings; and the annual Christmas broadcasts 'to all My People, everywhere' had brought this extraordinary relationship down to earth, bridging the gap created by courtiers and official classes between great personages and the masses, and revealing to people for the first time vividly the simple, straightforward, and constant concern for their welfare which had been King George's greatest characteristic.

The King himself was as surprised as anybody by the spontaneous enthusiasm shown in the week of the Jubilee celebrations. 'The greatest number of people in the streets that I have ever seen in my life', he wrote in his diary when he got back from the formal thanksgiving in St. Paul's: 'the enthusiasm was indeed most touching'. Even more impressive were the decorations and the cheers and clapping which greeted the King and Queen when they drove through the most densely populated areas of London, and especially in the East End. 'I'd no idea they felt like that about me,' he said at the end of one long, tiring day; 'I'm beginning to think they must really like me for myself.' The same rather charming note of diffidence marked his message of thanks broadcast to the Empire: 'The Queen and I thank you from the depths of our

hearts for all the loyalty and—may I say so?—the love with which this
day and always you have surrounded us.'

Only a nation so 'optimistic, phlegmatic, and self-confident', Sir
Harold Nicolson has written, could have staged such a demonstration of
its own pride in its past at such a moment in European history. He
might well have chosen more forceful adjectives than those. A blind
stupidity, a lethargy, and an unwillingness to make any further sacrifices
or face the implications of known facts afflicted the nation with a sort of
paralysis which became less excusable every month. The lessons to be
drawn from Manchuria had been obscure and complicated by special
circumstances. It was possible, too, to hope that power and responsibility might in a few years have some sobering effect on Hitler and to
believe for the moment that he meant what he said. For he had to move
cautiously towards the goal of total rearmament for fear of being caught
before he was ready. In particular he wanted the Saar plebiscite to decide on reunion with Germany to go through before he alarmed Europe
with any dramatic announcements. And, though well-informed people
knew that a crisis inevitably impended between Italy and Abyssinia,
Mussolini still seemed dependably anti-German and to represent no
serious threat to peace. The atrocities which had marked the Fascist rise
to power were conveniently forgotten. Well-travelled persons, remembering the chaos of post-war Italy, told each other comfortingly that,
whatever one thought of Mussolini, he had at least made Italian trains
run up to time.

All this made the wave of pacifism, which reached its climax in the
Fulham by-election, understandable. The clamour of those who
opposed armaments of any kind was loud and clear. 'I would close every
recruiting station,' Lansbury wrote in his message to the Fulham
electors, 'disband the Army and dismiss the Air Force. I would abolish
the whole dreadful equipment of war, and say to the world, "Do your
worst." ' On the other side there were only Churchill and his handful
of personal friends; and Churchill spoiled much of the effect of his
clear analysis of the threatening dangers by the very quality of his
oratory, which to the English mind made his views suspect: they were
not going to be carried away by mere words, as they believed he had
been. Yet the mere known facts of the world's relative air strengths,
measured in operational aircraft, should have carried their own warning.

Russia led with 1890 and France came next with 1665. Britain came only sixth, with 884 planes, well behind Italy, and equal to the combined forces of Poland and Jugoslavia. In the teeth of the facts another, even more shameless election pamphlet during the following year ran: 'The Unionist Party want war. Your husbands and sons will be cannon-fodder. More poison gas will mean dearer food. Register your distrust of the war-mongers by voting Labour.'[1] The government meanwhile, seriously misled on the essential facts by its intelligence services, spoke unfortunately with the uncertain voice of a tired and bewildered Baldwin. His reply to a Conservative attempt in November, 1933, at least to get the 1923 Air Force programme completed[2] muddled his friends as much as his opponents:

> One of my difficulties here, and of anyone indeed who has to speak on this matter, is that they cannot tell all they know. It is impossible. If I were to stand here and say where the difficulties are, and who are the people who raise those difficulties, it would be perfectly impossible to advance one inch with regard to disarmament. One's lips are sealed.

It was indeed at this point that the Conservative brand of pacifism, which they preferred to call appeasement, began to have a perhaps even more fatal influence in sapping the national morale. The extremists on that wing, obsessed already with the fear of Russian communism, openly welcomed the rise of Nazism and the rearmament of Germany as constituting a more effective barrier against Russian expansion westwards than had the Little Entente. Basically the Conservative line at its weakest was to let the rest of the world go hang, provided that Britain could keep out of trouble. Granted that the Socialist and Liberal encouragement of a hysterical pacifism broke the government's nerve and paralysed all efforts to rearm when rearmament might still have been effective in limiting the scope of disaster, it was a failure of Conservative nerve and a Conservative reluctance for self-sacrifice which in the later stages threw successively the Abyssinians, the Spanish Republicans, the Austrians, and the Czechs to the wolves in the hope that Britain might still be spared. Behind it all there was what Churchill called the 'fatalism and helplessness' which marked so many of Baldwin's utterances at this period. To tell 'the man in the street', as he did in 1932, that it would be

[1] Quoted G. M. Young, *op. cit.*, p. 78.
[2] The R.A.F. was still ten squadrons short of this.

'well to realise that there is no power on earth that can protect him from being bombed' was to foster the very spirit which he claimed to be exorcising. 'The bomber will always get through' was a poor slogan by which to call on the nation for rearmament and self-sacrifice in the cause of world peace.

By the time of the Jubilee any shadow of justification there had ever been for the Opposition line on rearmament had vanished, and complacency had become inexcusable. Hitler had not altogether marked time in 1934 while he waited for the Saar plebiscite. The annexation of Austria had been in the forefront of his programme from the first—it was postulated on the first page of *Mein Kampf*, and it was an obvious weak point at which to attack the Versailles Treaty. The refusal of the *Anschluss* in 1919, in flagrant breach of Wilson's principle of self-determination, was a major grievance in Germany with which English opinion much sympathised; and although the Hague International Court had refused to sanction a Customs Union in the closing days of the German Republic as a breach of treaty obligations, it would be difficult for Great Britain to oppose a renewed attempt. On the other hand the Austrians were much less enthusiastic for the *Anschluss* since the advent of Nazism; and their Chancellor, Dollfuss, himself virtually a dictator, had made it clear that he would put up a stout fight for the independence of his small Republic, strategically so important. Italy and Hungary had drawn together to preserve Austrian independence, and at Riccione, in August, 1933, Dollfuss obtained promises of full support from Mussolini.

Hitler clearly needed to postpone a decision on Austria until he was rearmed and could afford to defy Mussolini.[1] But he had loosed forces which he could not easily control. Helped by German money and arms and encouraged by propaganda broadcasts from Munich, the Austrians staged their coup on July 25th. Parties of armed Nazis seized the Chancellery and the Vienna wireless station, Dollfuss himself being wounded and left to bleed to death; and there were similar outbreaks in all the larger towns. But the Austrian government kept their heads. Dr. Schuschnigg assumed power and the army and police rallied to him. Above all, Mussolini promptly announced the despatch of three divi-

[1] For an analysis of Hitler's policy and intentions at this stage, see A. J. P. Taylor, *The Origins of the Second World War*, p. 83 *et seq.*

sions to the Brenner Pass. This created just the sort of crisis which Hitler at the moment had to avoid at all costs. But he had shown his hand and the methods he proposed to use in redressing Germany's grievances and proved that *Mein Kampf* was not merely a daydream, but a practical programme for action. There was no longer any shadow of excuse for misunderstanding him.

Once the Saar territory had been safely gathered in, Hitler moved further into the open. In March he announced that he was reintroducing conscription in flagrant defiance of Versailles and was bringing the army up to a total of 550,000, which was twice what he had previously declared to be Germany's maximum need. This did bring together Britain, France, and Italy into anxious conference at Stresa in April and produce the so-called Stresa Front. The three powers put forward a resolution to the Council of the League that Germany had 'failed in the obligation lying on all members of the international community to respect the undertakings they have contracted'. But Germany was no longer a member of the League, and the Stresa Front was in reality nothing but a façade. A frontier incident at Wal Wal had given Mussolini the excuse he needed for an attack on Abyssinia, and he was already concentrating troops and supplies for the purpose. Faction and intrigue had almost brought effective government in France to a standstill; and in England the pacifist tide was only reaching its climax. The League of Nations' Union had just launched its great Peace Ballot; and the results were to be announced in the Albert Hall on the 27th of June.

The Union had canvassed some 12 million people with five very carefully worded questions. Over 11 million had voted for Britain to stay in the League, and nearly 11 million for the, by then unattainable ideal of 'an all-round reduction of armaments by international agreement'. Very slightly smaller majorities were obtained for the abolition of nationally controlled military and naval aircraft, and for an international agreement prohibiting the manufacture and sale of arms for private profit. In fact it was only with the fifth question that the questionnaire touched reality at all. 'Do you consider', it ran, 'that, if a nation insists on attacking another, the other nations should combine to stop it by: (*a*) Economic and non-military measures? (*b*) If necessary, military measures?' It was this which most clearly revealed the muddle into which the country had been thrown by the casuistry of the Opposition leaders after Manchuria and the over-enthusiasm of the League of Nations' Union. For, while economic sanctions polled the usual 10 million votes, military sanctions were only advocated by just under 7 million. On this last issue 2,364,441 abstained, and 2,351,981 actually voted against. Thus the confusion created by the Japanese adventure in Manchuria was perpetuated to operate ruinously during the Abyssinian crisis; and Mr. Baldwin's reluctance to take decisive action in the teeth of so clearly declared a public opinion was confirmed, and prolonged.

Baldwin's pronouncements so far, though they carried the government's full support, had been made as Lord President of the Council. Ramsay MacDonald, in spite of his failing sight and dwindling vitality, still carried responsibility for policy and for a government which, both in the Cabinet and in the House of Commons, was overwhelmingly Conservative. Events had thus manœuvred Baldwin perilously near that of the Press Lords who had tried to dictate his policy to him in 1931. He had denounced them then, in a biting phrase, as men who were aiming at 'power without responsibility, the prerogative of the harlot throughout the ages'.[1] But this was precisely what was in danger of happening to him. He himself, like his nominal leader, was certainly a tiring man. He had never had much of the restless energy of a Churchill or a Chamberlain, and his occasional bursts of devastating activity had nearly always been followed by dangerous periods of languour in which he let events take their course with an almost oriental fatalism. 'Half the mistakes from 1918 on have been the work of tired men,' he had written to MacDonald in 1932, when the withdrawal of Samuel and his colleagues from the National Government threatened to interrupt the ritual of his holiday at Aix-les-Bains.[2] Yet for three years after that he maintained in office a leader whose exhaustion was apparent to the whole world. 'I am more and more carrying this government on my back,' Chamberlain wrote in his diary in March, 1935. 'The P.M. is ill and tired, S.B. is tired and won't apply his mind to problems.'[3] Yet when, at the beginning of June, MacDonald at last withdrew, via the office of Lord President, into the lonely obscurity of retirement it was the scarcely less exhausted Baldwin who took over from him.

In the sphere of home affairs this did not much matter. The enor-

---

[1] See, *inter alia*, G. M. Young, *op. cit.*, p. 162.
[2] *Ib.*, p. 172.   [3] Feiling, *op. cit.*, p. 242.

The End of the Baldwin-MacDonald Régime

mous, kindly tolerance of Baldwin—his determination to see both sides
of every question and, if possible, the best of both sides—were still
great assets. It was his greatest quality that he could take the sting out
of political controversy with a sort of sedative wisdom. It had been invaluable in ensuring the peaceful, orderly progress towards social justice
which, behind all the crises, had in fact been going on for fifteen years,
and was still going on in 1935, in spite of those who shouted that it was
too slow and the clamour of the die-hards who walked in fear of revolution. But foreign affairs had always bored and irritated him. He could
understand the unreasonableness of Englishmen, whether they were
employers or workers, and convince them that he understood. The
unreasonableness of foreigners was a sealed book to him, and he
lacked the machinery to get on terms with them. But by 1933 the international situation had reached a point where there was no longer a
possibility of finding a solution by compromise. Inadequate and in-
accurate though the available information about German armaments
seems to have been, Baldwin's own subsequent statements make it clear
that he knew enough to make it, to his mind, essential for Britain to
rearm. Whether it spoke through the League or harked back to the
traditional method of alliances, the Foreign Office could do nothing for
peace if it spoke from a position of total weakness. On the other hand
there was East Fulham and the declared determination of the British
electorate not to get involved in anything which could conceivably be
described as an armaments race.

Three years later, on November 12th, 1936, in a speech which has
since been subjected to much gross misrepresentation, Baldwin explained the 1933 situation clearly enough:

> I put before the House my own views with appalling frankness.
> From 1933 I and my friends were all very worried about what was
> happening in Europe. You will remember at that time the Disarm-
> ament Conference was sitting at Geneva. You will remember at
> that time there was probably a stronger pacifist feeling running
> through this country than at any time since the war. I am speaking
> of 1933 and 1934. You will remember the election at Fulham, in the
> autumn of 1933, when a seat which the National Government held
> was lost by about 7,000 votes on no issue but the pacifist. You will
> remember perhaps that the National Government candidate who
> made a most guarded reference to defence was mobbed for it.

232

That was the feeling in the country in 1933. My position as a leader of a great party was not altogether a comfortable one. I asked myself what chance was there—when that feeling which was given expression at Fulham was common throughout the country— what chance was there within the next year or two of that feeling being so changed that the country would give a mandate for re-armament. Supposing I had gone to the country and said that Germany was rearming and that we must rearm, does anybody think that this pacific democracy would have rallied to that cry at that moment? I cannot think of anything that would have made the loss of the election from my point of view more certain.[1]

The gist of that was clear enough. He did not feel justified in rearming there and then as, in view of his huge majority, he undoubtedly could, without a mandate from the electors. He was convinced that an election on the armament issue would put into power the Opposition leaders who would probably plunge the country into war, but would first strip it of the means of conducting one. Therefore he waited quietly for a turn in the tide of public opinion. He remarked on a different occasion that in matters of armament a democracy will always be two years behind the dictatorships; and he was thus far right, that he was able to seize such a tide in the autumn of 1935 and, in his own words, to get 'from the country—with a large majority—a mandate for doing a thing that no one, twelve months before, would have believed possible'.

The accusations which have been levelled at him, based universally on statements from the 1936 speech lifted from their context, that in 1935 he deliberately misled the British people on the strength of German rearmament and of the necessary scale of British rearmament, in order to ensure his own election, may be dismissed as calumnies. His remarks applied throughout to a hypothetical election in 1933. But, even accepting that, it is difficult to excuse him for not putting the issue at once to the electors, instead of leaving the vociferous pacifist case unanswered, save by the lonely voice of Mr. Churchill, whose facts and figures commanded little attention in the face of bland denials of ministers who might be presumed to be better informed. The obituary leading article in *The Times* in 1947 summed up the real case against Baldwin in 1933 very fairly:

[1] R. Bassett, *Telling the Truth to the People, The Myth of the Baldwin Confession, Cambridge Journal*, Vol. II, p. 84.

Democratic leadership demanded that he should go to the country with a frank acknowledgement of the dangers, challenging its illusions with inconvenient truth, and risking defeat. But he hesitated to take a course that might place the control of national policy in the hands of men who, in his view, were more likely to accelerate than retard the onset of war. He made the worst of two worlds. What he sacrificed to political expediency obscured the real issue, delayed the education of public opinion, and impeded the process of rearmament, on the speed of which the success of any conceivable foreign policy then depended.

It is, perhaps, in this context significant that Baldwin's favourite book, which he read and reread, was F. S. Oliver's *Endless Adventure*; and he may in 1933 have let himself be over-influenced by that passage in the chapter on Politics and Morals in which Oliver lays it down that 'the prime motive of the politician is not to do good to humanity, or even to his country, but simply to gain power for himself'.[1] But even Oliver goes on to insist that the ultimate judgement on a politician must be based on the use he makes of power when he has got it. Between 1933 and 1935 Baldwin had great power and made scarcely any use of it at all. If he and his friends were really as worried as he said they had been in 1933, it becomes hard to justify the reassuring reply he gave to Churchill's attack on the very modest Air Estimates in March, 1934:

> If all our efforts for agreement fail, and if it is not possible to obtain this equality in such matters as I have indicated, then any government of this country—a National Government more than any, and *this* government—will see to it that in air strength and air power this country shall no longer be in a position inferior to any country within striking distance of its shores.[2]

Even as late as October, 1935, on the eve of the election which was to give him the authority he knew he had been needing for two years, he still spoke reassuringly. 'I give you my word', he told the Peace Society, 'that there will be no great armaments.'[3] It was a promise which was to be all too faithfully kept.

Moreover, even before the election, there was begun that dangerous process of trying to shore up a situation of weakness by worthless agree-

---

[1] Oliver, *The Endless Adventure*, Vol. I, p. 17.
[2] Churchill, *op. cit.*, Vol. I, p. 89.
[3] Templewood in *Nine Troubled Years*, p. 195, strongly confirms both Baldwin's exhaustion and his unease in dealing with foreign affairs and foreigners.

ments with statesmen who had already proved clearly that they did not regard inconvenient promises as being in any way binding. It so happened that the terms of the Anglo-German Naval Treaty, limiting the Germans to 35% of the British tonnage, and signed in June, 1935, were observed by both parties down to the outbreak of war. But such a treaty was only necessitated by the unilateral denunciation of equally solemn earlier agreements; and as Sir Samuel Hoare, who negotiated it, himself admits, Hitler only forced his Admirals to respect it because he believed right up to the actual outbreak of war that, if he gave Britain a free hand on the seas and outside Europe, she would connive at his own plans for expansion on the Continent. Hoare argued none the less that his treaty had effectively limited a German expansion which would have taken place anyway, and bitterly reproached the French politicians for a policy of drift which had 'stopped agreements which would have restricted the German army to 300,000 men and the Luftwaffe to 300 first-line machines'.[1] It is inconceivable that Hitler, had he signed any such agreements, would have paid the slightest attention to them. Whereas the democratic statesmen, by persuading people that the paper promises of the dictators represented solid guarantees for the future, lulled them into a false sense of security and weakened the force of their own demand for an urgent policy of rearmament.

Hoare was new to the Foreign Office, having been transferred there from the Admiralty in the Cabinet reshuffle which followed MacDonald's resignation; and he, too, was unfortunately a very tired man after long years of strain at the India Office piloting through the enormous Government of India Bill. He was given Eden as a sort of assistant with a defined responsibility for League affairs. But even so the complicated responsibilities which were immediately thrust upon him were far more than an unfit man could possibly be expected to shoulder successfully. For no sooner had the naval treaty been rushed through than he found himself plunged into the long-expected crisis over Abyssinia.

The Covenant of the League of Nations had debarred from membership all territories 'inhabited by peoples not yet able to stand by themselves under the strenuous conditions of the modern world'; and it should have been clear to everybody in 1923 that Abyssinia fell well

[1] *Nine Troubled Years,* p. 145.

within that category. The authority of the Emperor, Haile Selassie, extended precariously only over those districts inhabited by his own Amharic tribesmen and scarcely at all into the recently conquered borderland tracts where powerful local chieftains or nomadic Somali tribes pursued an existence unchanged for centuries. There were scarcely the rudiments of a modern state, the slave trade flourished, and along the ill-defined frontiers there were incessant troubles over slave raiders and disputed wells and grazing lands. 'No one', said Churchill, when it was too late and the war had already begun, 'can keep up the pretence that Abyssinia is a fit, worthy and equal member of a league of civilised nations.' Nevertheless, she had been elected to the League in 1923, largely at the instance of the French who wished to forestall an Italian protectorate, and it was too late to argue about that when the crisis had actually come in 1935.

In a series of agreements stretching from 1906 to 1925 both the French and British had conceded large Italian claims to a special position in the development and exploitation of Abyssinia, and Italy had long regarded herself as entitled to pursue in that territory the same sort of policy as had involved Britain, fifty years earlier, in the virtual, if temporary annexation of Egypt and the Sudan. Mussolini had never regarded the election to the League as any bar to the extension of Italian influence, and a number of forces were now at work pushing him towards more speedy and dramatic action. There was the long-standing disgrace of the Italian defeat and massacre at Adowa in 1895 still to be avenged, and few more suitable objectives could be found for the showy, brittle military power which Fascism had been steadily building for the past ten years. There was a real need for raw materials and for territory sufficiently fertile to be colonised by the growing surplus of Italian population which her industry could not absorb and which was now denied its safety-valve of emigration to America. There were genuine grievances against the failure of the Abyssinian government to control its frontier tribes and so create conditions in which Italian trade could profitably expand. Above all, there was the prestige need for a spectacular triumph to justify the regimentation of the nation and the grandiose claims of a revived Roman imperialism.

There were also many reasons which made the winter of 1935–6 a particularly suitable moment for Italy to strike. M. Laval was working hard to lead the French government along his own appeasement line, and a solid understanding with Italy was a key element in his policy. He reckoned that the Anglo-German Naval Treaty, concluded by Britain in her own interests without consulting her Stresa allies, had set them free to make their own arrangements for security. With his Alpine frontier safe and a friendly Mussolini standing on the Brenner and securing the loyalty and independence of Austria, he hoped to be able to present a strong enough front on the Rhine to force Hitler to a settlement in the west and divert his expansionist ambitions eastwards, if necessary by the sacrifice of the Polish and Hungarian alliances of the Little Entente. For all this a promise to Mussolini of a free hand in Africa was a trivial price to pay. When Eden went out to Rome at the end of June in a last effort to bring Italy back into the field of negotiation he found Mussolini inflexible beyond the reach of any argument: secure in the knowledge that France would not interfere, contemptuous of any possible action by the League, and sceptical of any British intention to intervene so long as the interests of Egypt and the Sudan in the head waters of the Nile at Lake Tsana were safeguarded. Eden's offer to try to induce Abyssinia to make large cessions of territory to Italy in return for an outlet to the sea through British Somaliland interested him not at all. It also produced, when it was disclosed by an accidental indiscretion to the London press, an outburst from the right wing at any cession of British territory and simultaneous protests from the left at concessions to violence and threats at the expense of a fellow member of the League.

Deprived of the most obvious and certain way of stopping Italy by joint firm action with France, desperately anxious to preserve the Stresa Front as the only possible cover for British rearmament, the government was forced to fall back with the greatest reluctance on action through the League. For the attitude of Conservatives and of members of the government to the League and the question of sanctions was as muddled and dishonest as that of the Opposition. With the possible exception of Eden, not one member of the Cabinet believed that economic sanctions could be effective in deterring any but the smaller powers. Applied against a great power they must almost inevitably provoke hostilities if they threatened to be effective; and Conservative opinion was deeply averse from placing the armed forces of Great

Britain at the disposal of Geneva. If the collective responsibility and collective action so feelingly advocated by Hoare and his colleagues were to involve military sanctions, it was perfectly obvious that the brunt of League action would fall on one, or at the most two of the great powers. But to that they would vigorously object as being a wanton sacrifice of British lives and treasure in other people's quarrels. Thus in the end the National government faced the electors in November of 1935 with slogans which concealed the same basic dishonesty as that of the Opposition. Both made it clear that in no circumstances would they fight. Chamberlain's insistence to the voters of Edgbaston that the League had been founded to prevent war and not to spread it, and that there must be no military sanctions, was almost word for word what Lansbury and Cripps had said at the time of the Manchurian crisis.

Chamberlain had persuaded Baldwin that rearmament and not unemployment must be made the main issue of the election; and the electorate, faced with the indistinguishable slogans of both sides promising to uphold the Covenant, had to decide on the defence issue alone. In spite of Attlee's gibes at war-mongers and scare-mongers and of posters depicting babies in gas masks, the nation showed clearly that the wave of pacifist hysteria was passing. People were beginning to realise that even 'upholding the Covenant' might involve the use, or at least the threat of force. So, though Labour gained 95 seats and returned with 154 members, there were 385 Conservatives. Baldwin got his mandate, and it was essentially a Conservative government which carried responsibility for the next four years. National Labour and National Liberalism were dropping out of existence as the crisis which had called them into being receded into history, though both were still represented in the Cabinet by Simon and Thomas. But by the time the new government was safely in the saddle the Abyssinian crisis had reached the point where the degrading consequences of muddled thinking about the League could no longer be avoided.

So far all the comfort Haile Selassie had got by appealing to the League was a ban on the export of arms to both disputants which, as in the case of China, told only against the unarmed victim of aggression. Then, on September 12th, Hoare brought his government out into the open with a clarity which most of them were to find embarrassing in a speech to the League Assembly at Geneva. Though he strongly emphasised that responsibility must be genuinely collective and that all must act together, the phrase which caught the world's attention and which hit the headlines was that in which he pledged his government unconditionally to the collective maintenance of the Covenant in its entirety, and particularly to 'steady and collective resistance to all acts of unprovoked aggression'.[1] Laval covered himself with a more careful phrase, that France's obligations were 'inscribed in the Covenant', and that she would 'not evade them'. There were, after all, plenty of let-out clauses in Article XVI.

From then on events moved irresistibly forward in such a way as to do the maximum harm to all the various schemes the lovers of peace were nursing for halting the threatened aggressions of Germany, Italy, and Japan. A League Committee of Five produced with commendable speed a solution which should have satisfied everybody. League advisers, under supervision from Geneva, were to take over direction of Finance, Justice, Education, and Public Health in Abyssinia. A special gendarmerie was to be formed to suppress slavery once and for all, and there was to be financial assistance on a large scale for economic development. Territorial adjustments were to be made in favour of Italy, offset by cessions of territory and a port in Somaliland or Eritrea, and the special interest of Italy in the economic development of Ethiopia was handsomely acknowledged. Haile Selassie accepted what amounted to a League mandate; and there is evidence that the Fascist Grand Council would gladly have accepted too. But Mussolini wanted a more spectacular triumph. He had in his pocket the assurance that France would never countenance military sanctions. He did not believe that Britain would risk war without France; and he thought all the talk at Geneva a gigantic bluff. On October 3rd he invaded Abyssinia, using every ruthless expedient of modern warfare, including poison gas, to force a quick decision, and so brought all concerned face to face with the problem of what they meant by 'resistance to unprovoked aggression'.

Still under French and British leadership, the League reacted correctly enough. Italy was pronounced an aggressor and all export of war materials to her was forbidden. But oil was not included in the list of banned commodities, in the hope that France and Britain might still be

[1] This is the version as given in his own book, on p. 170.

able to negotiate a compromise; and oil was the crux of the whole matter. Mussolini could complete the conquest of Abyssinia and present the world with a *fait accompli* if all his foreign trade were cut off except the import of oil. On the one hand there was the fact that Mussolini had bluntly announced that he would treat an embargo on oil as an act of war, which brusquely demolished the illusion that economic sanctions would by themselves be so effective that military sanctions would never be needed. On the other there were the very tricky considerations that it would be difficult to ban the oil experts of the United States, who had already shipped twice as much to Italy as in any previous year; that France would not fight, nor even allow the use of her bases at Toulon and Bizerta; that to close the Suez Canal, which would also be instantly effective, would similarly inflame American public opinion; that Malta, without effective anti-aircraft protection, was an unsafe base for the fleet; and that if Britain alone had to bear the brunt she would be powerless to take action if a crisis threatened elsewhere—in the Rhineland or at Hong Kong.

In this jungle of dangers, possibilities and perplexities, the British government lost its nerve. Baldwin had all along stood for peace at any price, and he was haunted by the thought of Walpole's ruin, at the end of a long, brilliantly successful administration, because he let himself be stampeded into war against his better judgement. Hoare's health was failing and he was suffering from periodical fainting fits. Eden almost certainly would have stood by the League and followed the implications of its actions to their logical conclusion, but was too young and inexperienced to dissociate himself from colleagues so formidably senior. Chamberlain, surprisingly in view of later events, held out longest against moral collapse. In the Cabinet at the end of November he was still arguing that 'in the last resort, if necessary, we ought to give the lead ourselves, rather than let the question go by default': that the United States had already come half-way to meet us, and if we backed down at that point their government would be left at the mercy of their own oil firms.[1] But at the end of his argument he showed that he, too, was preoccupied in the last analysis with lines of retreat. For he suggested that if an oil embargo brought down an Italian attack, and Laval even then refused to come to Britain's aid, we could finally 'make it

[1] Diary, November 29th, 1935, quoted Feiling, p. 272.

clear at Geneva that France, and not we, were blocking oil sanctions'. There were in that sentence the germs of the failure to realise that if Britain failed, by action that was at least nominally collective, to halt an aggressor in circumstances in which it was perfectly possible to do so, she doomed herself eventually to a life-and-death struggle. The entry in Chamberlain's diary for December 8th, when Hoare was already in Paris negotiating with Laval, shows that he had made the right appreciation, if only he and his colleagues could summon up the nerve to apply it in action:

> By putting his great army the other side the Suez Canal, Mussolini has tied a noose round his own neck, and left the end hanging out for anyone with a Navy to pull. It would seem incredible that in such a position he should venture to attack us, and in the end I don't believe he would. . . . If only our defences were stronger, I should feel so much happier, but though we are working night and day, they aren't what I should like.

In the upshot Britain, and all those who were working for peace achieved the worst of all the possible worlds. Hoare, ordered to Switzerland for his health, stopped off at Paris with full Cabinet approval for a last attempt to find terms of compromise which would avoid facing the ultimate issues of oil and Suez and which the French would be prepared to back. Thus emerged the notorious Hoare-Laval Pact, which would have offered, subject to confirmation by the League, very much better terms for Italy than those of the Committee of Five. In the words, even, of a notable Tory apologist, 'they much affronted Article XVI by giving a rich reward to aggression'.[1] Hoare undoubtedly believed that he had found a solution basically acceptable to his colleagues, to the League, and to the Italians; and he went peacefully on to his skating holiday, incurring thereby an additional and undeserved humiliation by falling in a final blackout and breaking his nose. Unexpectedly enough his hopes were disappointed by one of those rare, unpredictable, and almost irresistible upheavals of British public opinion against which no government can prevail, however great its parliamentary majority. The public at large, the press, and even the younger Conservative M.P.s, could see only one simple fact: that the two governments were conspiring to sell the Abyssinians down the drain. How

[1] Feiling, p. 273.

many of those who refused point-blank to accept such a solution were prepared to face the only alternative which would save Abyssinia—a virtually single-handed war against Italy—can now never be known. Certainly Sir William Fisher, the commanding Admiral in the Mediterranean, was one. Whatever the deficiencies of the Malta base, he was, in Hoare's own words, 'rightly confident that he could drive the Italian fleet from the sea'.[1] Nor can anyone ever know what unified action the lesser powers at Geneva might have been shamed into by so decisive a lead from Britain as an open war against Italy on behalf of the Covenant, though the effect on the Americans might have been remarkable.

For in practice the Cabinet, though after some hesitation it bowed to the storm, repudiated the Pact, and threw Hoare overboard as the scapegoat for views and intentions which his colleagues had shared to the full, did not proceed to any heroic action. Hoare's Pact would have saved some shreds of honour and might just conceivably have achieved his overriding aim of keeping Mussolini out of Hitler's arms. The Cabinet did neither. There was no more talk of oil. Ineffectual sanctions, for which Italy held Britain to blame, inflamed Italian hostility without hampering the Italian war effort. The League, turning a deaf ear to repeated appeals from the Abyssinian Emperor, signed its own death warrant and read the funeral service over the Covenant in June, 1936, when Britain formally proposed the cancellations of sanctions—'the very midsummer of madness', Chamberlain called them. A month before that the Italians had entered Addis Ababa and the war was over. King Victor Emmanuel was proclaimed Emperor of Abyssinia, and Mussolini was left triumphing over the white flag which had been 'hoisted in the ranks of world-sanctionists'. What differentiated the Abyssinian crisis from the Manchurian was that in its case sanctions, properly applied, whether they led to war or not, would have been effective in foiling an aggressor. Hoare himself has admitted that Britain alone could 'of course have easily defeated Italy'.[2] The risks, made so much of since by apologists, were not very formidable. Hitler, still only half armed and half equipped, could have done little to exploit the situation; and Britain had long since made it clear that she did not intend to deploy

[1] Templewood, *Nine Troubled Years*, p. 191.
[2] *Ib.* Clearly neither Hoare nor Chamberlain saw the Admiralty memorandum, to which Mr. Taylor refers, stating that we could not single-handed defeat the Italian fleet.

any great naval strength in the Pacific to frustrate Japan's ambitions.

It is, indeed, difficult to see what greater advantage Hitler could have snatched from a Mediterranean war than he successfully snatched from its avoidance. On March 7th, 1936, he informed the powers that his troops were already marching into the demilitarised Rhineland. His generals had advised against it, and a mere parade of force by France and Britain would have turned him out again. The French generals demanded mobilisation, rightly believing that that would suffice. But their politicians, in their usual state of confusion, would not move without British support; and Britain, defeated and disillusioned, scarcely paid attention. So one more asset, which would have been of incalculable military value in saving France's allies in Central and Eastern Europe a year or two later, was thrown away. To the mild French suggestion that the issue might be referred to the Hague Court for arbitration Hitler scornfully retorted: 'Germany has no intention of being dragged into any international court, for no such court has the responsibility towards the German people that I have.' As for Locarno, he regarded that as a dead letter since the French had signed a pact for mutual defence with Russia, and so re-created the threat of 'encirclement'. British public opinion acquiesced in a rectification of an out-of-date clause in the Versailles Treaty and a reassertion of valid sovereign rights by Germany; and the German engineers set about constructing the West Wall—the so-called Siegfried Line—behind which international adventures further east could be conducted with impunity.

Baldwin's only answer to Hitler's Rhineland coup was to appoint Sir Thomas Inskip, an able and worthy, but very wordy lawyer, wholly without qualifications for the job, as Minister for the Co-ordination of Defence; and since his first pronouncement in his new capacity declared that he regarded it as no part of his business to interfere with the activities of the service chiefs, the general picture of British unpreparedness was not materially altered. More effective in waking the country from its lethargic belief that another European war was something which simply could not happen, was Hitler's bland assurance to Eden and Halifax, when they visited Berlin at the end of March to try to snatch something from the ruins of Locarno, that he had now achieved air parity with Britain. It may well not have been strictly true. But, if not, it was clear that it very soon would be, and Baldwin was forced at last to admit that Churchill had all along been right. He claimed, probably correctly, that he had not misled the country on the actual figures of front-line aircraft in the previous November, but admitted that the Cabinet must accept responsibility for having totally misjudged the pace of German rearmament.

Yet there was still no urgency in the response either of the government or the people in Britain. During these years ministers such as Chamberlain and Hoare were constantly to justify the feebleness of foreign policy and the abject surrenders to force which followed one another in dreary succession by the impossibility of effective diplomacy with no force behind it. But they themselves were criminally slow and half-hearted in the steps they took to remedy their own weakness. In the financial year of 1935–6, the year in which Mussolini overran Abyssinia and Hitler reoccupied the Rhineland, the British government spent on the defence services only £186 million—less than a fifth of the estimated German military expenditure that year. In February, 1937, the government took powers to borrow £400 million for defence and issued a warning that this figure might rise to £1,500 million. But this was to be spread over five years, and Chamberlain's 1937 budget only increased defence estimates to £198 million, so that he was still spending less than half the German sum. The Defence White Paper of March, 1936, had provided for the modernisation of the Army's equipment and a modest addition of four new battalions to its strength. The Navy was to get two new battleships and an aircraft-carrier, and the cruiser strength was to be raised from 51 to 70. The Air programme was expanded so as to aim at a total of 1,750 planes for home defence, while twelve new Squadrons were allocated to imperial defences elsewhere.

But this did not mean that Britain was recovering any ground. She was actually losing it still for at least two years after the critical state of affairs had been exposed and admitted. Even as late as the year 1938–9 the first-line aircraft available for home defence increased by only 124, while the German total rose by 742; and up to the actual outbreak of war German expenditure increased more each year than the British. It was of course true that, while we were being quantitatively outpaced in the vital sphere of the air, we were establishing a qualitative advantage which was to save the nation in the Battle of Britain. The defenders of the methods of British rearmament are entitled to point to the Spitfires and Hurricanes which outpaced their German opponents as to some extent the result of a slower and more cautious start. But a complacency about our own rearmament and a blindness to the scope and pace of German progress continued to mark the attitude of the British government even after the outbreak of war.

So the Baldwin-MacDonald régime limped sadly towards its end amidst failure and loss of confidence. On January 20th, 1936, King George's failing health at last suddenly gave way, and the nation listened, with a grief which was spontaneous and genuine and almost universal, to Lord Dawson's last bulletin, given out at intervals by the B.B.C., that 'the King's life is moving peacefully towards its close'. In spite of his long, almost fatal illness of 1928-9, George V had retained to the end a remarkable vigour and clarity of mind. But his last months had been clouded by anxiety and fears for the future. 'I am an old man,' he said to Hoare with a rather charming egotism at the time of the Abyssinian dispute. 'I have been through one world war. How can I go through another? If I am to go on you must keep us out of another one.'[1] Baldwin was ageing too, and extremely tired and ill. The personal humiliation he had suffered when he threw Hoare over did damage both to his prestige and self-esteem from which neither wholly recovered. He sat now, a huddled, miserable figure on the Treasury bench, under heavy fire from Churchill and Amery, Boothby and Lloyd George, with little to reply save for confessions and apologies.

But, after a wretched summer of international troubles, during which Chamberlain alone managed to instil some energy into the government's plans, Baldwin was to pull out one last effort and render the nation one last service. He had hung on to office largely in order to see the new King into the saddle. In the event he was compelled to stage-manage his abdication; and he did it with brilliant skill. Edward VIII had earned as Prince of Wales a popularity not only in Britain, but throughout the Empire, which verged on adulation. Though he was now 41, the fact that he was still unmarried, slim and remarkably youthful in appearance, preserved about him the Prince Charming atmosphere of his younger days, and no King ever shouldered his burdens with more universal goodwill. There were older and stuffier folk who shook their heads over innovations in Court routine and still more over the

[1] Templewood, *op. cit.*, p. 159.

type of person he chose for his personal friends; and there were elder statesmen who saw dangerous signs of Crown interference in politics when he said emphatically and publicly what he thought of the conditions he found among the unemployed of South Wales. The overwhelming majority welcomed a King who spoke with the voice of the present rather than the past and were prepared to tolerate even the rather raffish company he sometimes kept as an inevitable result of a modernisation of the Monarchy which, like everything else, must move with the times.

But the King's entanglement with a Mrs. Wallis Simpson, already once divorced, and preparing that autumn to divorce her second husband, was moving too fast with the times for the bulk of a very conservative public opinion. Throughout the summer the affair remained only a scandal in high society, much commented upon in the American press but, by a strangely well-kept self-denying ordinance, unmentioned in the English papers. With the opening of the divorce suit at Ipswich in October it became a constitutional crisis. Baldwin, whose inaction and procrastination had been such damaging factors in great affairs for the past year, suddenly braced himself to deal with a situation which, if allowed to drift, might do irreparable harm to the Monarchy and the Empire. It is clear from the long self-justification which he published in 1951,[1] that King Edward himself had little inkling of the probable impact of his plans. Whether he was fully informed of what was going on in the American press he does not say: of the headlines 'Edward Will Marry Wally', and of what one of the more sober letters to *The Times* from America described as 'unsavoury gobbets of news about the King and Mrs. Simpson', which in recent weeks had become 'a perfect avalanche of muck and slime'.[2] He seems to have treated Baldwin's first intervention, which was simply a request that the divorce proceedings might be dropped, as a mild impertinence; and he professed himself 'shocked and angry' when his Private Secretary, Sir Alexander Hardinge, wrote painfully and formally to inform him that the London papers could not be kept quiet much longer; that if the King persisted in his intention to marry Mrs. Simpson the government would probably resign and that there was reason to suppose that it would not be possible

[1] *A King's Story*, by H. R. H. the Duke of Windsor.
[2] Quoted in full in Evelyn Wrench, *Geoffrey Dawson and our Times*, p. 339.

to form an alternative one; and that the only possible salvation of the situation was for Mrs. Simpson to go abroad at once.

Fortunately Baldwin was able to get the issue all but settled before the press control broke, on December 2nd. The King had made it clear that he would marry at all costs, and that if that could not be done constitutionally, he was 'prepared to go'. Baldwin, equally, had established that the Cabinet would resign if there were any question of Mrs. Simpson as Queen, and that the Opposition leaders concurred in this. The King's last hope was that the Cabinet and the Dominions' governments would introduce legislation to make possible a morganatic marriage; and the answers from the Dominions, all unfavourable, were coming in when the scandal broke, touched off by some passing remarks in a Diocesan Address by the Bishop of Bradford who, as a matter of fact, had not heard about Mrs. Simpson at all, and merely expressed the hope that the King might 'give more positive signs of his awareness' of the need for God's Grace at his coronation.

Undoubtedly the King had expected his enormous personal popularity to carry the day in the teeth of Archbishops and Prime Minister, newspaper editors and Cabinet; and it is much to his credit that, in the last hectic week of his reign, he made no attempt to divide the country or to encourage the formation of a King's Party—an idea which captivated, among others, Sir Oswald Mosley, Lord Beaverbrook, and Mr. Churchill. During that week opinion in the country hardened against the King's project: it was noticeable that the attitude of the rank and file in the House of Commons stiffened considerably after a week-end among their constituents. On December 10th Baldwin formally communicated the King's decision to abdicate to the Commons, following up with one of the most masterly speeches of his career—an unrhetorical, conversational account of the whole development of the crisis, insisting that the King could not have behaved better, 'deeply regretting' that he had rejected the Cabinet's last-minute appeal to reconsider, and calling on the House and nation to rally to the new King.

Thus in the end Great Britain and its Monarchy emerged from a grave situation not with diminished, but with enhanced prestige. King George VI and his Queen slipped with miraculous ease into the position in which his father and mother had served so well, and soon found themselves well-loved and esteemed. Their coronation on May 12th,

1937, the last grand parade of the old order, drew the Commonwealth together in a real consciousness, as *The Times* put it, of 'a great Imperial and dynastic success'. It was also very widely seen as a personal triumph for Mr. Baldwin, who drew nearly as many cheers as the royal couple: a last personal tribute in a career of many vicissitudes. On May 28th he resigned, handing over to Neville Chamberlain, and in due course withdrawing to the House of Lords as Earl Baldwin of Bewdley. Ramsay MacDonald faded from the scene at the same moment; and with them went, in effect, the last of the post-war world, to the story of which the doings of Chamberlain's government down to its fall in 1940 form but an appendix.

CHAPTER 12

The Suicide of the Old World

Neither MacDonald nor Baldwin has so far received fair justice
at the hands of historians; and the failures, political and
social, of the era to which Churchill gave their name have
largely obscured its successes. The wave of admiration and gratitude for
MacDonald's courage and self-sacrifice in 1931 ebbed quickly, and he
died a lonely, broken man, ostracised by the friends and political associates of a lifetime and largely forgotten by the nation as a whole. His
enemies and detractors survived to write their versions of his story, and
it is only in recent years that historians have been able to modify and
correct their less balanced judgements. Baldwin's last years, immediately before and during the war, were poisoned by a stream of vilely
abusive letters and speeches accusing him of having deliberately de-
ceived the electors over German armaments to keep himself in power
and holding him directly responsible for the destructive air raids of
1940. The political and social achievements of the various governments
of these two men, measured by the impossible standards of the idealistic
daydreams of 1918, seemed meagre and trivial, and have since been
quite overshadowed by the spectacular advances made in the years
after 1945. That the unity, stamina, and moral courage of the nation
which stood firm behind Churchill in 1940 were largely their creation
has got forgotten.

In all the vital aspects of national life, where health and wealth and
social security were concerned, the picture presented by the Britain of
1938 was a mixed one, upon which judgements vary directly in accordance with the political outlook of the commentator. One contemporary
summed it up fairly enough when he wrote, in 1938, that 'compared

with what they were at the turn of the century, our social services are a miracle of collective care and collective kindness. Compared with what they might well be, they are in some respects paltry and mean.'[1] The more complacent type of Tory like Neville Chamberlain could point proudly to the rise of 12% in the average real value of wages since 1924; to the rising consumption of all the staple foods except flour, which for most of them had gone up by 50% since 1914; and to the housing programmes which had produced nearly 4½ million new dwellings in Great Britain since the war, so that there were now more houses than families, and most local authorities were within striking distance of clearing the last of their slums. Of the men medically examined for military service in 1940 twice as many were placed in the fittest class as in 1918. The death-rate from tuberculosis had dropped to little over half the 1922 rate, and even the figures for infant mortality, which had risen to an alarming peak in the 1931 depression, showed signs of improvement. An Act of 1938 went far to establish a week's holiday with pay as the standard industrial practice, and holiday homes and camps were appearing all round the coast to meet what was to be a rapidly growing demand. Butlin opened his first one at Skegness in 1937; and another, long overdue Act of Parliament had provided for the school-leaving age to be raised to 15 in 1939, though this belated good intention was frustrated by the outbreak of war.[2]

There was also some encouragement to be drawn from the steady rise in luxury spending, at any rate among those who were fortunate enough to be in full employment. The cinemas absorbed some £40 million a year of the nation's spare cash and contributed £7 million a year to the government in Entertainment Tax. Women were using some 1,300 tons of powder and rouge and 1,600 tons of face cream—about 1½ million pounds' worth—every year. There were £30 million annually available for investment in football pools. Eight out of ten men and four women in ten were smokers, and they spent £160 million a year on tobacco; and though the consumption of beer had dropped by half since 1900 and that of spirits by four-fifths, thanks to heavily

---

[1] John Hilton, *Rich Man, Poor Man*, from whom most of the statistics in the following passages are drawn.
[2] A very full analysis of the work of a large number of statisticians and economists who have investigated social conditions of this period is to be found in Mowat, *Britain Between the Wars*, Chapter 9.

increased taxation, £250 million—£5 a year per head of the population
—was still being spent on drink.[1]

But, as the more thoughtful writers of the time were beginning to
point out, it is unwise to draw too optimistic a conclusion from this
heavy spending on luxuries. If pawnbrokers had lost a third of their
business, the hire-purchase companies had taken their place, and the
bulk of the population was living on credit. By 1938 the total of instalment credit granted by shopkeepers and financing firms was £50 million
—twenty times what it had been in 1918—and about two-thirds of all
the manufactured goods sold in Britain were the subject of hire-purchase agreements. Moreover, families on or below the poverty line will
always tend to economise on necessities and will fight to the last to
preserve the few small comforts and luxuries which alone make the drab
struggle with want and unemployment tolerable.[2] And, in spite of all the
efforts and the undoubted progress made in the twenties and thirties, it
was still a dismal truth in 1938 that one-third of all the families in
Britain lived below that poverty line and another third scarcely above
it. In the areas of concentrated unemployment, in Durham and South
Wales and parts of South Yorkshire and Lancashire, and in London's
overcrowded East End, the bulk of the population was still under-
nourished, badly housed, and very ill-provided for in sickness and old
age. Contemporary statistics are incomplete and based in part on
variable standards. But it seems inescapable that, although the proportion of the population living actually below the subsistence level and in
acute want had dropped from roughly 10% in 1899 to 3% in 1938, in
round figures some 20% of the whole still lived at, or scarcely above,
that level, liable to be plunged into near-starvation by any sudden
temporary misfortune. Far too much of the medical help available
depended still on the haphazard distribution of hospital services supported by private charity, by subscriptions and bazaars and by London's
133 annual flag days. In London, Liverpool, Manchester and Sheffield,
where the slum clearance plans were not yet completed, there were still
back-to-back houses and tenements where some seven or eight families
shared the use of one insanitary water-closet.

It was from these areas that the children came whose condition so

---

[1] Hilton, *op. cit.*, pp. 117–21.
[2] See, e.g., George Orwell, *The Road to Wigan Pier*.

shocked their hostesses when the government's 1939 evacuation scheme distributed them widespread over the surrounding countryside. A great many people were then jerked out of the complacency with which they had contemplated recent social advances, as it became obvious that the statistics published by health authorities had been perfunctorily obtained and far too optimistically interpreted.[1] Of the $1\frac{1}{2}$ million mothers and children then moved it was found that the majority were verminous, at least to the extent of having lice or nits on their heads, and many of them had the sanitary standards and eating habits of animals. But it would not be fair to conclude that the prevailing mood at the end of the thirties was one of complacency. The events of 1931 seem to have given the old social order a shock from which it never wholly recovered. More and more thoughtful people were finding it impossible to ignore the social disaster which had overtaken the black areas and were beginning to echo King Edward VIII's passionate exclamation, which had so shocked the constitutional purists, that something must be done. The despair on the faces of the men who called every week at the Labour Exchanges, who stood about in silent groups at street corners or sat in chilly discomfort in workmen's clubs, and the ill health and undernourishment of their wives and children, could not be off-set, bookkeeping fashion, against the rising prosperity of employed workers elsewhere. The gains which had been made in social welfare and security were seen less and less as matters for self-satisfaction, but as a foundation only for a proper system. The clamour for a state health service and family allowances was strengthened by a mass of careful statistics which showed beyond all reasonable doubt that about half the population of Britain had barely enough to eat and that a tenth of it was seriously underfed.

The gradual collapse of Conservative complacency in face of facts like these was reflected clearly enough in the changing tone of literature. To the voices of men like G. D. H. Cole and R. H. Tawney, who had long been working to bring home to the educated world the still shocking inequalities of the British social structure, there was added now the clamour of the poets and the novelists. Auden and Spender, Isherwood, and Day-Lewis in their poems and plays and novels lumped together in a common condemnation the verse-forms and the books, the social

[1] Hilton, *op. cit.*, p. 133.

organisation and economic practices, the religion and the philosophy of the world in which they had grown up, and insisted that the contemporary artist could only emancipate himself and his art from outworn and valueless conventions by becoming identified with the cause of the working masses. In countless ways the writers of the Left Book Club and novelists like Orwell and Priestley pointed in the same general direction, towards Marxist solutions and revolutionary upheavals against 'the bosses', under which heading were included not only the silk-hatted Bradford millionaire, but Dons and Conservative politicians, the clergy of the Established Church, the literary critics, and all those who upheld the outdated values of the Public School system. At its worst this movement degenerated into a sort of fake, working-man toughness in clothes, speech, and manners; at its most muddled to the identification of the armaments' manufacturer as the sole cause of war and to the pacifism which, however sincere, was the main obstacle in the path of those who were struggling to avert another world calamity. But it represented, too, the valid social protest of the world which had failed to be born in 1918; which, indeed, seemed to them to have been deliberately strangled at birth by the old men, whether they were high-minded traditionalists or shameless profiteers.

By a curious twist of circumstance, it was the Spanish Civil War which largely fused these muddled currents of thought into an effective force, pierced the illusions of the pacifists, and forced into clear definition the real issues which divided Europe. It made Auden and Day-Lewis—and, indeed, the overwhelming majority of the Intellectuals—realise that the cause of freedom might, after all, demand that 'simple men who have no taste for carnage'[1] should kill and be killed, and even the gentle Spender to declare, mistakenly as it turned out, that somewhere in Spain there was a bullet for him. Strangely enough, its impact on the official politicians was comparatively slight. The Labour Party continued to oppose increases in the service estimates, reiterating faith in the League long after such a faith had lost all the basis it ever had. The government pursued that general policy of keeping out of trouble at any cost which was to make Conservative appeasement take the place of Socialist pacifism as the dictator's best friend. On public opinion outside the political world its effect was decisive. This was reflected not

[1] Day-Lewis, *Overtures to Death*, 1938.

so much by the comparatively trivial rise in the membership of the Communist Party,[1] but in the fact that it brought into a single alignment with all the leftist elements among the politically minded a great mass of non-political opinion. More than any other single issue, the Spanish war forced on the British people the knowledge that there were things happening in Europe which even a selfish and isolationist opinion could not safely ignore.

When the heterogeneous body of Spanish nationalists and militarists, Monarchists and Carlists, Churchmen and Falangists, banded somewhat precariously together under the leadership of General Francisco Franco, launched their military coup in July, 1936, they undoubtedly expected the government of 'the rabble', the Republic of 1931, to collapse without a struggle. But in central and western Spain, in Madrid, Valencia, and Barcelona, and in the Basque country in the north, equally heterogeneous masses of anarchists and syndicalists, Trotskyites and Socialists, communists and trade unionists, rallied to the Republic with fanatical enthusiasm; and had the timorous government of Señor Azana at once provided the clamorous mobs with arms, it is equally possible that the revolt might have been stamped out within a few days. But fumbling leadership allowed it to develop into a long-drawn-out civil war, fought with ferocious cruelty by both sides, which did not end until Madrid fell in 1939. As the issues crystallised, on the one side into a gallant battle for freedom and democracy, on the other into a holy war against communism and irreligion, it became a fight to the death; and the well-documented, profusely illustrated accounts put out by each side detailing the atrocities perpetrated by their enemies were equally horrifying and equally convincing.

Had the Spaniards been left to fight it out among themselves, the government would probably have won. But Mussolini had promised help for the Spanish monarchists as early as 1934; and once he was satisfied of the correctness of Franco's affiliations he sent his first and decisive contribution—the transport aircraft which, further reinforced by the Germans, alone enabled the Army of Africa to cross the Straits of Gibraltar at the end of July and consolidate the rebel hold on southern Spain. The Popular Front government in France arranged at the same time the sale of aircraft to Madrid, but dared not go too far

[1] From 7,500 in 1936 to 18,000 in 1939. Pelling, *op. cit.*

in providing help for fear of a rift with Britain, intent as ever on peace at any price. But neither Germany nor Russia was ready for the major war which must grow out of large-scale intervention. Stalin, intent on his second Five Year Plan and in the midst of a great purge eliminating thousands of senior officials and soldiers unsympathetic to his régime, would only send such grudging contributions as would prevent for the time being the actual defeat of the government forces. His tanks, and the International Brigades of volunteers, mostly communist, saved Madrid from capture in October of 1936. But there seem never to have been more than 500 Russians serving at any one time in Spain, mostly as staff officers or as technicians and instructors.[1]

Franco drew much more substantial help from abroad. Mussolini supplied him with not only some £88 million worth of equipment and munitions, but with two regular divisions and ultimately a whole Army Corps, complete with Headquarters, to whom he shamelessly wired congratulations on every victory. By July, 1937, there were some 50,000 Italians serving with Franco.[2] Hitler was at first more cautious. Like Stalin, he sent enough only to prevent his protégé's defeat. His generals used the Spanish theatre to try out their new weapons and tactics, and never committed more than 10,000 men to the task at any one time, though many more than that passed altogether through this baptism of fire. Only towards the end of 1938, convinced that France and Britain would not intervene whatever happened, did Hitler release supplies of war material on a scale large enough to enable Franco to win the war outright.[3] Long before then the western powers had made it impossible for themselves to affect the issue by the policy of Non-Intervention.

Non-Intervention in Spain was never anything but a face-saving farce. Like the arms embargoes in Manchuria and Abyssinia, it operated exclusively to the advantage of the enemies and disturbers of the peace. The governments of Germany and Italy cheerfully joined in a scheme to patrol the Spanish coasts and frontiers to keep out arms and volunteers for either side, since participation made it all the easier for them to avoid the blockade. The closing of the French frontier and the British arms embargo and prohibition of foreign enlistment effectively e duced aid to the Spanish government to what the Russians could fly

---

[1] Hugh Thomas, *The Spanish Civil War*, p. 637.
[2] *Ib.*, p. 634.   [3] *Ib.*, p. 612.

in clandestinely. Franco got what he needed to secure victory; and Mussolini, with a friendly power on the threshold of Gibraltar, could persuade himself that he had moved a perceptible step nearer the dream of a revived Roman Empire of the Mediterranean—*Mare Nostrum*. In the given circumstances there was little else a British government could do. The Opposition in Parliament clamoured for help for the Spanish government, which was to court a major war, but continued to oppose the rearmament which such a policy demanded. Official Conservatism opinion hardened against any kind of war until the nation was effectively rearmed and, accepting the popular view that this was a struggle between Fascism and Communism, became obstinately convinced that Communism was the greater danger. 'After all,' the current phrase of the day ran, 'there are worse things than Fascism.' Mistrust of Russia and a distaste for any kind of Communist alliance were to be main causes of the futility of government policy during the next two years and of Conservative apathy in the face of progressive aggressions by the two dictators.

Thus the gulf which the Spanish war opened up between public opinion in the country and its official representatives in Parliament steadily widened. Hitler's brutal suppression of his political opponents and the mounting persecution of the German Jews had already brought the Trade Union elements of Labour largely to the view that the dictators must be resisted by force; and the heroic fight of the masses in Madrid and Barcelona against overwhelming material odds strengthened this tendency. It also brought round to the same view much Liberal and moderate Conservative opinion. Nearly half the 500 British killed fighting with the International Brigade had no affiliations with the Communist Party; and intellectual opinion, whether Socialist or not, held more and more strongly that it was the cause of Liberalism and democracy, and not Bolshevism, which was being defended in the trenches round Madrid.

It was in the midst of this grim and bewildering muddle that a new King and, almost immediately, a new Prime Minister shouldered their unenviable responsibilities. All the values and principles which had determined political behaviour for nearly twenty years had shifted so suddenly that almost everybody who thought at all beyond the football pools and racing results, from the professional politicians to their humblest voters, found themselves torn by divided loyalties and faced with alternatives often equally distasteful. There has probably never been a period in a nation's history when political passions have run so high and politicians have failed so signally to give any effective lead to public opinion. At the great Albert Hall meeting which Churchill called in December, 1936, to clamour for rearmament, leaders of the League Peace Ballot found themselves sitting on the same platform as Liberals and Tories and Trade Unionists, while official Labour still preached pacifism. Die-hard Tories were coming round to the idea that the dictators could not be halted without Russian help, while their Party leaders allowed themselves to become identified with the cause of the dictators abroad and of the 'owners' at home. At such a moment few men could have been found more fitted for his office than King George VI; few less so than Neville Chamberlain.

The new Prime Minister was to be the third in succession to engulf in failure and recrimination a long career of disinterested and invaluable public service. For the age of peace and social reform which ought to have been dawning he would have been the ideal leader: immensely energetic, doggedly persistent, and with a business-like zeal for administrative efficiency still quite undimmed at the age of 68. But the world he understood was a world of business men, where contracts were sacred and enforceable without violence, and difficulties could be ironed out round the conference table; and where the keenest rivals could by hard bargaining reach mutually profitable agreements. He understood as little of foreigners as Baldwin did. The mixture of hysteria and shrewd duplicity in Hitler and Mussolini's paranoiac bombast belonged to a jungle world he could never understand. 'One of the things that comforted me when I gave up office', Baldwin said later, 'was that I should not have to meet French statesmen any more.' Unfortunately Chamberlain, unlike Baldwin, was unaware of this limitation, buoyantly confident of his own ability to reduce European passions to terms of common sense, and briskly determined to cut through the red tape of old-fashioned diplomacy and settle the world's problems in a series of frank, man-to-man talks with the other leaders. Moreover, the clarity of intellect which enabled him to move with skill and certainty through the intricacies of rating adjustments and pension schemes and budgetary calculations wholly deserted him when he came to con-

R

sider foreign affairs. Starting from false premises, he would persist, in the teeth of facts and experience, in policies long proved bankrupt; and his mind would harbour self-contradictory judgements with apparent unconcern. Thus it was that he, who had said as early as 1936 that he did not 'take Hitler's peace professions at their face value',[1] was two years later to offer a worthless scrap of paper with Hitler's signature on it as holding the promise of 'peace in our time'.

The Cabinet which he formed at the end of May, immediately after the coronation, was not a strong one; and its two ablest members, Eden at the Foreign Office and Duff-Cooper at the Admiralty, were to resign in disgust before two years were out. There was one provocative appointment—that of Leslie Hore-Belisha, a Jew and a Liberal, to the War Office, where he was to shock the 'bow and arrow brigade' out of their 1918 complacency. At the Home Office there was Hoare, generously intent on devoting the rest of a ruined career to the cause of prison reform. Simon brought an unparalleled intellect but no quality of strength or leadership to the Exchequer; and Inskip was to remain, incredibly, for nearly three more years in self-satisfied inaction, coordinating defence. There was indeed, as Churchill remarked, 'a marked and felt dearth of men of high ability'. Chamberlain towered above them in lonely, though not, it seems, distasteful eminence. There was in him an element of arrogance—a contempt for the opinions and motives of those who differed from him—which enabled him to face the appalling responsibilities of these two years with a resilient self-confidence which, in retrospect, it is hard to understand.

It can at least be laid to the credit of this government that it rearmed the nation to the just essential minimum needed to avoid total destruction in 1940. Before leaving the Exchequer, Chamberlain had planned defence expenditure of £500 million a year for five years, to be financed partly by a Defence Loan, and partly by a defence contribution from industry. The proposals of the Defence White Paper of March, 1936,[2] were implemented. With some creaking the naval programme went through and proved in the event just adequate to the needs of war, and a fighting Air Force was created which could and did stand up to the full assault of the *Luftwaffe*. Hore-Belisha, fortunately, went well beyond the provisions of the White Paper in achieving the 'drastic changes'

[1] Feiling, *op. cit.*, p. 297.   [2] See above, p. 244.

prescribed by the Prime Minister, overwhelming amidst much recrimination what Chamberlain called the 'incredible obstinacy of some of the army heads in sticking to obsolete methods'. Modernised conditions of living and more attractive terms of service, coupled with the growing sense of emergency in the country, raised the recruiting figures at last, both for the regular and territorial armies, to something approaching the required figure; the territorial army was, indeed, by a stroke of the pen, doubled in numbers. But industrial difficulties obstinately hampered the much needed re-equipment; nor, as experience was to show in 1940, had that re-equipment been planned on a sufficiently large or imaginative scale.

The crux of the whole problem, however, as everybody knew, was the speed of aircraft production; and here at last there was a sense of urgency strong enough to overcome Treasury scruples and hesitations. Between 1934 and 1938 the air budget had risen from £18 million to £126 million and the numbers employed in aircraft factories from 33,000 to 90,000. The output of trained pilots had also increased, from 300 a year to over 2,000. The R.A.F. was taking in 600 recruits a week; and there were 29 civilian schools turning out pilots for the auxiliary reserve. But far too much of the progress recorded was still preparatory only to a great expansion. Lord Nuffield was preparing to fulfil an initial order for 1,000 Spitfires. A. V. Roe's £1 million factory at Manchester was still being built; the Bristol works were in the midst of a £1 million expansion; and the huge Rolls Royce shadow factory at Crewe was not to be ready until the end of the year.[1] Everywhere there was glittering promise, but as yet little actual performance; and in fairness to the statesmen of the appeasement era it must be remembered that preoccupation with this situation was the background of all their thinking, blinding them sometimes to the solid valuable assets elsewhere which year by year they were throwing away.

If the policy of appeasement meant the improvement of the international atmosphere by the removal of justified grievances, there was much to be said for it; and this was no doubt what Eden had in mind when he first defined it as the government's policy in 1936. In Chamberlain's hands it became very much more than that. Passionately afraid of

[1] These facts and figures are taken from an unpublished Memorandum drawn up by Mr. Geoffrey de Havilland in 1938.

war, he was prepared to throw away solid assets one after the other in return for assurances of friendship and paper promises from men who had already shown a cynical disregard for their own most solemn undertakings. The cry of peace at any price might have made sense if there had been any price at which peace could be bought; but it was impossible to read *Mein Kampf* and believe that there was. Moreover, when the price was invariably paid by others—by Abyssinians and Spanish workers, Austrians and Czechs—it became on the lips of British statesmen a shameful cry. Even the generosity with which Conservative circles discussed the purchase of German friendship by returning her former colonies showed a cynical disregard for the welfare of the inhabitants of those territories. Nor was the claim really justified that Britain was buying time to rearm. Each progressively more abject surrender left the aggressors relatively stronger, the powers working for peace and reason sapped in morale and materially weakened. Each year of delay served only to make the coming war harder to win. Yet the overwhelming mass of British opinion enthusiastically endorsed the Chamberlain government's every move; and if Britain stood alone in 1940, it was at least partly because she had allowed those who might have stood with her to be crippled and demoralised or alienated during the fatal years of appeasement.

Whether the British people and the Dominions would have responded to a more vigorous and realistic leadership can now never be known. The allocation of responsibility between a democracy and the leaders it elects is not possible. But it is, perhaps, just to say that the British between 1937 and 1939 were not given a fair chance. Unpleasant facts were too often suppressed or garbled by statesmen anxious at all costs to avoid irritating the dictators or precipitating the issues. In the face of ministerial complacency and official belittlement of all that he said, Churchill inevitably remained a voice crying in a wilderness where men preferred to believe the government's palatable half-truths and cowardly evasions.

'Nothing could be more fatal', Harold Nicolson had written in 1919, 'than the habit (the at present persistent and pernicious habit) of personal contact between the statesmen of the world.' Chamberlain was to prove himself even more determined than Lloyd George to side-track the Foreign Office and handle all important negotiation at the summit, and with even more disastrous results. He carefully eliminated from his entourage anybody who showed any strong desire for a more robust policy than his. As his permanent and inseparable adviser in foreign affairs he took Sir Horace Wilson, whose brilliant career at the Treasury had in no way equipped him for diplomacy, but who surpassed even his chief in his willingness to meet German demands at almost any cost. Sir Eric Phipps, who took too objective a view of Nazi Germany, was shifted from Berlin to Paris and replaced, as luck would have it, by Sir Nevile Henderson,[1] nervous and unbalanced, hypnotised by the spectacle of German might, and genuinely convinced that Germany must be allowed to absorb without opposition the territory of all the weaker nations surrounding her frontiers. In the inner Cabinet there was Hoare, who had already shown his willingness to throw the Abyssinians to the wolves, Simon, whose great intellect was unhelpful in a crisis requiring strength of character, and Halifax, who succeeded Eden at the Foreign Office, and whose courage and integrity were unquestionable, but whose religious convictions made it difficult for him to enter with convincing enthusiasm into policies which presupposed any intimate collaboration with a godless Russia.[2] So supported, Chamberlain set himself to pay Danegeld, for as long as possible and mostly at other people's expense, in the belief that gradually personal contact with himself would wean Mussolini away from Hitler and Hitler from his unreasonable ways.

The summer of 1937 was a singularly unpropitious moment for the launching of any such policy. The two dictators, assertively conscious of their own power and of the self-confessed weakness and indecision of their opponents, had drawn together into what they called the Axis in November of 1936; and this a year later had become the triangular Anti-Comintern Pact by the inclusion of Japan. 'As for the British government,' so Lloyd George accurately summed the situation up that summer, 'they have now succeeded in quarrelling simultaneously with Germany, Japan, and Italy; in alienating Russia; and in being at least two years behind with armaments.'[3] Against all this, appeasement could

---

[1] For Vansittart's responsibility for this appointment, see Taylor, *op. cit.*, p. 158 n. Incidentally, Phipps lost much of his objectivity in the defeatist atmosphere of Paris.
[2] For the strained relations which developed between Chamberlain and the rest of the Cabinet, see Duff Cooper, *Old Men Forget*, pp. 207–42.
[3] Boothby, *op. cit.*, p. 32.

claim one small gain: a treaty with Egypt, signed in August, 1936, which restored her virtually to a position of sovereign independence and permitted the withdrawal of all British troops save from the Canal Zone, but ensured the use of all bases and facilities needed in any international emergency. Otherwise the horizon was black. France was torn by political feuds, and her industry, already gravely handicapped by the 40-hour week, was all but paralysed by a series of disastrous strikes. And when Japan launched the next phase of her Asiatic adventure, in July, 1937, with the invasion of China proper and the seizure of Shanghai and Peking, there was nothing at all the peace-loving nations could do. The Chinese government doggedly survived, precariously supplied along the Burma road; and in September, 1938, the League voted for sanctions. But not one single nation attempted to apply them, and in the mounting tension in Europe Japan's progress passed almost unnoticed.

Chamberlain set himself first to woo Italy. It was a hopeless task, for Mussolini had already moved the other way. Absorbed in dreams of Mediterranean Empire, to which France and Britain were likely to be the major obstacles, he was irrevocably committed to the Axis, and had already warned the Austrian Chancellor, Schuschnigg, in the spring of 1937 that he would not again mobilise on the Brenner to save Austria from Hitler. In such circumstances the negotiations which culminated in the signing of the Anglo-Italian agreement of April 16th, 1938, excited in Rome a merely cynical derision. Italy undertook to do what she had already promised to do eighteen months earlier in a so-called Gentlemen's Agreement—to withdraw her troops from Spain. They were in fact withdrawn, but only in Mussolini's own good time, and only when Franco's victory was finally assured. In return the Italians obtained a promise of the recognition by Great Britain of their conquest of Abyssinia. All this was too much for Chamberlain's Foreign Secretary, Anthony Eden, whom experience had convinced that the dictators responded only to firmness and a show of strength. He had uttered a warning speech at Llandudno in October, 1937, against trying to make new friends by throwing old ones overboard. When he found in the following January that Chamberlain had not only brusquely rejected, without consulting him, a tentative offer from Roosevelt to call some sort of international conference with a view to general pacification, but was also negotiating directly and behind his back with Count Grandi, the Italian ambassador,[1] for an agreement of which he wholly disapproved, he resigned. His departure was hailed as a diplomatic victory by both dictators; and in exchange Chamberlain got Halifax, who was a much more convinced appeaser and who had already assured Hitler on a visit to Berchtesgaden in November that the British government would look favourably on changes of the situation in Germany's favour in Danzig, Austria, and Czechoslovakia, provided they came 'through the course of peaceful evolution' and avoided methods 'which might cause far-reaching disturbances'.[2]

While the British government thus deluded itself that a start had been made in detaching Mussolini from the Axis, Hitler cashed in unexpectedly on that much more solid agreement. The Austrian Nazis, acting in fact against his orders, gave him his chance by an attempt to seize power in Vienna in January, 1938, which miscarried. On February 12th Schuschnigg went to Berchtesgaden, on his own initiative, to protest against Nazi illegalities, but was instead mercilessly bullied into legalising the Party in Austria and giving control of home affairs and the police to the local Nazi leader, Seyss-Inquart. He preserved, however, Austrian independence; and Hitler clearly believed that the 'course of peaceful evolution' was safely launched. But the immediate outbreak of riots and beatings-up by the Nazi minority everywhere in Austria,[3] clearly intended to culminate in a revolution, goaded Schuschnigg into changing his line. On March 9th, in the teeth of a warning from Mussolini and without encouragement from London or Paris, he announced a plebiscite, to be held on the 12th, in which the Austrians should decide whether they wished to remain independent or not. If he intended to force the issue, he certainly succeeded. 'Peaceful evolution' went by the board. Faced with the alternative of humiliation or force, Hitler ordered his wholly unprepared army to invade Austria on March 12th. On the 11th Schuschnigg tried to back down, but he was too late. France was in the throes of a Cabinet crisis. Britain, though protesting, was clearly not going to move. The Czechs, solemnly promised by Goering 'on his word of honour' that they had nothing to fear, hesitated

---

[1] Grandi's jubilant despatch recording this is printed in *Ciano's Diplomatic Papers*, ed. Malcolm Muggeridge, pp. 164–84.
[2] See Taylor, *op. cit.*, p. 137.
[3] The registered Party membership amounted to only 2% of the population. *Ib.*, p. 106.

and were lost; and Mussolini held his hand, earning thereby Hitler's hysterical gratitude. The western powers could only acquiesce in the *fait accompli*, and on March 13th, a day late owing to the mechanical breakdown of 70% of the German transport, Hitler made his triumphal entry into Vienna, bringing with him the Gestapo and the Jew-baiters and the concentration camps and all the apparatus of Nazi tyranny. The prevailing attitude of the governing class in Britain was that, as in the case of the Rhineland, Hitler had merely in Lord Lothian's phrase, 'walked into his own back garden'.

When Churchill told the Commons that Hitler was confronting the world with 'a programme of aggression, nicely calculated and timed, unfolding stage by stage', he was in fact mistaken. Hitler's conference with his service chiefs, which was the subject of the famous 'Hossbach Memorandum', laid down no hard and fast programme.[1] He only discussed the various diplomatic possibilities which might open the way to the 'territorial gains' which were his avowed objective: problems which as he frankly admitted, 'could only be solved by means of force'. These were the means to the end of German hegemony in Europe. Whether, ultimately, *Lebensraum* was to be found in the Ukraine or in the former colonies, the immediate prizes were obviously Austria, Czechoslovakia, Danzig and the Polish Corridor, where there were German inhabitants to do most of his work for him, and where British opinion would feel that his grievances were justified. British pressure, he reckoned, would be enough to prevent any armed intervention by France. He could therefore risk stirring up trouble in those areas without waiting for the German army to be ready for a major war. The threat was to be enough. He had probably intended to start with Czechoslovakia, geographically isolated and surrounded by enemies. As luck would have it, Austria had dropped into his lap first and long before he had really expected it. The obvious next move was to encourage the already wildly over-excited Sudeten Germans in Czechoslovakia and see what happened.

But before that crisis came, Chamberlain had just time for one more small but dangerous concession—this time to the Irish. De Valera had just implemented a new constitution for what was henceforth to be known as Eire, which became for all practical purposes an independent republic, though still nominally within the Commonwealth; and there

[1] Taylor, *op. cit.*, p. 164.

was everything to be said for Britain's accepting this and liquidating all the remaining ties and debts between the two countries. But the surrender of the naval bases at Queenstown, Berehaven, and Lough Swilly was a high price to pay for the problematical goodwill of Ireland, and was to be bitterly regretted by those responsible for fighting off German submarines from Britain's western approaches in 1941.

The facts concerning the liquidation of Czechoslavakia are not now difficult to elucidate nor much disputed. The conclusions to be drawn from them will probably continue to be hotly argued until the last survivor from that unfortunate era is dead. For the responsibility for that fiasco was not confined to Chamberlain and the inner Cabinet— Halifax, Hoare and Simon—who shared his decisions, but extended to the overwhelming majority of the British people, and, indeed, the peoples of the Dominions. A passionate self-justification thus distorts the issues still for all those who can remember those weeks of despair and hysteria.

The state of Czechoslovakia, though created in flagrant disregard of their own principle of self-determination, was much the most successful creation of the Versailles diplomats. It might, perhaps, have been wiser to safeguard the interests of the 2 million Slovaks, the 3 million Sudeten Germans, and the Poles, Ruthenians, and Magyars, by establishing a federal constitution modelled on that of the Swiss. As it was, in a unitary state the $7\frac{1}{2}$ million Czechs inevitably dominated, and there was some exploitation of minorities; but until western statesmen began feverishly to seek some justification for their impending betrayal of the Czechs it was universally agreed that these were the best treated of the many European minority populations. Czechoslovakia was much the most prosperous, the best governed, and the strongest of the succession states. Her frontiers were not only clearly defined, but strategically the most formidable in Europe, and so admirably fortified that the German generals who later inspected them reckoned that it would have taken them four months to batter their way through. She could mobilise a small but efficient air force and an army of 35 divisions, well equipped and highly mechanised, and more than adequately supplied by the great Skoda armaments' factories whose output at that time slightly exceeded the entire output of Great Britain. Nor was it true that the seizure of Austria had outflanked these defences and made it easy for the Germans to 'overrun' the country, as was and is so constantly stated by apologists for the Munich policy.[1] General Halder actually quoted the fact that Hitler shared this delusion as a supreme example of the Führer's military ineptitude.[2] Finally, the republic's military position was shored up by defensive alliances with France and Russia and an Arbitration Treaty with Germany.

The German general staff was under no illusions as to the formidable task presented by the Czech defences, even if skilful propaganda had generated a powerful fifth column in the frontier areas populated by the Sudetens. But it was equally clear that Czechoslovakia, thrusting deep into the heart of Germany, was a dangerous threat in the rear of any military operation against the French frontier, and an invaluable base for the Russian air force if Hitler's expansionist aims carried him first to the east. Plans for her elimination had therefore been in preparation since June of 1937.[3] The clamour of the Sudeten Germans for unity with the Fatherland, organised from Berlin through the Nazi agent in Czechoslovakia, Henlein, was never more than a pretext for this, though of course it had the great additional value of tangling the western statesmen up in their own principle of self-determination. So in April, once Austria was secure, Henlein opened his noisy campaign for autonomy for the Sudeten areas and the abandonment by Czechoslovakia of her French and Russian alliances. The immediate reaction of the British government was to begin that process of undermining the Czech and French will to resist which Chamberlain was to carry to a triumphant conclusion in September. Strong pressure was brought to bear at once on the Czechs to make concessions to Henlein and in conference with the French ministers, Daladier and Bonnet, in London on April 28th, the British stiffly refused to join in warning Hitler that an attack on Czechoslovakia would bring both western powers to her rescue. Had Halifax not been made of somewhat sterner stuff than his chief, the whole crisis would have come to a head in May. Border troubles in the Sudetenland, some sinister rumours of German troop movements[4] and a partial mobilisation of the Czech army brought Europe to the verge of war. But France and Russia both announced that they would

[1] E.g. Templewood, *op. cit.*, p. 288.
[2] Churchill, *op. cit.*, p. 219.
[3] See quotation from the Nürnberg documents in Churchill, *op. cit.*, p. 219.
[4] According to Taylor, *op. cit.*, p. 165, there were no such movements.

fight, and Halifax made it clear both to the German ambassador and his own ambassador in Berlin, Henderson, that it was unlikely that Britain would be able to keep out. An enraged Hitler was forced to accept the appearance of a diplomatic defeat, but only for the moment. On May 28th he gave orders that the whole question must be settled finally by October 1st.

The western powers spent the summer in a series of uneasy and futile manœuvres. Lord Runciman, coldly rational, insular, and remote, quite unfitted to deal with the passions and unreason of nationalism run mad, was sent out with a mission to Prague at the beginning of August to mediate between the Czechs and the Sudeten Germans, rather grumblingly accepted by both sides, and nominally independent of the British government. The German technique of raising the stakes and extending their demands every time a settlement seemed within reach was bound to defeat such an endeavour; and Chamberlain's dream of inducing the Czechs to agree to a solution so just that British and Dominion opinion would willingly fight for it was a chimera.[1] For Hitler had no intention of accepting or allowing a reasonable settlement. He wanted the Czech state destroyed, if possible without having to fight a major war to achieve its destruction. In this objective M. Bonnet and Mr. Chamberlain all too willingly collaborated. They feared all the consequences of a major war. They did not care for the Czechs; and they disliked intensely any suggestion of close co-operation with Russia which this particular war would inevitably involve. So, throughout the summer, the French will to resist, already shaky and uncertain in April was steadily weakened further: by suggestions that Russia would never move, and that if she did her army, after the recent purges, would be unenthusiastic and badly led; that Britain, even if she did not back out, would be ineffectual; and that Mussolini would seize the opportunity for a stab in the back. British opinion which might, given a lead, have reacted more vigorously, and which, even without a lead, was perceptibly stiffening, was largely kept in the dark. Chamberlain, obsessed with his ideal of appeasement and more and more rudely intolerant of criticism, partly avoided opposition by a secretive diplomacy which often left both Parliament and the public, and sometimes even the

---

[1] Henlein had defined these tactics to Hitler on March 28th: 'We must always demand so much that we can never be satisfied.' Taylor, *op. cit.*, p. 153.

Cabinet, uncertain of his intentions. 'Fortunately', he wrote, very characteristically, as early as May 1st, 'the papers have had no hint of how near we came to a break over Czechoslovakia.'[1] The general knowledge that firmness by Britain and France had then stopped Hitler in his tracks would have embarrassed his efforts to soothe and pacify Germany at all costs. Already, on August 24th, when fresh and threatening German troop movements were reported, he was instructing Henderson to prepare the way for a personal interview with Hitler. So he allowed the September crisis to burst on a British public largely unprepared, whose morale had been weakened rather than strengthened by every government pronouncement since the spring.

Throughout the summer the rumours multiplied and the tension mounted, while Runciman toiled to produce a settlement unacceptable to either side. It was generally expected that the crisis would come with Hitler's speech to the annual Nazi Party rally at Nürnberg on September 12; but in fact *The Times* touched it off with a disastrous leading article on the 7th, for which Dawson, the editor, took personal responsibility. It went far beyond anything that had yet been officially suggested in advising the Czechs to consider abandoning the idea of autonomy and ceding the Sudeten areas to Germany outright. The quasi-official standing of *The Times* and Dawson's known friendship for Chamberlain made this an even more damaging bombshell, encouraging both Hitler and Henlein to raise their terms, suggesting to the Czechs that their country was about to be dismembered, not by their enemies, but by their friends, and damping the already feeble will to resist aggression in Britain and France. A Foreign Office repudiation, toned down as it was by later pronouncements of Chamberlain and Halifax, did little to repair the damage; and the predominant reaction to Hitler's raging speech on the 12th was relief that he had stopped short of actually declaring war.

Events for the next fortnight seemed to move with bewildering rapidity, but the essentials of the situation did not change at all. Chamberlain sent his famous telegram asking for an interview on the 13th, and on the 15th met Hitler at Berchtesgaden, to find to his dismay that Germany had no concessions to make. All that Hitler would now discuss were ways and means of applying the principle of self-deter-

[1] Feiling, *op. cit.*, p. 353.

mination to the Sudetenland. It took Chamberlain three days to persuade first his Cabinet, and then the French ministers, who came to London again on the 18th, to agree to what he described in the House of Commons as 'a solution which would not automatically compel France to take action in accordance with her obligations'. This was the immediate handing over of all Czech territory where the German-speaking population exceeded 50%, Czech minorities and all. Such a plan, by depriving Czechoslovakia of her strategic frontiers, sealed her fate, with it that of France, and all too nearly Britain's too. For the guarantee of the new frontier by Britain, France, and Germany, with which the pill was gilded, was not worth the paper it was written on. But these were the terms Bonnet handed to the Czech ambassador in Paris with the brusque instruction: 'Acceptez'; and after 47 hours of remarkably courageous resistance, at 2 a.m. on September 21st, Benes accepted, faced by the brutal assurance from the British and French Ministers at Prague that he would otherwise be left to his fate.

Yet even this turned out to be too little for Hitler when he and Chamberlain met again at Godesberg on the 22nd. He presented what was in effect an ultimatum, demanding that German troops should immediately occupy such areas of Czech territory as he specified; and this was more than even Chamberlain could stomach. The Cabinet in London felt obliged to lift their ban on Czech mobilisation, and on the 24th the French decreed a partial mobilisation. The next day both Czechoslovakia and France rejected the 'de facto ultimatum, of the sort usually presented to a vanquished nation, and not a proposition to a sovereign state'. Chamberlain had tried to comfort himself with a slight modification of Hitler's timetable—he put off the date of the military occupation to October 1st, which was the day he had originally fixed anyway—and with an assurance that this was Germany's last territorial claim in Europe—which he had said before, equally solemnly, when he seized Austria. But even Chamberlain could no longer resist the tide of opinion which now saw the German demands as intolerable and war was inevitable. He, Simon, and Hoare had two final talks with Daladier and Bonnet on the 25th and 26th in which they did their best to sap the faith of the Frenchmen in their own military and air strength,[1] but they had to let the Foreign Office state categorically that 'if Czecho-

[1] See especially Templewood, *op. cit.*, pp. 312–15.

slovakia were attacked, France would be bound to come to her assistance, and Great Britain and Russia will certainly stand by France'. The fleet was mobilised, gas masks were distributed and such civil defence precautions as existed were put into operation.

For in that week there had taken place a remarkable turn-over of public opinion, ill-informed though it had been. The T.U.C., in session at Blackpool from September 5th–9th, had come out strongly for 'a positive and unmistakable lead for collective defence against aggression', and demanded that the government should 'leave no doubt in the mind of the German government that they will unite with the French and Soviet governments to resist any attack on Czechoslovakia'.[1] Churchill, who had asked for an ultimatum to Germany as early as the 10th, now found himself with some strange allies as the feeling against peace with dishonour hardened and the country braced itself for what seemed an inevitable war. Between September 21st and 28th the entire press, even including *The Times*, swung over against 'an abject and humiliating capitulation'.[2] The government could no longer shelter itself, as Baldwin had, behind the reluctance of a pacifist public opinion. The nation now was leading the government, not with any of the fervour of 1914, reluctant and fearful, but determined that appeasement had gone far enough. Chamberlain still prevented any useful contact with the Russians for whom he had, as he said himself, 'the most profound mistrust';[3] and on September 26th he sent off Sir Horace Wilson with a personal letter to Hitler assuring him that he could get 'all essentials without war and without delay', appealing at the same time to Mussolini for some mediating influence—an appeal strongly reinforced by President Roosevelt. His broadcast to the nation on the 27th, at the very moment when Hitler was rousing his followers in the Sportpalast to brutal frenzy, was no clarion call to a crusade, but a flat, tired confession of failure. 'How horrible, fantastic, incredible it is', he said, 'that we should be digging trenches and trying on gas masks here because of a quarrel in a far-away country between people of whom we know nothing.'

With equal sombreness on the 28th he started to prepare the hastily summoned House of Commons for what all now regarded as an in-

[1] G. D. H. Cole, *History of the Labour Party*, p. 335, and Mowat, *op. cit.*, p. 613.
[2] *Daily Telegraph*, September 24th.
[3] Feiling, *op. cit.*, p. 403.

evitable war; and it was probably one of the great accidents of history
that Hitler's answer to his letter, inviting him to meet him, Mussolini
and Daladier at Munich the following day, should have been handed to
him just as he reached his peroration.[1] For, thus dramatically presented,
it stampeded both the House and the nation out of all reason and
beyond the point of considered criticism. The relief to overstrung
nerves of this sudden, last-minute let-off inevitably produced a hysterical enthusiasm which engulfed the whole nation in uncritical adulation
and hope. Nobody paused to think what was really going to happen at
Munich: that the four powers—for nobody thought of inviting the
Russians and the Czechs were to be excluded—were going to agree on the
orderly method of implementing the German demands, so that Hitler
could get all the spoils of a victorious war without having to fight it and
the illusion could be maintained that this was a peacefully negotiated
settlement which had 'avoided the use of force'.

The hysteria lasted until the Prime Minister's triumphal return to
the waiting crowds at Heston Airport and Downing Street, bringing
with him what he described, as even he after a day or two of reflection
thought, somewhat rashly, as 'Peace with Honour'. Munich had given
the Czechs an additional week in which to evacuate their fortress line
and the frontier areas assigned to Germany. The fortifications and the
weapons defending them were to be left intact; and with the frontier
areas went the bulk of Czech mineral resources. Their treaties with
France and Russia were cancelled; and a merely insulting guarantee by
the Munich powers of the new frontiers, still to be defined by a commission under German chairmanship, was substituted. Czechoslavakia
was left in the end with nearly a quarter of a million Germans within
her new borders to make further trouble, and nearly a million Czechs
found themselves incorporated in the German Reich. For a short time
Chamberlain and many others were able to persuade themselves that
the Germans would play fair on the plebiscites and respect the rights of
the minorities. He even assured the House of Commons that the new
state, freed from its subversive German population and internationally
guaranteed, would really be stronger than the old. 'Some day', he wrote
to the Archbishop of Canterbury the day after he got back, 'the Czechs
will see that what we did was to save them for a happier future.'

[1] Taylor implies that this was deliberately staged, *op. cit.*, p. 183.

Then there was the piece of paper by which the Prime Minister set such store, which he flourished to the crowds as what he believed to be the guarantee of 'peace in our time', and in which he and Hitler had jointly recorded their determination to consult on all future difficulties and 'never to go to war with one another again'. This, it must be said, never carried much conviction, even among those who were blinded with enthusiasm for the Munich Treaty. It was, after all, not the first solemn assurance of his peaceful intentions Hitler had given, and all the others had been broken. Few could share Chamberlain's own naïve belief that this was different from other promises, because 'this time he has made the promises to me'.[1] In truth the rejoicing crowds in the streets and the 40,000 persons of all classes and nations who wrote to the Prime Minister to express their gratitude,[2] the journalists who 'thanked God and Mr. Chamberlain',[3] and the old ladies who demanded that the umbrella he had carried to Munich be broken up and the pieces sold as sacred relics—all these gave an illusion of a public opinion much more united than it was. Attlee, deploring 'one of Britain's greatest diplomatic defeats and a bitter humiliation', and Churchill denouncing 'a total and unmitigated defeat' spoke for many who kept off the streets on October 1st and nursed in private a bitter sense of shame. And this, as the excitement died down, quickly became the mood of the nation as a whole. Even the ministers who continued to affirm their belief in Munich belied it by the vigour with which they set themselves to rearm. The seriousness with which the nation forthwith started to prepare for a war which now seemed inevitable was its real verdict on Munich.

The arguments used by those who justified Munich have not changed from that day to this. The decisive factor in their minds was the consciousness of weakness in the air. They knew that Britain had only five squadrons re-equipped with modern eight-gunned fighters, that there were few heavy A.A. guns available for the defence of London and none elsewhere, and that there was a universal shortage of fire pumps. They believed that the French could put no more than 750 planes into the air and the German front-line strength was put at over 2,000. They had a profound mistrust of Russia politically and a profound contempt for her recently purged army, and no faith at all in the ability of the Czechs to

[1] Quoted Mowat, *op. cit.*, p. 619.
[2] See Feiling, *op. cit.*, p. 378.
[3] Godfrey Winn.

hold their own defence line. They did not think the French army capable of an offensive and they were convinced that the Dominions would refuse to support action on behalf of a remote people they had never heard of. The year's breathing-space, which was all that was gained, was enough, they claim, to give us the bare minimum of necessary defence equipment, and to enable ministers to lead a united and determined Empire in 1939 into a conflict indisputably just and unavoidable.

It is easier to counter these arguments today than it was in 1938.[1] In the light of the events of 1940 the heavily mechanised and well-equipped Czech army of some 35 divisions looks much more formidable; and the skilled resistance offered by the Russians to the German assault in 1941 removed another set of misconceptions. We know now how impressed the German generals were with the Czech fortifications and that they had only thirteen divisions left, of which only five were fully trained and equipped, for the defence of their West Wall when they had allotted what they thought necessary for the defeat of the Czechs. The senior German generals were, indeed, so appalled by the risk that they were prepared to remove Hitler from power rather than let him take it, though whether their nerve would have held had Chamberlain not decided at the critical moment to go to Berchtesgaden will never be known. By 1939 the German army could face the French on equal terms. Only two additional British divisions had been added to replace the lost Czech 35 together with a Polish army whose tactics and equipment were wholly out of date; and the relative air superiority of Germany had increased, not diminished, in the intervening year. The turnover of military power produced by the rapid German army expansion and the overwhelming German tank output, supplemented as it was by the Skoda production and the captured Czech equipment, was in the event the decisive factor in making 1940 possible. For, unless they could defeat the French army, the Germans could not acquire the bases needed to provide fighter cover for a concentrated bomber assault on Britain.

Certainly the government was ill served by its expert advisers, both

[1] We now have all the information revealed in, inter alia, *Documents on British Foreign Policy*, ed. Woodward and Rohan Butler, J. W. Wheeler-Bennett's two books, *Munich: Prologue to Tragedy* and *Nemesis of Power*, and L. B. Namier's *Diplomatic Prelude* and *Europe in Decay*.

military and diplomatic. In 1939 the War Office was still 'unanimous' in the opinion that the Polish army was superior to the Russian and likely on the 'excellent terrain' of Poland to give a very good account of itself.[1] Henderson at Berlin constantly infected the Cabinet with his own hypnotised conviction of German invincibility; and when Phipps wrote from Paris, at the critical moment on September 24th, that 'all that is best in France is against war, *almost* at any price',[2] it is difficult not to feel that his 'best' people were those right-wing elements who feared revolution more than Nazism and were to provide the backbone of Vichy. In their suspicions of Russian intentions they may well have been right; for, though she continued to assure Benes of her support to the very last, there is evidence that Russia never moved a man or a gun in support of her assurances.[3] But nobody can argue that Stalin had any better reason to trust the western statesmen, whose publicly expressed opinion of Russia was frequently contemptuous and sometimes insulting; and the ignoring of Litvinov's last-minute appeal for joint action at Geneva on September 21st and the studied exclusion of Russia from the Munich four-power conference undoubtedly played their part in preventing any understanding at Moscow the following summer.

But, when all the excuses have been made, it seems likely that the considered judgement of historians will be more nearly that of Churchill than that of the many apologists for Munich, who themselves supply some of the most convincing evidence of their own failure of nerve and judgement.[4] This was indeed the root cause of the débâcle, as the veteran Thomas Jones, himself a convinced peace-at-any-price man, wrote sadly to Lady Grigg at the very start of the crisis: 'I wish', he wrote, 'I felt more confidence in the collective wisdom and strength of the Cabinet. Nobody does—they don't themselves.'[5]

[1] Templewood, *op. cit.*, p. 344.
[2] Quoted Templewood, *op. cit.*, p. 310.
[3] Mowat, *op. cit.*, p. 609 n., giving the conclusions of Max Beloff in his *Foreign Policy of Soviet Russia*.
[4] See e.g. Templewood, *op. cit.*, and Sir Nevile Henderson's *Failure of a Mission*.
[5] Thomas Jones, *A Diary with Letters*, p. 408.

CHAPTER 13

Epilogue. Phoney Peace and Phoney War

'If you have sacrificed my nation to preserve the peace of the world,' said Masaryk, the Czech ambassador, to Chamberlain and Halifax on the night before Munich, 'I will be the first to applaud you. But if not, gentlemen, God help your souls.'[1] It was to be six months before Chamberlain was forced by hard facts to admit that his bid to save peace by throwing the Czechs to the wolves had failed; and he never to the end admitted that his policy had been mistaken or ill-judged. The nation as a whole reacted more rapidly and more honestly. The hysterical relief of the week after Munich died quickly away, to be followed by a period of even less attractive recrimination and vituperation in which everybody, parties and individuals alike, sought to lay the blame on everybody else. But out of it all there emerged with surprising speed and unanimity a sense of shame and shortcoming: a feeling that feebleness and self-indulgence and cowardice had led Britain to a great betrayal; and, more important, a growing determination that it must never happen again. Abruptly the nation stopped trying to live in an idealised past and prepared to face and assume responsibility for the extremely unpleasant world in which it found itself living. By April of 1939, when even Chamberlain had abandoned his hopes of appeasement, it even accepted what had before seemed inconceivable—the introduction of military conscription in time of peace—though not without vigorous protests from both Liberals and Socialists. It was at this point that the era of 'Between the Wars' really came to an end; and the years of 1939 and 1940 were perhaps even more a prelude to a new age than an epilogue to one that was past.

---

[1] Wheeler-Bennett, *Munich*, p. 178.

Epilogue. Phoney Peace and Phoney War

For a brief space appeasement held its disastrous course. While the nation rearmed and reorganised itself for a struggle which more and more people saw to be unavoidable, the pathetic attempts to detach the Duce from the Axis, at whatever humiliating price, were continued. The Anglo-Italian agreement of the previous April was implemented regardless of the continuance of the Spanish war, since, as Halifax ruefully admitted, Mussolini had always made it clear that he would only withdraw his troops when Franco's victory was assured. As France and Italy drifted towards an open breach over Spain and over North African colonial ambitions, Chamberlain, on December 12th, contributed the public observation that Britain was under no obligation to support France against Italy, though he added, somewhat vaguely, that Anglo-French friendship was beyond 'mere legal definition'. The following month he and Halifax paid a humiliating visit to Rome, in the course of which they had to toast the King of Italy as Emperor of Ethiopia, and which achieved nothing. The last entry in Ciano's accounts of the conversations runs: 'Chamberlain informs him (Mussolini) that Great Britain will take part in the World Exhibition in Rome in 1942.'

Meanwhile the remains of Czechoslovakia—that state which was to be so much stronger and happier after Munich—were quietly devoured with apparent British acquiescence. The British and French ambassadors in Berlin, who should have sat on an international commission to determine the new frontier with Germany, coldly ignored the Czech request that they should interfere with the German arrangements, which were a travesty of justice. When the Polish and Hungarian 'vultures descended upon the carcase',[1] the four-power conference to settle the new boundaries was never even mentioned: an 'award' by Ribbentrop and Ciano gave the Poles Teschen, which they had already taken, and the Hungarians the Ruthenian territories they demanded. Of the guarantee of the new state by which Chamberlain had set such store in September nothing more was heard save for a tentative enquiry by the British government on March 2nd, 1939, which was insolently rejected as an unwarrantable interference in a German 'sphere of influence'. Finally, by the somewhat premature recognition of Franco as the Spanish government on February 27th, when the war was not yet over

---

[1] Churchill, op. cit., Vol. I, p. 252.

and Parliament had just been led to believe that no such step was contemplated, the policy of appeasement reached its climax. A purring self-satisfaction, wholly out of tune with the known state of the world, pervaded ministerial speeches. 'No man that I know is less tempted than Mr. Chamberlain to cherish illusions,' Halifax told the world in February; and Mr. Chamberlain on March 10th was assuring a press conference at the House of Commons that 'Europe is settling down to a period of tranquillity' and holding out hopes of resumed discussions on disarmament before the end of the year. Hoare, after consulting his chief, denounced 'Jitterbugs' who were prophesying war to his constituents at Chelsea on the same day and expressed the hope for a golden age of peace and prosperity if only Hitler, Chamberlain, Daladier and Stalin could get together round a table. But when Russia, a week later, proposed a conference of Britain, France, Russia, Poland, Rumania, and Turkey, to discuss means of resisting aggression, Chamberlain, under strong pressure from Simon, rejected the overture as 'premature', and thereby doomed to failure any further attempt to reach an understanding with Stalin.

The rejection of this suggestion was all the more surprising because by then the Ides of March had come and gone. On that day, March 15th, the *Punch* cartoon showed John Bull in an Air Raid Warden's helmet waking from a nightmare as the threat of war vanished through the window, and Hitler occupied Prague, using as his pretext carefully fomented disorders in Slovakia and Ruthenia. This was the event which completed the turn-over of British opinion, since it put the future beyond argument. Even *The Times* was forced to admit that Hitler had here no 'moral case'. Only Chamberlain seemed to waver for a moment. 'Internal disruption', he told the House of Commons that afternoon, had disintegrated the new Czech state and there was therefore nothing left for us to guarantee. He found the 'manner and method' of Hitler's action at variance with the principles of Munich, but that was all. At Birmingham two days later, after being stiffened by Halifax, his tone at last hardened. There ran through what he then said a bitter note of personal disillusionment. He had staked so much on his first, Berchtesgaden impression of Hitler as 'a man who could be relied upon when he had given his word',[1] and his sense of personal outrage permeated

[1] Feiling, p. 367.

everything he said. But the reversal of policy thereby precipitated was startling and complete. On March 31st he gave to Poland, unasked, what he had so obstinately refused to Czechoslovakia: a more or less unconditional guarantee of British support against any foreign aggression, which was in due course translated into a reciprocal treaty and to which the French then subscribed. But even this change of heart did not prevent the government from handing over to the Germans the unspent balance lying in the London banks of the £30 million which had been lent to the Czechs after Munich to help in their reconstruction.

The guarantee to Poland, extended within a few weeks to Rumania and Greece after Mussolini's sudden attack on Albania on Good Friday, April 7th, ushered in a new period—the period in which there was no longer any hope of avoiding war. For nothing could stop Hitler from pushing his next demands, for Danzig and a corridor to East Prussia, especially as he no longer took Anglo-French guarantees at all seriously. The new policy was welcomed by Churchill and his friends in the House, and indeed by most of the public, if only because it at last pledged Great Britain unequivocally to make a stand against further German aggression. As Churchill said, 'God helping us, we can do no other.' But, as Lloyd George also pointed out, such a guarantee made no sense at all unless accompanied by a close understanding with Russia. Every argument used by the Munichers to justify the abandonment of the Czechs applied a hundred-fold to the Poles. They were more remote, politically and socially far less developed, and militarily twenty years out of date. Moreover, the simultaneous collapse of Germany and Russia at the end of the first world war had enabled the restored Polish state to maintain an arrogant independence which they could not see was doomed as soon as both powers recovered. They would therefore neither make concessions to Hitler nor allow Russian troops on their soil even as allies. They had furthermore, like the British War Office, a misplaced confidence in their own military strength and there would be no persuading them to back down in a crisis.

A military alliance with Russia was in fact the only condition on which the coming war in Europe could be fought out on approximately equal terms. The studious cold-shouldering of Russia since the beginning of the Munich crisis had probably made any such arrangement already impossible. Stalin said himself that he was not prepared to pull the western powers' chestnuts out of the fire for them and the replacement of Litvinov by Molotov in May signalised a reorientation of Russian policy away from the League and from western commitments. Moreover the negotiations in Moscow, when they did get started in April, were conducted as offensively as possible. Neither Chamberlain nor Halifax would condescend to visit Stalin personally, and the senior Russian leaders were expected to deal with Foreign Office officials and soldiers of secondary rank. Since, on top of all this, Poland and Rumania steadfastly refused to tolerate Russian troops on their soil in any circumstances there was never any justification for hoping that an effective alliance could be secured. Stalin in fact seems to have used the negotiations, as they dragged on through the summer, as a means of forcing better terms out of the Germans, who were at least prepared to allow him a free hand in the Baltic states, Bessarabia, and eastern Poland. On August 23rd he signed with Ribbentrop the Non-Aggression Pact which precipitated the war. Freed from danger in the east and certain that the western powers were again bluffing, Hitler could proceed to the dismemberment of Poland.

Actually, there seems to have been a moment when Hitler hesitated. Letters poured in on him, from Chamberlain and Daladier insisting that an attack on Poland meant general war; from Roosevelt and the Pope and King Leopold of Belgium begging him to hold his hand. But what seems to have given him pause was the unmistakable temper of the House of Commons on hearing of the Russian pact and the similarly hardening mood in France. When, on August 25th, the Anglo-Polish Treaty was renewed and Mussolini at the same time informed the Germans that he was not yet ready for a major war and would not march, the orders for the attack on Poland, timed for 4.40 a.m. the next morning, were cancelled. Almost immediately, however, the heat was turned on again. Reports of fictitious atrocities by the Poles against their German minorities multiplied in the German press, and the Poles ordered a general mobilisation on August 31st. In the end the outward decencies of diplomacy were scarcely observed at all. The Poles were presented with an ultimatum and the attack went in, at 4.45 a.m. on September 1st, before they had even seen its detailed terms. For a day both France and Britain seemed to waver. An exchange of notes with

Germany, a mediation attempt by Mussolini, and various procedural difficulties were made the excuse for doing nothing throughout Saturday, September 2nd, and there were fears when the Commons met that evening that another retreat was being prepared. When Arthur Greenwood rose to speak in place of the absent Attlee, Amery's voice came from the back benches opposite—'Speak for England'; and Greenwood, protesting that after 38 hours of war in Poland nothing had been done to implement our promises, undoubtedly voiced the nation's feelings. At 9 the next morning Hitler, Goering, and Goebbels received from Henderson with, it is said, 'stunned surprise' the British ultimatum which meant that by 11 we were at war. By that evening France had followed suit, and during the next few days every member of the Commonwealth save Eire came in too.

It might perhaps be argued that the six months of so-called phoney war which followed the last year of very phoney peace should be included in any study of Britain between the wars: that the era did not really come to an end until that stormy scene in the House of Commons on the afternoon of May 7th, 1940; when the Norwegian campaign had been lost and the Blitzkrieg let loose on France, Belgium, and Holland; and men of all parties rose to protest at the government's ineffectual direction of the war. From the artistic point of view the tragedy might well end with Amery thundering at the government front bench in Cromwell's words: 'You have sat here too long for any good you have been doing. Depart, I say, and let us have done with you. In the name of God, go.' It was, indeed, Churchill's dynamic courage which set the tone for a new age; and in the Battle of Britain the nation expiated the sins of omission of a decade. But it was the shock of Munich which really brought the period of self-interested complacency to an end, and it was out of the recriminations and self-reproaches of the following months that the new spirit was born.

The record of British effort and achievement between the two wars is not a proud one; and its tragic ending has perhaps caused too much stress to be laid on the lessons which were not learnt and the great opportunities which were missed. But it should not be concluded entirely as a story of failure. That the social system and the constitutional machinery of the nation were able to adapt themselves to rapidly and vastly changing conditions without violent upheaval, that the essential

tolerances and liberties were preserved and unity and prosperity maintained without recourse to the extremist ideologies fashionable in the
XX-century world, were not mean achievements. They could not have
occurred without much skill and hard work and an immense patience
on the part of all kinds and classes of people. The faults of the age were
glaring and the penalties exacted for them spectacular. What was successfully accomplished was not spectacular and fell far short of the
dreams and intentions of 1918. But it was because of these same unspectacular achievements that Churchill was able to lead a united
nation to ultimate victory—a nation, moreover, which still survives the
dogged struggle for post-war recovery with its perhaps even more
severe tests of patience and discipline.

Bibliography

This list of books does not pretend to be exhaustive. It consists only of those which have been found useful in the preparation of this study. It is divided into two parts, the first consisting of those essential for a detailed study of the period; the second of those useful only in a supplementary sense for filling in the background of particular aspects and incidents.

PART I

C. L. Mowat, *Britain Between the Wars, 1918–1940,* is long, comprehensive, and scholarly, and indispensable as a work of reference. D. C. Somervell, *The Reign of King George V,* is also valuable as a consecutive narrative of the events as they appeared in 1935. There is a number of biographies which, because they cover the whole period in great and scholarly detail, are essential reading: Harold Nicolson, *King George V*; Keith Feiling, *The Life of Neville Chamberlain*; R. F. Harrod, *The Life of John Maynard Keynes*; Alan Bullock, *The Life and Times of Ernest Bevin,* are in this category. More restricted in scope, but also valuable are Robert Blake, *The Unknown Prime Minister*; Malcolm Thomson, *David Lloyd George*; John Bowle, *Viscount Samuel*; and J. A. Spender and Cyril Asquith, *Life of Lord Oxford and Asquith.* Essential reading for the political, social and economic development of Britain in these years are G. D. H. Cole, *History of the Labour Party*; Julian Symons, *The General Strike*; R. Bassett's two unnecessarily long but irreplaceable volumes, *The 1931 Political Crisis,* and *Democracy and Foreign Policy,* a study of public opinion during the Manchurian episode; Robert Graves and Alan Hodge, *The Long Week-end*; Malcolm Muggeridge, *The Thirties*; John Hilton, *Rich Man Poor Man*; Thomas Jones, *A Diary with Letters, 1931–1950*; and A. J. P. Taylor, *The Trouble Makers*.

On the history of foreign affairs during this period the most important single book, because the only one so far based on a close study of the recently published documents, is A. J. P. Taylor's *The Origins of the Second World War*. As a survey it is, however, highly selective and it does not altogether replace any of the following: W. S. Churchill, *The World Crisis* (last vol.) and *The History of the Second World War* (first vol.); G. Medlicott, *British Foreign Policy since Versailles*; R. B. McCallum, *Public Opinion and the Last Peace*; Harold Nicolson, *Peacemaking, 1919*; J. M. Keynes, *The Economic Consequences of the Peace*; David Lloyd George, *The Truth about the Peace Treaties* and *The Truth about Reparations and War Debts*; L. B. Namier, *Diplomatic Prelude,1938–39* and *Europe in Decay, 1936–40*; J. W. Wheeler-Bennett, *Nemesis of Power, the German Army in Politics, 1918–1945* and *Munich, Prologue to Tragedy*, and *Ciano's Diplomatic Papers* (ed. M. Muggeridge).

PART II

In this category I have placed almost all the Memoirs and Autobiographies since, valuable and entertaining though many of them are, they are not reliable evidence for the historian, being permeated still with the prejudices and beliefs of an earlier period. Of the great number available, Viscount Templewood (Sir Samuel Hoare), *Nine Troubled Years;* M. A. Hamilton, *Remembering My Good Friends*; R. Boothby, *I Fight to Live*; L. S. Amery, *My Political Life*; Duff Cooper, *Old Men Forget*; Bishop Hensley Henson, *Retrospect of an Unimportant Life*; and Sir Nevile Henderson, *Failure of a Mission*, are all for different reasons good reading. Less valuable are, C. R. Attlee, *As it Happened*; Philip Snowden, *Autobiography*; Hugh Dalton, *Call Back Yesterday*; Margot Asquith, *Autobiography* (second vol.); Sir Norman Angell, *After All*; Sir Herbert Samuel, *Memoirs*; H. L. Stimson, *The Far Eastern Crisis* and, with M. Bundy, *On Active Service*; and Herbert Morrison, *Autobiography*.

Bibliography

There is a number of biographies of varying interest and importance, of which some are: Sarah Gertrude Millin, *General Smuts*; Lord Ronaldshay, *Life of Lord Curzon*; Harold Nicolson, *Curzon, the Last Phase*; Raymond Postgate, *Life of George Lansbury*; John Evelyn Wrench, *Geoffrey Dawson and Our Times*; J. C. Smuts, *Jan Christian Smuts*; M. A. Hamilton, *Arthur Henderson*; Malcolm Thomson, *Life and Times of Winston Churchill*; J. W. Wheeler Bennett, *Life of King George VI*; Dennis Bardens, *Portrait of a Statesman, The Personal History of Sir Anthony Eden*; Tom Driberg, *Lord Beaverbrook*. The later chapters of C. K. A. Bell's monumental *Randall Davidson*; Antonia Valentin, *Frustrations: Stresemann's Race with Death*, and Sir Henry Clay, *Lord Norman*. There is no satisfactory life of Baldwin. A. W. Baldwin, *My Father: the True Story*, corrects the perspective of G. M. Young's unsatisfactory *Stanley Baldwin*, but gives no coherent picture; nor do Arthur Bryant, *Stanley Baldwin, A Tribute*; and Adam Gowans Whyte, *Stanley Baldwin*. L. McN. Weir's *The Tragedy of Ramsay MacDonald* is merely a vicious attack.

For those who like by-ways or who have highly specialised interests, there are, among much else, H. Pelling, *The History of the British Communist Party*; Ramsay MacDonald, *The Foreign Policy of the Labour Party*; J. M. Keynes, *Treatise of Money, The General Theory of Employment, Interest, and Money*, the pamphlet of 1926, *The Economic Consequences of Mr. Churchill*, and *Two Memoirs*; Etienne Mantoux, *The Carthaginian Peace*; B. H. Liddell Hart, *Foch, Man of Orleans*; S. Gwynne, *The History of Partition*; Lord Beaverbrook, *Men and Power*; Ferdinand Czernin, *Europe, Going Going Gone*; Cyril Connolly, *Enemies of Promise*; George Orwell, *The Road to Wigan Pier*; Gerald Macmillan, *Honours for Sale*; J. H. Morgan, *Assize of Arms*; K. Zilliacus, *Inquest on Peace*; H.R.H. the Duke of Windsor, *A King's Story*; and Hugh Thomas, *The Spanish Civil War*.

But such a miscellaneous list could go on for ever. The specialist in economic and social history is recommended to study the footnotes in Mowat's *Britain Between the Wars* for a very complete bibliography. The complete list of first-hand sources for the foreign history of the period is to be found in Taylor's *Origins of the Second World War*.

Index

Index

Index

Index

Index

Lawrence, Col. T. E., 35
League of Nations, Covenant of the,
26, 35–6, 46–7, 105–6, 145–6, 210–
11, 214, 218–19, 235–6, 238–9, 242;
Manchurian policy, 209–14, 216,
219, 230, 241–2, 262; misc. refs., 75,
106, 142–4, 148–9, 161, 207, 232
League of Nations' Union and Man-
churia, 214, 217, 219; the Peace
Ballot, 230–1; misc. refs., 26, 147
Leeds, 55
Ledru-Rollin, M., 116
Lenin, 54, 97
Leningrad, 54
Leopold II of the Belgians, 279
Liddell-Hart, Capt. B. H., 27
Litvinov, Maxim, 144, 274, 279
Liverpool, 53, 251
Llandudno, 262
Lloyd, Lord, 161
Lloyd George, David, part in Ver-
sailles Treaty, 29–30, 32–3, 37–40;
on reparations, 40–3, 48; the
Sankey Commission, 55–7; the
Irish settlement, 65, 67; the
honours scandal, 68–9; fall from
power, 70–4, 76–82; in 1931 crisis,
177; misc. refs., 13–16, 18–20, 22–4,
49, 50, 53, 58–9, 62–4, 83–4, 91,
98, 101, 110, 154, 158, 164–6, 190,
245, 260–1, 278
Lloyd-Graeme, Sir Philip, *see* Cun-
liffe-Lister
Locarno, Treaties of, 111–12, 142–3,
243
London, police strike, 53; con-
ference of 1921, 70–2; misc. refs.,
160, 167, 169, 193, 251, 263, 269,
272
Long, Walter, 21, 79
Loos, Battle of, 27
Loucheur, M., 41
Lough Swilly, 265
Lothian, Lord, 264
Lowther, Col. Charles, 42–3, 49
Lusitania, ship, 14
Luton, 51
Lyons, Messrs., 127
Lytton, Lord, 212, 218–19; his report,
212–14

MacDonald, Ramsay, as Prime
Minister, 1923, 102, 104–7; in the

General Strike, 115, 119, 124, 132;
as Prime Minister, 1929, 156–8,
161–6, 168; on India, 159; in the
crisis of 1931, 171–2, 174–86; as
Prime Minister of National Govern-
ment, 186, 188–94, 196–200, 204–5,
231, 235; misc. refs., 22–3, 82, 89,
93, 96–8, 150, 155, 245, 248–9
McKenna, Reginald, 20, 81, 86, 112
MacLean, Sir Donald, 175
Macquisten, F. A., 117, 140
Madrid, 254–6
Maginot Line, 33
Maisky, M., 206
Malta, 240, 242
Manchester, 80, 251, 259
Manchester Guardian, 186, 214
Manchuria, 74, 209–13, 215, 217, 219–
20, 227, 231, 238, 255
Mander, Sir Geoffrey, 215, 219
Marshall Plan, 83
Mary, Queen, 225–7
Masaryk, Jan, 275
Maxton, James, 157
May, Sir George, 168; his committee,
169–73
Mein Kampf, 229–30, 260
Minseito Government, of Japan, 214
Molotov, M., 279
Mond, Sir Alfred, 141, 157
Montacute, 88
Moore-Brabazon, Colonel, 149
Montagu, E. S., 20, 64–5, 148, 158
Morgan, Messrs. J. P., 177–9
Morning Post, 127
Morrison, Herbert, later Lord, 183, 198
Moscow, 54, 107, 129, 274, 279
Mosley, Sir Oswald, 158, 165, 247
Mudania, Armistice of, 77–8
Munich, 229, 266, 271–2, 274–8, 280
Murray, Prof. Gilbert, 27
Mussolini, Benito, and Corfu, 99;
policy to Austria, 229–30, 237, 264;
to Abyssinia, 236–7, 239–42; to
Spain, 254–6, 261, 271; to the
Munich Crisis, 267, 271; to Al-
bania, 278; misc. refs., 208, 227,
244, 257, 262–3, 276, 279–80
Mustapha Kemal, 76–7

Napoleon I, Emperor, 34
National Industrial Council, 14, 157–
8, 219

Index

National Peace Council, 146, 219, 234
National Union of Railwaymen, 52–3,
  61, 118, 121, 136, 139
Neuilly, Treaty of, 47
New York, 177–8, 188
Newcastle, 130
Newport, 80
Nicolson, Sir Harold, 227, 260
Nile, R., 237
Nivelle, General, 16
Noel-Buxton, Lord, 165
Norman, Montagu, later Lord, 27,
  171
Northcliffe, Lord, 15–16, 29, 42
Nottingham, 192
Nuffield, Lord, 259
Nürnberg, 268

Observer, The, 152
O'Connor, Rory, 67
Oliver, F. S., 234
Olympic, ship, 86
Orlando, Signor, 41, 99
Orwell, George, 253
Ottawa Conference, 193, 197, 200
Owen, Wilfred, 27
Oxford, Union Society, 220; trousers,
  151; Movement, 152

Page, Walter, 85
Pakistan, 194–5
Pankhurst, Sylvia, 54
Papen, Franz von, 207
Paris, 30–1, 39, 70–1, 73, 76, 188, 241,
  261, 263, 269
Parmoor, Lord, 105, 108
Passchendaele, Battle of, 27, 150
Paul, William, 54
Peel, Sir Robert, 79
Peking, 262
Pétain, Marshal, 34
Pethwick-Lawrence, Mrs., 191
Philippines, 75
Phipps, Sir Eric, 261, 274
Pitt, William, Earl of Chatham, 19
Plymouth, 101, 134
Poincaré, President, and the Cannes
  Conference, 72–3; misc. refs., 77,
  82–3, 104
Ponsonby, Arthur, 105
Poplar and Poplarism, 59–60, 110
Postgate, Raymond, 135, 166
Prague, 267, 269, 277

Prayer Book, 152
Priestley, J. B., 253
P'u, Mr. Henry, 213
Pugh, Arthur, 116, 126, 133

Queenstown, 265

Radek, Karl, 129
Raleigh, Sir Walter, 20
Rapallo, Treaty of, 74
Rathenau, Walther, 72–4
Reading, Lord, 185, 193
Redmayne, Sir Richard, 55, 61–2
Reform Bill of 1832, 91
Reichstag fire, 220
Rhine, R., 33–4
Ribbentrop, Joachim von, 276, 279
Riccione, 229
Rivera, General Primo de, 203
Robinson, Sir Joseph, 69
Roe, A. V., 259
Rome, 237, 276
Roosevelt, President Franklin, 202,
  205–6, 262, 270, 279
Roosevelt, President, Theodore, 17
Rothermere, Lord, 148, 158
Ruhr, the, 72–3, 82–3, 99, 104, 115,
  220
Ruhrort, 71
Rumbold, Sir Horace, 77
Runciman, Lord, 20, 267–8
Ruthenia, 276

Saar territory, 44, 227, 229–30
St. Germain, Treaty of, 33, 47
Saklatvala, G., 55, 154
Salisbury, Lord, 69, 81, 114
Salvidge, Sir Arthur, 79–80
Samuel, Sir Herbert, later Lord, his
  commission and the General Strike,
  119, 123–5, 131–3; part in the 1931
  crisis, 172, 175–7, 179, 182–3, 185;
  part in the National Government,
  190, 193, 197, 208, 231; attitude to
  rearmament, 223; misc. refs., 20,
  158, 190
Sandringham, 182
Sankey, Lord, and Sankey Commis-
  sion, 55–7, 61–2, 118; his part in
  the 1931 crisis, 183, 185
Sassoon, Siegfried, 15, 27
Scapa Flow, 74
Scarborough, 122

Index